TROUBLE-FREE MENOPAUSE

TROUBLE-FREE MENOPAUSE

MANAGE YOUR SYMPTOMS AND YOUR WEIGHT

Judy E. Marshel, M.B.A., R.D.
and Linda Konner

AVON BOOKS  NEW YORK

This book was current to the best of the authors' knowledge at publication, but before acting on information herein, the consumer should, of course, verify the information with an appropriate physician or health care provider.

AVON BOOKS
A division of
The Hearst Corporation
1350 Avenue of the Americas
New York, New York 10019

Copyright © 1995, 1998 by Judy E. Marshel, M.B.A., R.D., and Linda Konner
Published by arrangement with the authors

ISBN: 0-7394-0026-6

Printed in the U.S.A.

Contents

Acknowledgments

Many thanks to the following people for their support and encouragement and for generously sharing information: Maria Alessi, M.S.; Salvatore Ambrosino, M.D.; Karen Argula; David A. Baker, M.D.; Patty Barnett, M.A.; Elda Bertagna, R.N.; Kate Broome; Wayne Callaway, M.D.; Virbala Chokshi, M.D.; Janis and Jerry Cohen; Julie Conner, M.S., R.D.; Michael Corpeal, M.S.; Mary Costello; Janine O'Leary Cobb, M.Sc.; Robert Crayhon, M.S.; Alice Cutler, M.A.; Joan Dobbs, Ph.D.; Arlene Dym, M.S., R.D.; Debbie Elezovic, R.N.; Esther and Arthur Ellner; Susan Eno, M.S., R.D.; Reva T. Frankle, Ed.D., R.D.; Craig Frischling; Renee Frengut, Ph.D.; Beverly Fuscaldo, R.N.; Ann Louise Gittleman, M.S.; Alan Geliebter, Ph.D.; H. Michael Grant, M.D.; Kathy Hager, M.S., R.N.; Steve Heymsfield, M.D.; Ronna Kabatznick, Ph.D.; Francis Kreb; Natividad LaGuerre; Ida LaQuatra, Ph.D.; Marion Levine, Ph.D.; Linda Lizzotte, R.D.; Sonja McKinlay, Ph.D.; Anita Mandato, M.S.; Phyllis Marks, M.D.; Arnold Marshel; Doris Marshel; Renee Marshel, Ph.D.; Richard Marshel; Bonnie Minsky; Elly Munsinger, AAFA; Nik Nekelieff; William D. McArdle, Ph.D.; Lynette McEvoy; F. Xavier Pi-Sunyer, M.D.; Harriet and Jules Pollock; Terry Polonus, Ph.D.; Ceil Quirk; Maxine Rumack; Janet Schebendach, M.A., R.D.; Melinda and Michael Sims; Jean Perry Spodnik; Charles Stringfellow, M.D.; Paula Szilart, M.S.; Rodney Taft,

vii

M.D.; David Tasaka; Alan Titchenal, Ph.D.; Cheryl Wacher; Lila Wallis, M.D.; Christine Wells, Ph.D.; Dorothy Wheeler; Jane Weston Wilson; Judith Wurtman, Ph.D.; Marc Zimmer, Ph.D.; the Paerdegat Athletic staff; and all my clients.

—Judy E. Marshel, M.B.A., R.D.

Author's Note

The information presented in this book combines "conventional" with "natural" or "alternative" treatments, with the aim of enhancing health, preventing or minimizing menopausal symptoms, and when appropriate, producing weight and fat loss. This book is designed to help you make informed decisions about your lifestyle, diet, and exercise. However, none of the recommendations should be used as a substitute for any advice or treatment prescribed by your own doctor or nutritionist. If you decide to follow any treatments or weight loss advice described in this book, be sure to consult your physician first.

It is my belief that controllable lifestyle factors, such as what you eat, the vitamins and minerals you take, how much you exercise and the type you do, and how you respond to stress directly affect the incidence and severity of age- and menopause-related symptoms. These symptoms can include hot flashes, vaginal dryness, and fatigue, as well as weight gain. Your lifestyle decisions may also impact *when* you begin menopause and how susceptible you are to diseases such as heart disease, osteoporosis, and breast cancer.

Since weight gain can be an all-too-frequent symptom of aging and menopause, this book is replete with information about how to shed unwanted pounds. You'll also learn that your weight and the percent body fat you maintain at this stage of life may be more under your control than you thought. What you eat to sustain your weight or to lose weight and satisfy the needs of your ever-changing body may need to be "revisited" and modified. That's why three nutritious eating plans, along with an exercise and stress management plan, are provided in this book.

Because it is my belief that diets don't work, the three weight-loss eating plans described in this book are not intended to be "diets." Rather, they are guidelines to help you learn about healthy eating and different eating styles. For effective weight control, you need to evaluate the eating-and-exercise options presented in the book and determine which ones are most effective for you, and put them into action. Over time, it's important for you to make necessary adjustments as your needs and lifestyle change. If weight loss is your goal, you are strongly urged to reject any rapid-weight-loss programs and to adhere as I do to the New York City Department of Consumer Affairs Weight Loss Bill of Rights, which issues the following warning:

"Rapid weight loss may cause serious health problems. (Rapid weight loss is weight loss of more than 1½ to 2 pounds per week, or more than 1 percent of body weight per week after the second week of participation in a weight loss program.) Only permanent lifestyle changes, such as making healthful food choices and increasing physical activity, promote long-term weight loss."

Keep in mind also that the case histories presented in this book clearly demonstrate that your metabolism, dietary needs, vitamin and mineral requirements, food sensitivities, and a host of other factors vary from person to person. Just as no two women have precisely the same menopause, your body's responses to food, herbal treatment, vitamin and mineral supplementation, and the like may be different from those described in these pages. Therefore, you may have to make certain adjustments to see the results you desire.

—Judy E. Marshel, M.B.A., R.D.

Introduction

Change is the only true constant in life. Just as you start feeling comfortable with some new aspect of your routine or the way you feel . . . something changes.

Many of the changes and new beginnings you face throughout life involve choice. You can choose to marry or to stay single; to have children or not; to live in one part of the world or another; to follow a lifestyle similar to that of your parents and grandparents or to seek different role models and new paths; to be sedentary or active; to choose to lose weight or to accept your figure as it is; to be selective about the food you eat or to make a habit of grabbing whatever is quick and easy.

However, other new beginnings and changes *can't* be controlled or avoided—nor can your reactions to them be predicted. These phases include the beginning and end of menstruation. At its start, you slowly move into "womanhood" as you leave childhood behind and watch your body assume a new shape and purpose. Suddenly, you are a fertile being. Decades later, in menopause, you experience the loss of fertility and many changes in the way your body looks, feels, and behaves. New opportunities may come your way, as may new concerns.

Some of these changes can be exciting—for example, you may no longer have to think about birth control, and so find this time of your life sexually liberating. Yet other changes may be temporarily scary—after all, your body and emotions are shifting in many unexpected ways. But none of these changes need to be worrisome, when you understand what is happening to you.

Here in the pages of *Trouble-Free Menopause*, you will learn more about yourself and your body before, during, and after menopause. You'll gain a greater insight into the possible long-term health risks that may take place, such as osteoporosis, heart disease, and breast cancer, as well as those you may be much more aware of right now, including hot flashes, vaginal dryness, and changes in or the end of your monthly menstrual periods. You'll come to understand which symptoms are menopause-related, which are age-related, and which may be the result of lifestyle choices you've been making for months or even years. With increased awareness of what's happening to you and why, you'll feel much more comfortable and confident. What's more, armed with the facts, you'll be able to make informed decisions about things you may want to do to further ease the transition to the next phase of your life, such as whether or not to embark on hormone replacement therapy or more natural modalities.

To help you deal with one common symptom in particular—weight gain—which you may have always had difficulty with but is more pronounced now, or perhaps it's become a more recent problem as you move through menopause and get older—I've devised an eating-and-exercise plan that should not only enable you to shed the extra pounds and excess body fat, but also help you to feel good, every day. In addition, I'll share some smart strategies for coping in a healthful way, with the stresses that may now be part of your life, possibly for the first time.

Over the last two decades, I've had ample opportunity to observe and work with menopausal women and I've learned which lifestyle and eating-style changes work for them—and which don't. For the first fourteen years of my career, I was the senior nutritionist at Weight Watchers International, where I met women from all over the world, many of whom were menopausal. I saw firsthand how the Weight Watchers eating plan affected them, and one conclusion I drew is that not everyone benefits from the standard American diet—a high-carbohydrate, low-fat diet. I've learned even more about what types of eating plans do and don't work over the past seven years. During this time I've been a nutritionist in private practice as well as a health consultant in corporate settings, working with menopausal women in one-on-one and group settings, focusing on health, lifestyle, and weight-management issues. I've provided them with information and the support tools to help them maintain a healthy mind and body and to prevent or minimize menopause symptoms, including weight gain.

Several of the women I've worked with over the years share their frank and often-revealing personal stories in these pages. Many of my clients had been lucky enough to sail through life with few or no hormone-related problems such as PMS, nor did they have any real health or weight issues. For some of them, menopause changed all that. Those who had a tendency toward high blood cholesterol found that they had to work harder than before to keep their cholesterol at a healthy level. Others who prided themselves on being able to eat and drink anything they wanted, with little adverse effect, found that they couldn't do that any longer. Now, a glass of wine triggered a hot flash, for example, or eating too much sugar on a regular basis led to a yeast infection.

For many, weight became another new issue to deal with. Those women who were thin prior to menopause and never had to worry about what went into their mouth or how much (or little) exercise they did suddenly found themselves coping with bulges that were never there before. Other clients had battled weight problems all their lives. Once they reached menopause, these women either experienced greater difficulty in losing weight or gained even more. Still others, who had been resigned to accepting their overweight bodies, got a menopausal wake-up call, and for health or emotional reasons finally decided to do something about their excess weight. By teaching them about good nutrition, exercise, and stress management, I helped them *help themselves* finally lose the weight they wanted to lose, as well as ease their transition into menopause.

And you can do the same by following the guidelines described in the pages of this book. There's no magic about any of this—except for the magic that lies within *you*. Once you know what to do—and begin to do it—you'll be astonished at the results you're likely to see, both in your overall well-being and in your weight. Here, in *Trouble-Free Menopause*, you'll learn the techniques for getting and staying healthy, for staying as symptom-free as possible, and for ridding your body of any unwanted pounds during this liberating new time of your life.

—Judy E. Marshel, M.B.A., R.D.

TROUBLE-FREE
MENOPAUSE

1

❧

What's Happening to Your Body?

"HOW DO I KNOW IT'S MENOPAUSE?"
TAKE THE MENOPAUSE SELF-TEST

- Forty-five-year-old Brenda, always the picture of health, has suddenly started waking up in the middle of the night with her heart racing, drenched in perspiration.
- Nancy, who's forty-seven, is trying to cope with a menstrual cycle that now has a mind of its own. Her periods, which used to come every twenty-eight days like clockwork, seem to arrive whenever they feel like it, and whatever tampon or pad she uses is never right anymore.
- Jennifer, who just hit the big Five-O, finds that she cries at the drop of a hat these days. As if *that* weren't bad enough, she's put on six pounds over the past eight months and hates her heavier body.

"Is it hot in here, or is it me?" has become your new catch-phrase. And your menstrual cycle has become somewhat erratic. Is what you experience the very first signs of menopause—or something else unrelated to it? This self-test will help you find out. Just answer these questions Yes or No.

1. Are you approaching the age when your mother began menopause?

2. Has your menstrual cycle changed?
3. Are you bleeding more heavily (or more lightly) than before?
4. If you've experienced PMS in the past, have those symptoms changed or worsened?
5. Are you experiencing any of the following symptoms for the first time?

   • chronic anxiety
   • abdominal bloating
   • aching joints and muscles
   • breast tenderness/loss of fullness in breasts
   • chronic fatigue
   • excessive hair loss/balding on scalp
   • growth of facial hair
   • frequent headaches
   • insomnia/sleep disturbances
   • irritability/crying spells
   • itching or tingling, as if ants are crawling over your body
   • memory lapses
   • frequent nausea
   • heart palpitations
   • prolonged sadness or mild depression
   • weight gain

6. Do you experience sudden sensations of heat or find yourself perspiring in the absence of stress or physical exertion?
7. Do you have to urinate more often than usual?
8. Do you find that you frequently have the urge to urinate, yet when you try, your bladder is empty?
9. Does your bladder leak urine when you laugh, jump, sneeze, or feel stressed?
10. Are you getting more frequent bladder infections?
11. Does it take longer than usual for you to become lubricated during sex?
12. Has your interest in sex declined?

13. Has your vagina become drier than usual during intercourse?

14. Do you get vaginal infections more often?

15. Has your vagina become itchier or more irritated than before?

16. Do you experience sudden waves of heat, perspiration, or redness of the skin?

17. Is your skin getting substantially drier?

18. Has your weight shifted from your thighs and buttocks to your abdomen?

19. Have you had a hysterectomy (removal of the uterus) that has disrupted your menstrual cycle?

20. Have you had radiation or chemotherapy that has disrupted your menstrual cycle?

21. Have you had a bilateral oophorectomy (removal of both ovaries)?

TOTAL: Yes_____   No_____

Count up the number of "Yes" answers. The more you have, the greater the likelihood that you've started menopause, although even one or two "Yes" responses might indicate the onset of menopause. (A "Yes" answer to question 21 means you are definitely menopausal. If your total blood supply to your ovaries after a hysterectomy or during radiation chemotherapy was permanently cut off, then a "Yes" response to question 19 or 20 would also indicate menopause.) Also keep in mind that this list is not all-inclusive. You may have other menopausal signs that are not specified above.

Although some of these changes may be related purely to aging, this might be a good time to talk to your gynecologist to confirm that the changes you are seeing are in fact connected to menopause and not to some other condition. For example, abnormally heavy or prolonged vaginal bleeding can be associated with a benign condition such as fibroids or polyps, or may be more serious, indicating such conditions as cancer of the cervix or ovary, or endometrial hyperplasia (overthickening of the lining of the uterus), which may be the forerunner of endometrial cancer. So do have a checkup.

Menstrual Flow Chart

Day	Jan	Feb	Mar	Apr	May	Jun	Jul	Aug	Sep	Oct	Nov	Dec
1												
2												
3												
4												
5												
6												
7												
8												
9												
10												
11												
12												
13												
14												
15												
16												
17												

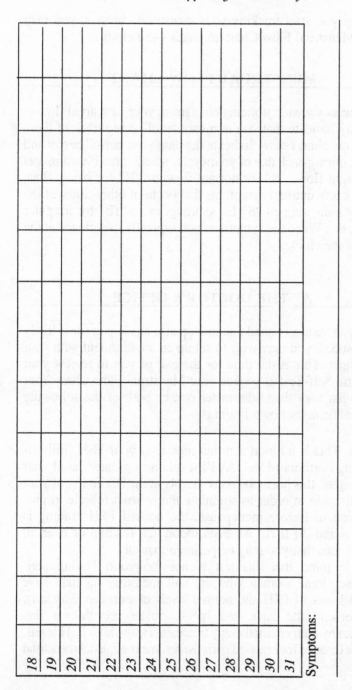

	18	19	20	21	22	23	24	25	26	27	28	29	30	31

Symptoms:

Abbreviations:

To help you start tracking your menstrual changes, you may find the Menstrual Flow Chart on pages 4–5 helpful.

MENSTRUAL FLOW CHART

As soon as you start noticing changes in your menstrual flow—which may indicate that you're menopausal—keep track of them by using the chart below. Indicate the date your period began and jot down, during each day of your cycle, whether the bleeding was "L" for light flow, "N" for normal flow, or "H" for heavy flow. Also track any unusual symptoms that occur at other times of the month by indicating an "S" for spotting, or an "IB" for irregular bleeding, etc. Write the symptoms you typically experience at the bottom of the chart.

AT THE DOCTOR'S OFFICE

Once you've established that menopause has begun (or is likely to occur soon), you may wish to set up an appointment with your gynecologist. This is the time for the two of you to review your Menopause Self-Test as well as your Menstrual Flow Chart. Your gynecologist may then administer one or both of the following tests to confirm your own findings:

FSH test. This is a blood test that measures your FSH (follicle-stimulating hormone) level. As I'll explain in greater detail later in this chapter, this hormone rises sharply at the beginning of your menstrual cycle in order to stimulate the ovarian follicle to produce estrogen. Before menopause, the normal FSH reading is between 5 and 30 IU/L. An FSH blood test reading of over 30 IU/L indicates that you may be perimenopausal.

Keep in mind that this test is not foolproof. During perimenopause, some women who are still menstruating may have increased levels of FSH and normal levels of estrogen. Similarly, some women who have had breast cancer are thrown into menopause by their chemotherapy treatments show high FSH levels, then, after three or four missed periods, resume their usual menstrual

---

The Stages of Menopause

The female reproductive system is controlled by a delicate balance of hormones produced by the ovaries, mainly estrogen and progesterone. As the production of these hormones shifts (more about this on pages 12–15), your body will go through three stages of menopause:

Perimenopause. The transitional state between fertility and menopause that lasts from several months to several years, from when you first start to experience physical changes (such as irregular periods and hot flashes) until your menstrual periods stop.

Menopause. The cessation of menstruation and, along with it, fertility, caused by the decline of estrogen and progesterone production. Menopause has officially occurred when twelve consecutive months have passed without a menstrual period.

Postmenopause. The days, months, and years that follow menopause.

The word "menopause" will be used throughout this book to refer collectively to all three stages.

---

cycle. This test is most reliable for those women who naturally stopped menstruating for several months.

Vaginal smear. This useful but less-common test for menopause involves scraping some cells from the vaginal walls and examining them under a microscope. Estrogen-nourished cells are thick and lush, while estrogen-depleted cells are thin and pale; a vaginal smear can give your gynecologist a good indication of whether you're at or near menopause.

Be sure to ask your gynecologist about anything that may concern you about your symptoms. Symptoms vary from woman to woman, and your doctor will be able to recommend the best course of action for you based on what's currently happening to your body and your personal medical history.

WHY ME . . . AND WHY NOW?

If you're just starting to exhibit some of the typical signs of menopause, you may be wondering: why *now?* After all, although the average age of menopause onset in the U.S. is fifty-one, some women may enter menopause in their early forties, while others may not do so until their mid-to-late fifties. A very few women even go through menopause in their thirties. A wide range of factors may influence the age you start menopause:

Genetics. Heredity plays a key role in the onset of menopause, and you're likely to start at or about the time your mother started. You're also apt to experience many of the same menopausal symptoms she did.

Environment. What some researchers attribute to heredity, others link to a combination of heredity *and* environment. In other words, it's possible that you and your mom started menopause at very different ages because you had very different habits that would affect the onset of menopause. For example, if you smoke cigarettes, you may enter menopause at a much earlier age than your nonsmoking mother did. Environmental factors may be at least as important as inherited ones.

Children. If you've never had children *or* if you've had twins, you may begin menopause earlier than other women. And if you didn't have your first child until late in life—after age forty—you may be more likely to start menopause later than usual.

Diseases and surgery/treatment. Research indicates that certain conditions and illnesses—fibroids, diabetes, cancer of the uterus and breast, and diseases of the pituitary gland—may cause the endocrine system to extend estrogen production, thereby delaying the onset of menopause. On the other hand, women whose ovaries are irreparably damaged (for example, due to trauma or disease) or who have had both ovaries removed (bilateral oophorectomy) will begin menopause immediately, since ovaries are the primary producers of estrogen and progesterone, the hormones needed to ensure regular menstrual cycles. Also, some women who have had a hysterectomy may also experience an early menopause if they have had complications such as a compromised or irregular blood flow to the ovaries (or instant menopause, if the blood flow to their ovaries has been cut off). Similarly, if ovaries have been affected during radiation or chemotherapy treatments for cancer, that, too, may trigger an instant or early menopause. Additionally, a defective autoimmune system, in which antibodies that destroy the eggs in the ovaries are produced, might bring on menopause.

Cholesterol levels. Low total cholesterol levels often trigger an early menopause.

Socioeconomic status. Women from a higher socioeconomic status tend to experience menopause later, presumably because of a nutritionally superior diet. Studies conducted in New Guinea in the 1970s revealed that undernourished women began menopause several years earlier than better-nourished women.

Weight. In general, thinner women (women with low body fat) may have an earlier-than-usual menopause. Marathon runners, anorexics, and stick-thin fashion models tend to enter menopause earlier than others.

WHAT'S HAPPENING TO MY BODY?

To better understand the changes going on in your body right now, let's look at how menopause fits into your entire life cycle:

Not All Estrogen Is Created Equal

Estrogen is present in your body in three different forms. Each has a different effect on the body. Let's take a look at the three forms: estradiol, estrone and estriol.

Estradiol is the name of the estrogen produced mainly by the follicles of your ovaries and, to a much lesser degree, by your adrenal glands. Typically, estradiol is approximately 10–20% of circulating estrogens. Estradiol is chemically active. It binds to many tissues including those of the uterus, breast, ovaries, brain and heart, organ systems in the body that have receptors that allow the estradiol to enter into their cells. But if estradiol is present in *too high an amount* for *a prolonged period of time*, it can cause adverse reactions, such as estrogen-related cancers, bloating, breast tenderness, blood sugar fluctuations, headaches and heavy periods. However, to prevent this excessive buildup, the body has a mechanism that allows estradiol to be converted in the liver into estrone.

Estrone, approximately 10–20% of your circulating estrogens, is a less active form of estrogen. Estrone is produced by the conversion of estradiol to estrone in the liver. It is also produced by the adrenal glands. The adrenal glands produce the hormone androstenedione, which can be converted into estrone in the adipose (fat) tissue as well as in muscle. Estrone is less likely to cause estrogen-related cancer. Yet too much of this form of estrogen can cause fluid retention and blood sugar fluctuations. To prevent an excess manufacture of estrone, the liver will break down estrone into estriol.

Unlike the other two types of estrogen, *estriol* offers a *protective* effect on your body. Typically, estriol makes up approximately 60–80% of circulating estrogens. This form of estrogen, while retaining its property as a female hormone, loses the ability to overstimulate responsive tissues like those of the breast and uterus. As a result, it protects against many types of cancers and menopausal symptoms.

YOUR REPRODUCTIVE SYSTEM: THE FERTILE YEARS

You are born with about 1–2 million egg cells, which will be your total supply for life. They are contained in your ovaries, the almond-shaped glands on either side of your uterus, and are cushioned by a protective layer of follicles. Only a tiny fraction of your egg cells (about five hundred) will ever have a chance to mature enough to be released (and possibly fertilized) during your menstrual cycle.

The function of the ovaries is regulated by the hypothalamus area of your brain, which oversees the brain's pituitary gland, which, in turn, makes sure the ovaries function as they should. The pituitary produces two hormones: 1) follicle-stimulating hormone, or FSH, which tells the ovaries how much estrogen to produce and when, and 2) luteinizing hormone, or LH, which does the same with progesterone.

Let's take a closer look at the role of each of these players during a typical twenty-eight-day menstrual cycle:

Days 1–14. On Day 1 of your cycle, you start bleeding. It's also the time when your hormone levels are very low. The hypothalamus senses that estrogen levels are too low, and so it signals the pituitary gland to begin producing FSH. Estrogen levels then rise.

Over the next few days one follicle, generally carrying one egg within it, grows and grows until it dominates all the other follicles. As the follicle grows it produces estrogen, which promotes the thickening of the lining of the uterus. By about Day 14—roughly the halfway point of the menstrual cycle—the follicle has reached its peak of maturity, and the egg within it is ready to be released. The pituitary is alerted to turn off FSH and produce a surge of LH. When LH peaks, ovulation—the release of the mature egg from the follicle into the fallopian tube—can occur. From there, the egg makes its way to the uterus for possible fertilization.

Days 15–28. At the place where the egg falls away from the follicle a new, temporary gland, called the corpus luteum, forms. This gland stimulates the production of a very small amount of estrogen and large amounts of progesterone, to further help prepare the uterus for the fertilized egg, or embryo. Once a certain amount of progesterone has been produced, the pituitary is alerted to halt production of LH. But even though FSH and LH have both been shut off, the corpus luteum keeps pumping out small amounts of estrogen and progesterone. If fertilization occurs, progesterone levels will continue to increase. If not, the levels of both hormones will taper off until about Day 28, when they will again be very low. That's when cells from the inner lining of the uterus will dissolve, causing some of the blood vessels supplying them to leak. This flow of blood is menstruation, and with it, the entire cycle begins again, as the hypothalamus alerts the pituitary gland to start pumping out the hormones once more.

This pattern continues for the length of your fertile life, interrupted by pregnancy, the surgical removal of your ovaries or uterus, and/or a hormonal imbalance caused by factors such as stress.

YOUR REPRODUCTIVE SYSTEM: THE APPROACH OF MENOPAUSE

Although you may start out with approximately 1–2 million egg cells in your ovaries, that number diminishes as you get older. By the time you reach puberty, you're down to about 300,000 eggs, and by age forty you're down to just a few thousand. Once you start menopause, you've got only a few hundred eggs left.

Several factors cause your egg supply to shrink over time— depletion of eggs and/or follicles, defective eggs, defective follicles, or erratic levels of hormone production, to name but a few. But your hypothalamus doesn't know when these aberrations occur and keeps doing its thing as if nothing were wrong. Sometimes, in its quest to maintain proper ovary function, the hypothalamus will continue to pour out FSH to levels 10–20 times as much as usual, and LH production may triple.

Yet once you start going through menopause, even extraordinary amounts of FSH and LH are insufficient to stimulate the few remaining follicles to produce significant quantities of estrogen and thicken the uterine lining in preparation for the fertilized egg. No ovulation occurs, and menstruation eventually stops. This is a gradual process; it can take years as your periods grow farther and farther apart until they disappear completely. There might, in the midst of all this, be episodes of heavier-than-usual bleeding. Or perhaps you might not experience any noticeable change in your cycle. But when twelve consecutive months without a period have elapsed, you have gone through menopause.

REACHING A NEW HORMONAL BALANCE

After menopause, estrogen is still produced, although the form and amount has for the most part changed, as has the source. Estrogen levels are a tiny fraction of what they were previously and, as time goes on, diminish still further.

Although you may think that, other than taking hormones, you're pretty powerless when it comes to your estrogen supply, there are actually four steps you can take that may help your adrenal glands boost androstenedione production and, along with it, boost your estrogen levels, easing your transition into menopause and minimizing your symptoms:

- *Exercise*, which speeds the conversion of androstenedione, a hormone produced mainly by the adrenal glands, into estrogen. This occurs in lean body mass (muscles).
- *Maintain a reasonable level of body fat*—ideally somewhere between eighteen and twenty-five percent, since body fat is also where this conversion takes place.
- *Eat a healthy diet*. Your goal is to ensure healthy adrenal glands. Whole grains, fruits, vegetables, and protein—low-fat sources of animal protein as well as vegetable sources of protein are the best choices for nourishing the adrenals. On the other hand, alcohol, sugar, and caffeinated foods such as chocolate, coffee, and colas can put extra stress on the adrenals.

  Keep in mind that as hormone levels drop, the pituitary gland sends signals to the adrenal glands to produce hormones. They can secrete significant amounts of hormones after menopause. The good news is that when the back-up system is working properly, you are likely to experience few if any menopausal sysptoms.

What About Hysterectomy and Surgical Menopause?

Surgical procedures involving ovaries can affect when and how menopause will take place. In a hysterectomy the uterus is removed and the ovaries remain. Since there is no uterus, menstruation stops immediately. However, providing that the ovaries—the body's main sources of estrogen and progesterone—remain intact, you should otherwise have a natural menopause. However, if surgery disrupts the blood supply to the ovaries, women may experience an earlier menopause or some menopausal symptoms, such as depression, a decrease in sexual pleasure, and problems with loss of urine control (urinary incontinence).

The above scenario also holds true for an oophorectomy (when just one ovary has been removed). However, in a bilateral oophorectomy, when both ovaries are removed, menopause will begin immediately and abruptly, and your symptoms are likely to be more intense than if you'd experienced menopause naturally.

A woman whose ovaries stop functioning following radiation or chemotherapy will also experience a sudden menopause. Yet some women undergoing these treatments find that their period may stop for 3 or 4 months, only to find them returning regularly. Although this isn't the norm, it does happen on occasion.

Foods such as tofu, soybeans, miso, licorice, and yams, which are rich in phytoestrogens, contain hormonelike substances that mimic the action of estrogen. They may offer many of the beneficial effects of estrogen without the negative side effects. Plant estrogens are 2% as strong as estradiol and they bind to the estrogen receptors of your cells. If you have too much estrogen, plant estrogens block its stronger effects. If you have too little estrogen, when they bind to the receptor sites they themselves act as estrogen and therefore counterbalance the low estrogen effect. As one example of phytoestrogen consumption, Japanese women—who generally eat a lot of soy products—rarely complain of hot flashes, which are quite common in the U.S. So you'd be wise to fill up on foods rich in phytoestrogens. Although these foods don't directly affect your adrenal glands and your supply of estrogen, they may help to reduce your menopausal symptoms.

• *Maintain a healthy liver.* It is here that potent estrogen is deactivated and then eliminated from the body.

• *Manage your response to stress*, because stress wears out the adrenal glands, which can lead to lower androstenedione production and, therefore, lower estrogen levels.

All the how-tos will be described in the pages ahead.

2

The Basics of Good Nutrition

"These hot flashes are driving me crazy! What can I do?"
*"Help me lose weight, Judy! I don't care what I have to do to
get off this weight that I've recently gained! Just get this fat
off me!"*

My menopausal clients want results—*now*. Some clients are
unhappy with the symptoms they're experiencing. Night sweats
are disrupting their sleep. Changes in their figure or their larger
dress size are making them uncomfortable. Many are desperate to
do *something*—even, they say, if it means throwing sensible eating out the window. I understand their dilemma—after all, I am
going through menopause myself and experienced hot flashes. I
have to work harder at keeping my weight in check, which is very
important to me, since I've struggled with my weight for many
years of my life. But I am *also* a nutritionist, and my primary concern is to help clients get and *stay* healthy.

Clients who've worked with me for months or years eventually
come to realize that a healthy lifestyle can help to relieve or eliminate uncomfortable symptoms, such as hot flashes, and to get rid
of unwanted pounds. They have found, to their delight, that by
eating a smart, balanced diet and exercising regularly, they've
eased their menopausal symptoms and slowly lost excess weight.
They actually felt that they were taking control over their destiny
by making positive changes that could potentially ward off long-
term diseases such as osteoporosis and heart disease.

16

They also learned that these lifestyle changes were more than simply eating less or differently for the short term. Rather, maintaining good health and a comfortable weight required a comprehensive approach—a nutritious diet, full of low-calorie, low-fat, nutrient-rich foods; regular exercise; stress-management techniques; and a behavioral/psychological component to encourage habit and attitude changes that sustain good habits for a lifetime. And that's precisely the combination of techniques you'll find in this book.

Your present menopausal symptoms, including any excess weight you may be carrying now, might well be the result of the eating habits you developed during the last years or even decades of your life. Just as a healthy prepregnancy diet and a program of regular exercise can make pregnancy and delivery easier, eating well prior to menopause enables a woman to get through these mid-life years more comfortably. If you entered your forties and fifties with a history of smart eating behind you—if you kept up your intake of vitamins, calcium, and other health- and bone-enhancing minerals, and focused on high-fiber, low-fat meals and if you exercised regularly—chances are you're having an easier time with menopause than some other women you know. On the other hand, if you've been a junk-food junkie most of your life, or if your weight loss chart looks like a day on Space Mountain, you may have a tougher time of things now that you want to lessen your menopausal symptoms or lose your menopause or post-menopause pounds. That's because your body's nutrient supply may first need to be restored before you can get relief from your symptoms or lose any weight. And you're going to need to learn (or relearn) *and apply* the basics of good nutrition consistently to get the results you want.

On the next pages you'll learn about the energy-producing nutrients—protein, carbohydrates, and fat—and how much your body needs. You'll also get the facts about water and why it is important at this crucial time. Don't beat yourself up if your eating habits have been less-than-great all along—be assured that you *can* reverse the damage. With an eating plan that suits your physical and emotional needs—along with a regular program of exercise—you *can* feel good, get relief from menopausal symptoms, and lose that excess fat. If you think your usual pattern of eating has clogged your arteries with fat or caused damage to your heart, don't despair! It's never too late to turn things around and give your health a big boost . . . starting with a change in diet.

YOU ARE WHAT YOU EAT

Probably ever since you were in elementary school you've been hearing, "Eat a balanced diet." If you're like most people, you wondered, "What's the big deal about a balanced diet? Why can't I just eat my Twinkies in peace?"

As you've gotten older, you've gotten smarter about a lot of things, including healthy eating. Slowly you came to understand why foods like broccoli and yogurt and apples are good for you, that the way you eat affects the way you look *and* feel. Once you realize that your body requires about *forty-five different nutrients* to maintain good health, suddenly the concept of a "balanced diet" makes perfect sense. As you may be trying to convince your children (or grandchildren) these days, a steady diet of Twinkies (or any other single food) just won't cut it.

Of the forty-five-odd nutrients you regularly require, some are needed in tiny amounts, while others have to be consumed in fairly large quantities for maximum health. Like a well-run company, all the nutrients must work together as a team to keep your body fit and functioning. Six of them—known as the essential nutrients—should be part of your diet regularly to ensure good health, and they come from the foods you eat and the beverages you drink and from vitamin and mineral supplements. Three of these six—protein, carbohydrates, and fat—provide calories necessary to fuel the body. The other three—water, vitamins, and minerals—don't themselves supply calories but nevertheless play important roles, including helping the other three nutrients do their job.

THE ENERGY-PRODUCING NUTRIENTS

Although calories—units of energy for the body—are provided by protein, carbohydrates, and fat, not all calories are alike. Protein and carbohydrates provide just four calories per gram, while fat provides more than twice as much—nine calories per gram. This is why the higher the fat content of a serving of a particular food, the higher the calorie count as well—and this is one of the reasons I'll be emphasizing low-fat eating.

So, while you won't get fat eating four heads of lettuce every day, you *may* put on a couple of pounds if you routinely gobble down several Snickers bars, as an addition to what you normally eat.

Foods contain varying amounts of protein, carbohydrates, and fat. That's why health experts always urge you to eat a variety of foods—including low-fat or nonfat dairy products, fruits and vegetables, whole grains, low-fat animal protein and/or plant protein, and a bit of heart-healthy fat—to help ensure that your body gets enough of *each* of the three vital nutrients along with important vitamins and minerals. Why are these nutrients so important to the body? The answers follow:

PROTEIN

Proteins are made up of building blocks called amino acids. Some amino acids are manufactured by the body and others are not, and can be obtained only by eating protein-rich foods. Protein forms part of every cell in your body. It's used to build, repair, and maintain muscle and all other tissue; it forms the core of your bones and teeth, the filaments of your hair, and the basic material of your fingernails; it is needed to transport nutrients in and out of your cells; and it is important in maintaining a healthy immune system. After water, protein is the most abundant material found in the body, and many essential body substances are made of protein, including insulin, a hormone that helps regulate your blood sugar; enzymes, including digestive enzymes that help break down food; and antibodies that fight disease and ward off potentially harmful invaders.

Protein is also important in many other ways, particularly for menopausal women. First, the thermic effect of food (TEF) found in protein is higher than that found in carbohydrate- or fat-rich foods. Translation: after you eat a "pure" protein-packed meal, calorie burning may be stepped up by 15–20 percent for your body to process it (compared to about just 3–5 percent for fat and

6–10 percent for carbs). So if you focus on meals comprised of very pure protein—for instance, omelettes made with egg whites only—or other high-protein foods like very lean fish or turkey, you're giving your metabolism a boost. Keep in mind that if your meal contains protein, carbohydrate, *and* fat—a "mixed" meal— the TEF decreases to about 10 percent. This is particularly good for those trying to lose excess fat, since over time, *that* should translate into a nice, steady weight loss.

Protein-rich foods are valuable sources of iron. Although you need less iron now than you did while you were menstruating, it's still important for keeping energy levels high, warding off disease, and helping you better handle your response to stress.

And because protein helps stabilize blood sugar, it may also prevent mood swings and minimize food cravings.

In addition to the protein they supply, low-fat and nonfat dairy products are believed by some researchers to be among the richest sources of calcium—a mineral you need to help you head off osteoporosis. While you *can* get calcium from lower-calorie plant sources, such as broccoli, you'd need to consume far more of these types of protein than you would from animal sources. For instance, one 8-fluid-ounce glass of fortified low-fat milk provides 300 mg of calcium, plus 400 IU of vitamin D, one of the nutrients necessary to help you absorb the calcium. To get that much calcium from cooked broccoli, you'd need to eat about *3 cups* of it. While some researchers believe that milk and other dairy products are a necessary part of the diet because of the large amount of calcium supplied, others believe that cow's milk and dairy products are fit for calves only. Why the controversy? Those against milk and dairy products contend that: (See the chart on page 26 for good sources of calcium-rich foods.)

- Milk is a highly allergic food. Many individuals are allergic to milk protein such as casein, lactalbumin, and lactoglobulin.
- Many people have a condition known as lactose intolerance, which causes gastrointestinal distress including gas, bloating, and diarrhea whenever dairy products are consumed. These people do not produce enough of the enzyme lactase to digest lactose (milk sugar).

- Because of its high level of animal protein, milk may cause greater calcium loss than gain.
- When milk is homogenized, the enzyme xanthine oxidase is absorbed in the bloodstream. This enzyme injures the arterial wall and may be a potential cause of heart disease.
- While dairy products are abundant in calcium, they are also rich in phosphorus. High-phosphorus foods like cheese and milk decrease calcium absorption.
- The high level of calcium to magnesium found in milk can interfere with magnesium absorption.
- Milk comes from cows, which may have been given growth hormones to enhance their milk yield. When we drink milk, there's the danger that we might ingest these hormones.
- Dairy products are mucus producing and can exacerbate phlegm production.

Remember that you don't have to use dairy products to get your calcium. If they tend to do you more harm than good, go for the vegetable sources of dairy.

ARE YOUR PROTEINS COMPLETE (AND DOES IT REALLY MATTER)?

You may have heard the expressions "complete proteins" and "incomplete proteins." Proteins from animal sources—meat, fish, chicken, turkey, and the like, as well as milk and dairy products—are complete proteins, because they provide all the essential amino acids. Incomplete proteins—those that lack one or more of the essential amino acids—include rice; dried beans, peas and lentils; tofu; nuts and seeds; peanut butter; and meat substitutes made of soy or textured vegetable protein.

It's possible—and common—to make a tasty, complete-protein meal by combining two incomplete proteins (such as beans and rice) or one incomplete protein with one complete protein (such as a lentils-and-chicken dish). *But you don't have to worry about getting a complete protein at any given meal as long as you eat a variety of protein-containing foods—as whole grains, dried peas/beans/lentils, seeds and nuts, vegetables, tofu, yogurt, etc.— throughout the day.*

PROTEIN: THE PROS AND CONS

A lot has been written lately about dietary protein—how much you really need and whether you may actually be ODing on protein, causing more harm than good to your body. I discussed the "pros" of protein above, and it is a critical nutrient. Yet as vital as protein is, some health professionals believe that too much protein from animal sources can lead to anything from heart disease to breast cancer, from weak bones to kidney damage.

For example, John McDougall, M.D., medical director of the McDougall Program at St. Helena Hospital in Deer Park, California, claims in his book *The McDougall Plan* that our love of protein in the form of red meat has led to a nation of brittle bones, allegedly because all that protein eventually causes the kidneys to filter calcium out of the body. In addition, Dean Ornish, M.D., director of the Preventive Medicine Research Institute in Sausalito, California, claims in his bestselling book *Eat More, Weigh Less* that a diet less than ten percent in fat—a drastic cut in fat as well as animal sources of protein—can prevent and/or reverse heart disease.

How real are these health risks? Let's start with heart disease. The concern about protein's link to heart disease appears valid when you realize that animal products do contain saturated fat, known to clog coronary arteries. However, *if* you choose moderate amounts of animal protein and stick with the lean varieties, you shouldn't put yourself at increased risk for heart disease. If you do the supermarket shopping, you are probably aware there are many more cuts of meat with much less fat available today than ever before. Read package labels so you'll know just what you're getting and how you can enjoy animal sources of protein foods without loading up on your total fat, as well as saturated fat. As a general rule, look for "Select" grade and lean cuts like the loin, sirloin, round, and leg. Also, if you make a point of trimming visible fat from lean beef, veal, or pork before cooking it—and if you keep the portions small—you're helping to reduce its level of saturated fat to that of skinless chicken and seafood, which is rather low. You can also regulate the amount of fat you consume from dairy and other products by choosing only low-fat or fat-free varieties: skim milk or low-fat milk instead of whole milk, low-fat or fat-free cheese instead of regular cheese, water-packed instead of oil-packed tuna. So it's quite possible to get the best of all worlds with a diet that includes reasonable amounts of low-fat, protein-rich animal sources of protein. And if you want further protection from the risk of heart disease, you can always divide your protein intake between the animal variety and protein derived from plant sources—dried beans (pinto, kidney, and lima beans) and peas (chickpeas, split peas), lentils, tofu, tempeh, and protein-rich grains like quinoa, amaranth, etc.—or rely totally on plant sources of protein. (See the chart on page 25.)

As for the possibility of developing breast or kidney cancer from eating too much protein, the 1982 *National Academy of Sciences Report: Diet, Nutrition and Cancer* indicates that "protein may be associated with an increased risk of cancers at certain sites," although other research has failed to consistently confirm that claim.

What about the notion that too much animal protein robs the body of calcium, leading to osteoporosis? Although it is true that the more animal protein you consume, the more calcium your kidneys filter out of your blood and into your urine, the amount of calcium lost is believed to be small. If you are concerned, make certain to eat a calcium-rich diet and be moderate in your consumption of animal proteins. Or, you can always opt for plant sources of protein or a combination of plant and animal sources of protein. And remember to look at the total picture. In addition to animal sources of protein, there are many other foods, beverages, and lifestyle habits that can rob your body of calcium, as well as those that favor calcium absorption, which is described in Chapter 4, in the section on osteoporosis.

The bottom line: keep in mind the bigger picture—balance, variety, and moderation of all foods, from the six different food groups—protein (poultry, meat, fish, dried cooked beans, peas and lentils, tofu, cheese, etc.), starch (bread, pasta, etc.), vegetables, fruit, dairy, and fat.

HOW MUCH PROTEIN IS ENOUGH?

Protein requirements vary, depending on your age and weight, as well as the weight you'd *like* to be. The National Research Council's Recommended Dietary Allowances (RDAs)

Food Sources of Unhealthy Hormones

Another real concern many clients express has to do with the hormones—estrogen, progesterone, and testosterone—that are routinely fed to livestock to speed their growth or the growth hormone that is given to cows to enhance their milk yield, as well as antibiotics and other chemicals given to them. Residues can remain in the meat or milk and if you eat a lot of them, you may be exposed to them as secondhand substances. What should you do? If this is a major concern, go for organically grown meats and poultry that are not fed these substances, and cows (and dairy products from cows) that are not given any hormones.

suggests .36 grams of protein per pound of body weight. Thus, if you weigh 150 pounds, you'd be urged to eat 54 grams of protein per day. In real terms, that translates to about 4 oz. (cooked) of animal protein (or for those who don't eat animal products, 4 oz. cooked kidney beans and 6 oz. tofu), 2 cups of skim milk or calcium-fortified soy milk, and the balance from starch and vegetables.

Are you surprised that milk, starch, and vegetables provide protein as do meat, fish, and poultry? In fact, 1 cup of milk has around 8 grams of protein, 1 slice bread about 3 grams, ½ cup vegetables around 2 grams, and 1 ounce of chicken, turkey, fish, beef, etc. provides about 7 grams.

Keep in mind that the suggested amount of daily protein intake is an *average* value, and that you may need more because you feel better eating more low-fat protein. Many of my clients were on high-carb, low-protein diets when they first came to see me. Some of them complained of low energy levels, constant food cravings, and an inability to lose weight eating this way. Eating more low-fat, protein-rich foods and reducing their carbs helped to turn this around. In Chapter 8, one of the Eating Plans, the Protein-Packed Plan, shows you how to eat a low-fat, protein-rich diet.

PROTEIN-PACKED PLANTS

Food	Protein gm (approx.)	Fat gm (approx.)	Calories (approx.)
LEGUMES, NUTS AND SEEDS			
Almonds, 1 oz.	5	16	180
Cashews, 1 oz.	5	15	170
Chickpeas (garbanzos), 2 oz. cooked	6	1	95
Lentils, 2 oz. cooked	5	trace	60
Lima beans, 2 oz. cooked	4	0.3	65
Peanut butter (smooth), 1 tbsp.	4	8	95
Peanuts, 1 oz.	8	14	170
Pistachio nuts, 1 oz.	6	16	175
Red kidney beans, 2 oz. cooked	5	0.3	65
Split peas, 2 oz. cooked	5	0.2	65
Sunflower seeds, 1, oz.	7	13	160
Tahini (sesame butter), 1 tbsp.	3	8	90
Tempeh, 2oz.	12	4.8	114
Tofu, 2 oz.	5	3	45
GRAINS (COOKED)			
Amaranth, ½ cup	8	2	105
Barley, ½ cup	2	0.5	95
Brown rice, ½ cup	3	1	110
Bulgur, ½ cup	3	0.5	75
Millet, ½ cup	4	1	143
Oatmeal, ½ cup	3	1	65
Pasta, ½ cup	3	0.5	110
Potato, white, 3 oz.	3	0.05	95
Rolled oats, ½ cup	3	1	65
Quinoa, ½ cup	8	1.5	106
Tortilla, flour, 1, 1 oz.	3	2	95
Whole wheat bread, 1 slice	3	0.7	70

CALCIUM-RICH FOODS

(Note: what should you aim for? About 1500 mg calcium per day. If you are taking hormone replacement therapy or estrogen replacement therapy, 1000 mg can satisfy your needs.)

Food	Calcium content mg (approx.)	Calories (approx.)
CHEESE		
Cheddar, 1 oz.	205	115
Cottage (2% fat), 2 oz.	40	50
Mozzarella, part-skim, 1 oz.	185	75
Muenster, 1 oz.	205	105
Ricotta, part-skim, 2 oz.	155	80
FISH/SHELLFISH		
Salmon, canned, drained, including bone, 3 oz.	160	155
Salmon, fresh, 3 oz.	10	180
Sardines, canned, in oil, drained, including bone, 3 oz.	335	180
Shrimp, canned, drained, 3 oz.	45	90
ICE CREAM/ICE MILK		
Ice cream, hard, (10% fat) ½ cup	85	135
Ice cream, soft serve, ½ cup	120	185
Ice milk, hard, ½ cup	90	90
Ice milk, soft serve, ½ cup	135	115
Milk/Yogurt		
Low fat (1%) milk, 8 fluid oz.	300	100
Low fat (2%) milk, 8 fluid oz.	300	120
Skim milk, 8 fluid oz.	300	85
Whole milk, 8 fluid oz.	290	150
Yogurt, nonfat, plain, 8 oz.	400	100
Yogurt, low-fat, plain, 8 oz.	400	150
Yogurt, low-fat plain, fruited, 8 oz.	340	250
VEGETABLES		
Bok choy (fresh), cooked, 1 cup	160	20
Broccoli (fresh), cooked, 1 cup	175	55
Broccoli (frozen), cooked, 1 cup	110	55
Brussels sprouts (frozen), cooked, 1 cup	60	55
Carrots (fresh), cooked, 1 cup	50	50
Collards (fresh), cooked, 1 cup	305	60

Food	Calcium content mg (approx.)	Calories (approx.)
Soybeans (fresh), cooked, 1 cup	145	260
Turnip greens (fresh), cooked, leaves and stems, 1 cup	275	60
OTHER		
Almond, 1 oz.	75	180
Tofu, plain, 2 oz.	70	45
Tofu, with added calcium salts, 2 oz.	150	45

CARBOHYDRATES

The main function of carbs is to provide energy for the body. There are two types of carbohydrates: "simple" sugars, which include white and brown sugar, molasses, and honey, as well as fruit and milk; and "complex" carbohydrates, such as bread, pasta, rice, potatoes, and vegetables. As you can see, these two categories are wide-ranging, including nutrient- and fiber-packed foods like whole grain bread, fruit, and veggies, as well as ones like refined sugar, which provides little more than empty calories. So it's important to be selective as you choose the carbohydrates you'll eat each day.

You may not realize that when you eat certain carbohydrates, you're *also* consuming some protein, so you get an extra nutritional bang for your buck. For example, a slice of bread provides about fifteen grams of carbohydrate plus three grams of protein. One cup of vegetables provides, on average, five grams of carbs plus two grams of protein. One glass of milk provides twelve grams of carbs plus eight grams of protein.

Simple Sugars

Odds are, when you think of sugar, you think: junk food. But there's sugar . . . and there's sugar. You can get a good idea of what makes *two* simple sugars so valuable for your diet by taking a closer look at the two nutrient-rich simple sugars, fruit and milk. That one simple apple or peach is packed with the vitamins, minerals, and fiber missing from the refined-sugar candy or soda. Also, the fructose (natural fruit sugar) found in fruit gives it its satisfying sweet taste.

Some folks still believe that a sugar fix is great for giving you a burst of energy, which might lead you to conclude that a handful of M&Ms is the perfect remedy for a midday slump. While it *is* true that refined sugars break down in no time and give your bloodstream a quick jolt of energy, once they leave your system you'll experience a sudden *drop* in energy levels, that letdown, tired feeling—and possibly even a craving for *more* sugary food. And as you already know, too much candy and other sweets don't do your waistline any good either. However, the sugars found in fresh fruit, for example, have a less dramatic impact on the body, since when fruit is broken down, the fiber in it slows down its digestion—making the process easier on the body and generally keeping you satisfied longer than sugar-laden foods.

COMPLEX CARBOHYDRATES

Just as simple sugars vary, so do complex carbs. You've probably heard a lot about the importance of eating whole-grain foods, and this is the category where you'll find such whole-grain complex carbohydrates as brown rice, whole-wheat bread, and whole-wheat pasta. This is *also* where you'll find the less-desirable refined complex carbs, such as white rice and enriched white bread, which have had most of their essential nutrients removed during milling. If your white bread or cereal is labeled "enriched," then B vitamins and iron have been put back, but you're still better off sticking to whole-grain foods whenever you have the choice because they are loaded with other valuable vitamins, minerals, and fiber.

Whole-grain complex carbs are great for maintaining your health and weight. They enter the digestive system slowly and, for that reason, they keep you satisfied longer than most other kinds of food, so you usually end up eating less. Part of that has to do with the presence in complex carbs of dietary fiber, which has been touted for years as a remedy for everything from irregularity to colon cancer.

Indeed, fiber—the indigestible portion of plants that is found in two forms, insoluble and soluble—should be an important part of your diet, probably more so now than ever. Woody-looking insoluble fiber absorbs water as it moves through the digestive tract, keeping body functions running smoothly by speeding up elimination. This helps prevent constipation, a problem you may experience more as you age. Also, insoluble fiber is believed to protect you against colon cancer. That's because it speeds up transit through the colon, thereby decreasing the time the bowel is exposed to potential carcinogens. Good sources of insoluble fiber include whole-grain breads and cereal, wheat bran cereals, and some fruit and vegetables.

Unlike insoluble fiber, soluble fiber looks like a gel when it's combined with water. Soluble fiber in your diet helps stabilize your blood sugar, which is important in helping to protect against diabetes and hypoglycemia, as well as reducing your risk of heart disease by helping to lower blood cholesterol. And those concerned about their waistlines, take note: not only does soluble fiber keep you satisfied longer by taking longer to chew and be digested by the body, it can easily replace certain high-fat ingredients in your cooking because of its gel-like consistency. For example, try substituting chopped prunes for butter or oil to get a moist cake without a lot of fat. Other good sources of soluble fiber are apples, beans (such as kidney and pinto), oats, oat bran, psyllium, flax seeds, and barley.

HOW MUCH CARBOHYDRATE IS ENOUGH?

If you are not carbohydrate-sensitive—for example, you don't have sugar or starch intolerance, allergies, or cravings or find yourself hungrier after you've eaten a carbohydrate-rich meal—you should aim for between 50 and 60 percent of your daily intake from carbs. The specific ways to accomplish this are described in the Carbohydrate-Packed Eating Plan in Chapter 8.

As for fiber requirements, the National Cancer Institute recommends that you consume between 20 and 35 grams of fiber a day, and that you aim for a variety of fiber-rich carbs so that you're sure to get both the insoluble and soluble kinds. If you haven't been eating reasonable amounts of fiber all along, introduce it into your diet gradually until you build up to the recommended levels, and don't forget to drink 6–8 glasses of water daily to help avoid any potential side effects from the fiber, such as bloating or gassiness. If you still experience gas after taking these measures, iden-

---

Quick Fiber Tip

Remember that the *form* of food you choose can greatly affect the amount of fiber you consume. For example, while a small-sized apple (with the skin) and a half cup of apple juice have about the same number of calories, the apple has about eighteen times more fiber than the juice. So whenever possible, choose the *whole* fruit or vegetable over the juice or sauce versions.

---

tify those foods causing the problem and reduce their intake. If you are cooking dried beans, soak the beans overnight. Then dump out the water and cook the beans in fresh water. Some clients find that charcoal tablets available in health food stores provide relief. Others find that an over-the-counter product called Beano, in tablet or drop form, when used with their beans, peas and lentils, cabbage, broccoli, carrots, and other vegetables eliminates or reduces flatulence. You may have to experiment with different fiber-rich foods to see which ones work best for you.

FAT

Why is it that fat is considered the biggest culprit when it comes to weight woes? Because it's the single most concentrated source of calories you take in. As I noted earlier, fat supplies more than twice the number of calories you would get from an equal amount of protein or carbohydrate, and that's true of *all* fat—whether it's butter or extra-virgin olive oil, margarine or mayonnaise. And the body doesn't have to work so hard to store excess fat.

If you take in excess calories, whether it is in the form of protein, carbohydrate, or fat, the body stores it as fat. For the body to store excess calories as fat, it has to process it and convert it into a suitable fat storage form. Your body expends calories doing this. If it's excess carbohydrates you are eating, to change it to fat is an energy-expensive process. For example, if you have 100 excess carbohydrate calories, the body uses about 23 calories to process it, so 77 calories are stored as fat. Yet, if you take in too much fat and have to store it, it is a simpler process. Your body would only expend about 3 calories in the storage process of the 100 calories consumed! So, 97 calories would be stored as fat! The bottom line: *too much fat can make you fat*—it's as basic as that—and too much is bad for your health. And too few essential fatty acids are bad for your health and weight loss.That's why you're urged to select reasonable amounts of heart-healthy and immune-enhancing fats each day.

There are three different types of dietary fat, some types helpful, and others more harmful:

1. *Saturated fat.* Saturated fat is found mainly in animal products, such as beef, veal, lamb, pork, chicken, turkey, whole and low-fat milk and milk products, and anything made from these foods. You'll also find these fats in natural fats such as palm and coconut oils, which are often hidden away in foods like crackers, granola bars, and store-bought cakes and cookies, as well as in such processed fats as shortening and lard. To make shortening or lard, an unsaturated liquid vegetable oil, like canola or soybean oil, is heated to high temperatures. This process is called "hydrogenation," and converts the liquid vegetable oil into a more solid form. Not only does this process convert some of the unsaturated fats into saturated fats, but it changes the arrangement of some of the molecules to a form called "trans" fatty acids.

   Why is this bad? Studies show that both saturated fat and "trans" fatty acids can put you at increased risk for heart disease because these fats can raise blood levels of "bad" low-density lipoprotein (LDL) cholesterol, which clogs your arteries with fat, and lower "good" high-density lipoprotein (HDL) cholesterol. So watch out for the words "hydrogenated" or "partially hydrogenated" on the ingredient listing on a food label. Saturated fat has also been linked with a higher risk of colon and breast cancer.

   Start reading labels. Limit your daily intake of saturated fat to less than ten percent of your total calories. Since the new labeling guidelines don't require that "trans" fatty acids be listed on the label, limit foods that contain "partially hydrogenated" ingredients, since "trans" fats are present. If you are a margarine lover, always look for a margarine with "liquid" oil listed, not "hydrogenated" or "partially hydrogenated" oils. These are usually available in tubs or squeeze bottles, not in stick form. They don't contain "trans" fat the way margarines generally do.

2. *Monounsaturated fat.* Monounsaturated fats are liquid at room temperature, and they actually *lower* cholesterol levels by lowering the level of harmful LDLs, while not impacting your HDLs, the "good" cholesterol. Peanut, olive, and canola oils, as well as avocados and olives, contain a good deal of monounsaturated fat.

3. *Polyunsaturated fat.* This type of fat—liquid at room temperature, like monounsaturated fats—is also frequently recommended because it lowers total blood cholesterol even more than monounsaturates do. However, polyunsaturates *also* lower "good" HLD cholesterol and, when eaten in large quantities, have been implicated in cancer, so as with all fats you should limit your intake. Polyunsaturated fats are essential fatty acids. They come in two forms. Omega-6 oils (also known as linoleic acid—LA) are derived mainly from such vegetable oils as safflower, sunflower, corn, canola, soybean, and sesame. Botanicals such as borage oil and evening primrose oil are good sources of LA. Omega-3 oils (or alpha-linolenic acid [A—LNA]) come from marine and fatty fish (such as anchovies, rainbow trout, salmon, mackerel, sardines, and herring), walnuts and walnut oil, flaxseed and flax oil, and pumpkin seeds, as well as canola and soy oil.

Although too much fat is clearly to be avoided, it's important to include *some* unsaturated fat in your diet each day because there are definite health benefits to be derived from small amounts of it. What you want to aim for is to reduce your fat intake to between 15 and 30 percent of your total calories. That equates to about one tablespoon of heart-healthy, immune system-enhancing fat per 1000–1200 calories. So if you are on a 1200-calorie diet, one tablespoon would contribute about 10 percent of your total calories from fat, as would 2 tablespoons on a 2400-calorie diet. Keep the rest of your diet low-fat and you can certainly keep your fat intake to 15–30 percent of your total calories. With a little planning you can keep your fat down.

As mentioned earlier, polyunsaturated fat provides essential fatty acids. Essential fatty acids help produce hormones, promote cell growth, lower cholesterol and triglyceride levels, and may play a protective role in preventing heart disease. Other reasons you need some dietary fat each day: Fat . . .

- aids in the absorption of fat-soluble vitamins and carries them to the body where needed
- helps make calcium available to the bones and teeth by aiding in the body's absorption of fat-soluble vitamin D
- cushions the body's vital organs
- helps prevent heat loss
- is a good source of energy
- is necessary for converting beta-carotene to vitamin A
- is necessary for maintaining healthy skin and hair
- is important for maintaining a healthy nervous system
- slows down digestion and the emptying of food from the stomach, and so produces a longer-lasting sensation of fullness after a meal

You can see that they don't call fat a critical nutrient for no reason—and why going on a fat-free diet is unwise and unhealthy. Just a little bit of fat does a lot of good . . . and goes a long way. While there is no RDA for fat established by the National Research Council, health experts suggest that you keep fat calories to no more than 15–30 percent of your daily total, leaning toward the lower range if you want to lose weight.

WHAT'S CHOLESTEROL AND HOW DO I KNOW IF MINE IS HIGH?

You hear a lot of talk about cholesterol, yet many people don't quite understand what it is. Many consider it a fat, but it isn't. Instead, it's a fatlike substance found only in animal products and manufactured by your own liver. It's a good thing—within limits. Our body uses cholesterol to manufacture cell membranes, produce some sex hormones, and help the body manufacture vitamin D. If you were to consciously attempt to eat a cholesterol-free diet for the rest of your life, that would be fine, because your body makes all it needs for good health. But since it's practically impossible to keep cholesterol out of your diet completely (unless you are a vegetarian), it's important to become aware of six blood lipid (fat) values:

- *Total cholesterol*. This number represents the total amount of cholesterol in your blood, and you probably already know yours. The National Cholesterol Education Program considers a reading of under 200 mg/dl (milligrams per deciliter of blood) desirable; 200–239 mg/dl borderline; and 240 mg/dl or higher indicative of heart disease.

- *High-density lipoproteins (HDLs)*. These are considered "good" cholesterol, as they help the body remove cholesterol from arterial walls and tissues. Regardless of what your total cholesterol is, you should aim for an HDL reading of 35 mg/dl or higher. Levels under 35 mg/dl decrease your risk of cardiovascular disease, while levels over 60 mg/dl add heart protection. Since estrogen, which helps raise HDL levels, diminishes significantly during menopause, you have to make sure to maintain adequate HDLs now through diet, exercise, and, if you choose, estrogen replacement therapy (ERT)/hormone replacement therapy (HRT).

- *Low-density lipoproteins (LDLs)*. These are considered "bad" cholesterol. They carry cholesterol to your blood vessels, tissues, and organs. However, they don't become dangerous until they become oxidized by joining with "free radicals," unstable forms of oxygen produced by such things as eating fried foods, being exposed to sunlight and X rays, and through nutritional deficiencies. Antioxidants in your diet will help prevent free radical oxidation and damage. As with HDL levels, the decline in estrogen during menopause can cause LDL to worsen—in this case, rise. You should aim for an LDL of less than 130 mg/dl.

- *Blood cholesterol ratio.* This is your total cholesterol divided by your HDL. Therefore, if your total cholesterol is 200 and your HDL is 40, your blood cholesterol ratio is 5. You should aim for a number of 4.5 or lower.
- *Lipoprotein (a).* This fat is similar to LDL, and high levels have recently been considered a heart attack risk factor, particularly when LDL levels are also high. A lipoprotein (a) level greater than 0.3 grams per liter of blood increases susceptibility to heart attack.
- *Trigylcerides.* High levels of these body fats—anything over 150 mg/dl—can also put you at risk for heart attack.

Your doctor may warn you that your cholesterol level is too high, but be sure to ask for the exact numbers so you can know what's going on. Since LDL cholesterol is affected by diet, you can lower it by cutting down the amount of total fat, saturated fat, and cholesterol by decreasing the amount of egg yolks, red meat, whole milk dairy products, and shrimp you eat, eliminating the skin on chicken, and increasing the amount of soluble fiber as in oat bran, fruits, some vegetables, cooked dried beans and peas, including some essential fatty acids in your diet. The National Cholesterol Education Program recommends that you keep your intake of cholesterol to under 300 mg a day. (See the following chart.) HDL cholesterol may be directly affected by the food you eat and beverages you drink. For example, too much polyunsaturated fat may reduce your HDLs, while alcoholic beverages can raise HDL levels. You can also boost your HDL number by losing any excess weight, exercising regularly, not smoking, and possibly through ERT/HRT. You may want to track your cholesterol levels to see your pattern over time. Refer to the chart Blood Pressure/Cholesterol Tracking in Chapter 11.

CHOLESTEROL AND SATURATED FAT
CONTENTS OF SELECTED FOODS
(ROUNDED VALUES/PER 100 CALORIES)

Food	Cholesterol (mg)	Saturated fat (g)
Apple, 1	0	0.10
Beef, "select" grade, cooked, 1½ oz.	40	1.5
Bread, whole wheat, 1 slice	0	0.5
Butter, 1 tablespoon	35	7.5
Cheddar cheese, 1 oz.	30	6.0
Chicken, roasted, 2 oz.	45	0.5
Egg, 1, poached	213	1.5
Flounder, baked, 3 oz.	60	0.3
Ice cream, (10% fat), ⅓ cup	20	3.0
Ice cream, (16% fat), ¼ cup	22	3.5
Lentils, cooked, ⅓ cup	0	0
Lettuce, 12 cups	0	0.15
Liver, 2 oz., cooked	220	1.0
Lobster, 4 oz., cooked	80	0.1
Mayonnaise, 1 tablespoon	8	1.5
Milk, nonfat or skim, 1 cup	4	0.3
Milk, whole, ¾ cup	25	4.0
Pasta, cooked, ½ cup	0	0.05
Peanuts, ½ oz.	0	1.0
Pork tenderloin, lean, 2 oz.	50	1.0
Salad dressing, French, 1½ tablespoon	3	2.5
Salmon, canned, 2 oz.	25	1.0
Salmon, cooked, 2 oz.	30	1.0
Shrimp, 3 oz., cooked	165	0.5
Soybean (dried), cooked, 3 oz.	35	0.35
Tofu, 4 oz., hot cooked	0	0
Vegetable oil, (safflower), 1 tablespoon	0	1.0

WATER, WATER EVERYWHERE!

You squeeze your arm or your calf—or pinch your stomach—and you conclude: Yup! That's pretty solid. But the reality is that our bodies are more than half water, with water comprising 80 percent of our blood, 70 percent of our brain, and even 20 percent of our bones. We could survive for weeks without food, but only a few days without water. That's because water is crucial for all bodily functions, from digestion and absorption to the elimination of wastes. Water helps lubricate our joints, carry nutrients throughout the body, regulate body temperature, and keep skin soft and moist.

HOW MUCH WATER IS ENOUGH?

"Six to eight glasses of water a day." That seems to be the magic number we always keep hearing—but how was that number arrived at? It's perfectly logical and mathematical. First off, through perspiration, urination, bowel movements, and just breathing, the body loses about 10–12 cups of water a day. Providing you eat a healthy diet, you'll take in about 3½ cups of water from food. (Vegetables and fruit are about 90 percent water, meat is anywhere from 60–75 percent water, and even dried foods like figs and raisins contain about 20 percent water.) Your body also makes an additional half cup or so of water each day as a by-product of metabolism. Therefore, if you lose about 10 or 12 cups a day, and you restore 4 cups of water through food and metabolism, then you need to drink 6–8 cups more to ensure proper body functioning. If you're an active person, you probably need to drink even more.

How to fulfill your daily quota of water? With filtered or bottled water, or alternate them with such drinks as herbal tea. Don't count caffeinated drinks like coffee, caffeinated tea, or colas toward your daily intake, though. They act as diuretics, and as such they can cause you to urinate—and therefore lose even more water than you just took in.

If you're not much of a water drinker and the thought of 8 cups of water a day is a bit hard to swallow, build up to that level gradually. Start with 3 glasses each day (one with each meal) for a week, then 4 the following week, until you're up to 8. How can you tell if you're taking in enough water? One way . . . if your urine has been dark yellow lately (and you're not taking vitamins), that's a sign that your level of water consumption may be too low. By the time you're up to 8 cups a day, you'll probably see that your urine is pale yellow, as it should be.

Water: A Good Friend, Not Only For Good Health, But If You Want To Lose Weight

Along with all the benefits just described, drinking plenty of water each day may prove to be your biggest support tool in your weight-loss program. While it may *not* directly help you lose fat, drinking plenty of water *does* flush out waste products created when your body breaks down fat. Drinking water also provides a nice feeling of fullness, which can help you keep your appetite under better control. Many of my clients have a couple of glasses of water when they wake up, plus another glass or two before lunch and dinner. This practice not only starts their day off on a positive note but it also helps remind them that they're taking good care of themselves by doing something very healthful. Since water can curb the appetite and create a sense of fullness—and is calorie-free—plain water can support their weight-loss efforts.

In fact, I've noticed in working over the years with menopausal women who are trying to lose weight that, initially, many of them have the tendency to confuse thirst with hunger. So they *eat* when they should really be *drinking water.* In time, they learn to recognize that their bodies are actually craving water, not food. So, if you ever find yourself standing in front of an open refrigerator, scanning the shelves and wondering, "What do I feel like eating?" try *drinking* a glass of water first. That may be all you need to feel satisfied.

BETTER IN A BOTTLE?

These days it's hard to walk down a street or around a mall without seeing one or more women—usually young and fit—toting a bottle of brand-name water. Yes, drinking "designer" water is "in"—but is it superior to what flows for free from your faucet? Not necessarily.

For example, mineral water, well water, and spring water all come from underground sources, and some of it is naturally carbonated. Depending on where the source is, the water will contain varying minerals. Distilled water is water that has been boiled so all the chemicals, minerals, pollutants, bacteria, etc. are removed. Other bottled water, such as seltzer and club soda, is merely processed tap water. Seltzer water is tap water that has added carbonation, while club soda has added carbonation plus salts and minerals. And the quality of both of these will be determined largely by the quality of the tap water used to make them.

As for your *own* tap water, it's possible that contaminants like lead, copper, and cadmium have seeped in, especially if you live in a house or apartment with old plumbing. But letting the water run at full force for about three minutes before you drink the water (or use it for cooking) may clear out any impurities that may have dissolved in it over time. Better yet, a high-quality water filter may get rid of the impurities. Be aware though, that this method doesn't eliminate pesticides, bacteria, or parasites that may be present in the tap water.

In any case, don't let your concern over the purity of what you're drinking interfere with meeting your daily quota of water. You should still aim for six to eight glasses a day.

Vitamins and minerals are essential nutrients too, and I discuss them in the next chapter.

3

Optimizing the Program:
Vitamins and Minerals

Before health food and vitamin stores became fixtures on the American landscape, people generally didn't take vitamin pills or other nutritional supplements. They lived in a "purer" environment and believed that as long as they were eating a "healthy" diet and a variety of foods, they were getting all the nutrients they needed—and, for the most part, they were right. Around the turn of the century, most folks ate more nutrient-rich, whole-grain, unprocessed food, grown in nutrient-rich soil, and they were more physically active. Today, though, it's quite a different story.

Supermarkets of the nineties are brimming with processed food, many of their nutrients stripped from them and their ingredient lists so long and unintelligible that it's often impossible to figure out just what's in that can or bottle, and what vitamins and minerals—if any—remain. Women trying to eat healthfully, yet keep their calories down, are particularly concerned about this situation because with fewer calories, even if their diet is super-healthy, they'll most likely fall short on some important nutrients. Additionally, in today's fast-paced society, you're probably experiencing some stress that goes above and beyond the usual stress of daily living—which, if prolonged, may be digging into your nutritional stores even further. What's more, as you age you generally don't digest, absorb, or use some nutrients as effectively as you did when you were younger. When you put it all together it's little wonder today's woman may be lacking in some critical nutrients and possibly enduring uncomfortable menopausal symptoms.

Hence, the importance of vitamin and mineral supplements. Because it's virtually impossible to obtain all the vitamins and minerals you need from food alone, supplements can make a big difference. But the crucial questions are: how much and what kinds are right for you, at this stage of your life?

THE SUPPLEMENT CONTROVERSY

While large segments of the population feel that there's no doubt about the value of vitamin/mineral supplementation, not everyone has jumped on the supplement bandwagon. There's still a good deal of conflicting information and advice on how best to satisfy one's nutritional needs, ranging from U.S. government recommendations to what your neighborhood health food store suggests. The National Research Council's Food and Nutrition Board has established its recommendations in the form of Recommended Dietary Allowances (RDAs).

Today's RDAs spell out the types and amounts of nutrients the government believes will meet the nutrient needs of healthy people—to prevent deficiency disease—based on age and gender. The RDAs are *not* designed to meet the additional nutrient needs of people who have medical problems or who are stressed, taking medication, or dealing with other particular conditions. The government's stance is that for healthy individuals the recommended amounts of nutrients can be obtained by eating a well-balanced diet, without requiring vitamin/mineral supplementation.

The RDAs are considered by many nutrition experts to be adequate for most adults eating healthy, balanced meals. For example, Wayne Callaway, M.D., an obesity expert who teaches at George Washington University, believes that vitamin and mineral supplements are unnecessary. "I don't generally recommend them unless there is a particular reason," he says. "I feel the RDAs are sufficient for meeting nutritional requirements. The RDAs have built into them a margin of safety of about two to three times what you would need."

Other experts believe that the RDAs are inadequate and much too low. For example, the Alliance for Aging Research, in Washington, D.C., a public health organization, has recently made an official recommendation that older people follow a regimen of vitamin/mineral supplementation as a way to ward off certain life-threatening diseases, such as heart disease and cancer. Their recommendations include, for example, 100–400 International Units (IU) of vitamin E per day—up to 50 times the RDA; and for Vitamin C, 250–1000 milligrams (mg)—up to 16 times the RDA.

As someone trying to lose weight, you should keep in mind, too, that the RDAs are based on about a *2000-calorie-per-day* diet—nearly twice the number of calories you're probably consuming. Which is why F. Xavier Pi-Sunyer, M.D., the director of the Obesity Research Center at St. Luke's-Roosevelt Hospital Center in New York City, believes that any woman who's cutting her calories to lose weight is not getting adequate nutrition from her food. "It is nearly impossible to get all your nutrients if you're on a weight-reducing, 1200-calorie-a-day diet," he insists, and he urges women on weight-reducing programs to take a daily vitamin/mineral supplement with as much as 100 percent of the RDAs. If you're eating 1500 calories a day or more, however, Dr. Pi-Sunyer feels that you're probably getting adequate nutrition from your food and therefore don't require supplements.

There are also doctors and nutritionists who recommend vitamin/minerals pretty much across the board, and I'm one of them. Even if my clients' caloric intake is reasonable and they're eating healthy foods, I feel it's possible that they may not be getting enough nutrients for optimum health, and so I generally recommend supplementation. I also tend to recommend certain vitamins, minerals, and herbs to my menopausal clients as a way to help alleviate their symptoms, including hot flashes, insomnia, and vaginal dryness. And, indeed, many of these women report significant relief from taking vitamin/mineral supplements in either the amounts stated in the RDAs or in higher amounts.

SHOULD YOU TAKE VITAMIN/MINERAL SUPPLEMENTS?

The recommendations offered in the two sections that follow are for menopausal women. You—along with your doctor or nutritionist—are the best judge of what will help you optimize your health and ease your particular menopausal symptoms. In making your decision, you'll both want to take into consideration such factors as your diet history, your (and your family's) medical history (see the list of medical problems on page 44), the results of your complete nutritional laboratory analysis, any medications you may be taking, the severity of your symptoms, and such lifestyle habits as smoking and drinking alcohol. Remember, too, that unlike medication, vitamin/mineral supplements may not be quick-acting—in some cases, you may not feel the impact for weeks or even months. So you need to be patient. If you don't feel the results, you may want to vary your intake until you come up with a formula that works well for you.

And always keep in mind that these are *supplements* to—not replacements for—a sound diet and healthy lifestyle. Whatever supplements you decide to take should not be an excuse to continue or lapse into poor dietary habits. If your goal is to live a long healthy life and ease any menopausal symptoms, you need all your nutrients, working together on a regular basis.

SUPPLEMENTS AND YOUR HEALTH

What could be safer for you than a vitamin pill, right? *Maybe.* You may have a particular health condition that would rule out even the most innocent-looking Flintstone vitamin. Before following any vitamin/mineral regimen, see your doctor and make certain to mention any severe or long-term health problems you may have as well as any medications you may be taking, to make certain supplements won't interfere with their effectiveness. For now, check the partial list that follows. If you suffer from any of these problems, you'll need to take special precautions before using any vitamins and minerals.

- aplastic anemia
- cheilosis (if a result of pellagra)
- diabetes
- gout
- G-6PD deficiency
- hemochromatosis (an iron metabolism disorder)
- hemorrhage
- kidney stones (or a family history of them)
- liver dysfunction
- low or high blood pressure (if active and severe)
- malabsorption syndrome
- normocytic anemia
- peptic ulcer
- polyneuritis
- refractory anemia
- sickle-cell anemia

VITAMIN/MINERAL Q & A

If you haven't been taking supplements all along, you may have a few questions about doing so. Chances are you'll find the answers on the following pages:

Q. How much of any given vitamin or mineral should I be taking now?

A. In the vitamin and mineral charts on pages 51–80 there are suggested ranges within the "conventional" and "alternative" categories. In most cases, the amount provided in the "conventional" category is in line with the RDAs, and provides a good insurance policy to keep the healthy person free from disease. Keep in mind that the intent of the RDAs, as previously stated, is to consume the stated amount of this nutrient through food, not supplementation, as the source of the nutrient. Yet, I am using their stated amount for a different purpose—as the basis for "conventional" vitamin/mineral supplementation.

"Conventional" vs. "Alternative" Medicine

If your idea of what a medical practitioner should be comes closer to Marcus Welby than to Gary Null, then you might be reluctant to follow any recommendation that even hints at "alternative medicine." But if that's the case, you might be closing your eyes to some simple, centuries-old health-care methods that might do you and your health a world of good. A survey by researchers at the Harvard Medical School and reported in the January 28, 1993 issue of the *New England Journal of Medicine* revealed that about one-third of all American adults reported using at least one alternative treatment.

Even the federal government has gotten into the act. Responding to increasing pressure, Congress established the Office of Alternative Medicine (OAM), at the National Institutes of Health in 1992. Although its $2 million budget is considered by many to be a shoestring as far as federal budgets, the OAM is an important acknowledgment by the medical establishment that there's room and, indeed, a need for the exploration and use of alternative practices. A good deal of the research currently being conducted by the OAM involves nutritional healing and includes antioxidant vitamins for treating tumors and herbs in the treatment of Parkinson's disease. After all, what is today considered "alternative" might become common medical practice in the near future.

The values in the "alternative" category are higher and are designed not merely to prevent disease, but to provide optimal intake for health promotion and relief of menopausal symptoms. Keep in mind that these values are averages; some alternative practitioners suggest larger amounts, others smaller amounts.

You should follow your doctor's advice, of course, but I generally recommend that my clients start at the low end of the "alternative" range, providing that there is no contraindication. If you see results, stay with that amount; if not, start increasing the amounts, over a period of several weeks, working your way up to the high end of the range. If, at any time, you find that your system gets upset, cut back your dosages and discuss what you're taking with your doctor or nutritionist.

Q. Should I take all my pills at once?

A. No. Since your body can absorb and use only a limited amount a vitamin or mineral at a time, it's best to divide the dose throughout the day to maximize your body's use of the nutrients. For instance, if you're taking 750 mg of vitamin C each day, take 250 mg at breakfast and the rest with lunch or dinner. In fact, you should take just about all your supplements with your meals. It's a good idea to drink some water when taking a supplement to avoid the possibility of it "repeating" on you.

Q. Why is it best to take supplements with meals?

A. You're more likely to develop indigestion if you take supplements on an empty stomach. Also, taking supplements with food aids in their absorption. Take supplements a few minutes before a meal or up to 30 minutes after. One exception is calcium citrate, which can be taken at any time. Some people take some in the morning and prefer to take the rest right before bed, as it can sometimes relieve insomnia.

Q. What's the difference between natural and synthetic vitamins? Is one type better than the other?

A. "Natural" vitamins are ones made without ingredients such as artificial coloring, preservatives, sugars, starches, or coal tars, while the synthetic kinds may have some of these "extras." The body is believed to use both more or less equally, except for vitamin E; the natural form of vitamin E, called d-alpha tocopherol, may be more absorbable than the synthetic form. (The charts that follow indicate the most absorbable forms of any given vitamin or mineral.) It's always a good idea to go for the natural kind. Be aware that the word "natural" on a label doesn't necessarily mean that the vitamin is extracted *completely* from a natural food source; it might actually be a blend of natural and synthetic, called "co-natural," and therefore cheaper to produce.

Q. What is a "chelated" mineral?

A. A chelated mineral is a mineral that is surrounded by a carrier protein that transports the mineral to the bloodstream. This is done to increase the mineral's absorbability. Generally, chelated minerals are more expensive, and it has yet to be proved definitively that they make a big difference. Besides, when you take a mineral with your meal, your stomach should naturally chelate the mineral during digestion.

Q. What about time-released vitamins?

A. Time-released vitamins are designed to be absorbed and released in the body more slowly, to prolong the availability of the nutrients to the tissues. However, research to date has failed to prove that time-released vitamins offer any real advantage over others.

Q. How can I tell if my supplements are working?

A. That's easy—by the way you feel. If you're taking supplements for general health and disease prevention—and, all other things being equal, you feel better, are more energetic, and have fewer colds, then they're working. Similarly, if you've started taking vitamin E for your hot flashes and they last for a shorter period of time, are less intense, or disappear altogether, then it appears that the vitamins are working. Remember, unlike "quick-relief" pills or powders, vitamins and minerals don't work overnight. You may have to take them for several weeks before you start noticing a positive effect.

Q. Should I start taking all my vitamins and minerals at once?

A. No. It's best to introduce one supplement at a time, then wait two days before introducing the next. This way, if a supplement doesn't agree with you, you'll be able to identify it, and eliminate it or replace it with a different form (e.g., capsule rather than tablet).

VITAMINS

Vitamins are organic compounds required by every part of your body to maintain health and prevent disease. Although needed in only tiny amounts, vitamins are nevertheless vital to life and good health. In most cases they are not produced by the body or are produced in insufficient quantities and so must be obtained from food or supplements. Vitamins help the body digest, absorb, and metabolize the protein, carbohydrates, and fats you eat as well as help regulate growth, metabolism, and cell reproduction. They also ensure the proper functioning of the heart and nervous system.

Vitamins are broken down into two categories, water-soluble and fat-soluble. Water-soluble vitamins include vitamin C and B-complex vitamins—thiamin (B_1), riboflavin (B_2), niacin (B_3), pyridoxine (B_6), folic acid, (B_{12}), pantothenic acid, and biotin. Fat-soluble vitamins include A, D, E, and K. The distinction is important because water-soluble vitamins are absorbed directly into the bloodstream, and any excess is generally eliminated in the urine. This holds true for all the water-soluble vitamins, except B_6, which if consumed in large quantities for long periods of time, may result in toxic-ity symptoms. Fat-soluble vitamins are best absorbed when eaten with fat. However, they can be stored in the body—usually in the liver or tissues—and, when taken in large quantities for long periods of time, may build up to toxic levels. That's why it's important to use them in reasonable and not excessive quantities.

How About Herbs?

You already know that herbs do wonders for perking up meals— a little fresh garlic, a touch of ginger can make for a memorable dish. But lots of people also know that herbs can do wonders for perking up their *health*.

It's really no secret that herbs can be amazingly effective in easing all kinds of physical problems—after all, they've been used by cultures around the world for thousands of years. The Chinese started using herbs to treat illness as early as 5,000 years ago, and today they still do; in fact, there are currently some 6,000 different herbs in the Chinese medicinal repertoire.

You may scoff at the idea of herbal therapy, and prefer prescription drugs, but when you think about it, a drug is just the chemical re-creation of the active ingredient of a plant—the part believed to promote healing. The good news is that drugs are often effective and that the amount of the effective ingredient is controlled and reliable. The bad news is that they can be accompanied by side effects that may be avoided when one uses the whole natural plant.

If you've never thought about trying an herbal remedy for your menopausal symptoms, now may be the time. Consider *dong quai*, a Chinese herb containing estrogen-like plant sterols that may be useful against hot flashes. It comes in capsule form with the suggested dose of 1–3 tablets daily. Or you might want to try ginseng, 1 capsule up to 3 times a day, which may relieve hot flashes and increase your energy. Or try an already-prepared blend of herbs, like the product Liberty Tea, a natural blend of dong quai, licorice root, wild yam, and other plants with estrogen-like properties that is available as a tea. Vitex (agnus castus) is also helpful in reducing discomfort caused by menopause. You may want to try each of these herbs for a couple of weeks, introducing one at a time, to see which works best for you. Remember to always check with your doctor before using any herbs.

In addition to the water- and fat-soluble vitamins listed above, I've included bioflavonoids, choline, inositol, and para-amino-benzoic acid (PABA) in the vitamin section. Although they are not considered true vitamins by the Food and Nutrition Board, they are important "nonvitamins," performing vital functions in the body.

The body requires about 13 different vitamins on a regular basis, and each one is present in varying amounts in specific foods. So for example, let's say you wanted to try to get a daily intake of 100 IU of vitamin E to help with hot flashes, an amount that's midway between the "conventional" thinking and the "alternative" recommendations. To get that strictly from your diet, you'd need to eat:

- 2½ cups of sweet potatoes
- ½ cup wheat germ (2 oz.)
- 2 oz. of almonds
- 4 tablespoons of safflower oil

That combination would pack about 1800 calories—*and* that wouldn't even be your total day's intake. Clearly, it would be nearly impossible to take in 100 IU of vitamin E through food alone *and* try to lose weight at the same time.

Furthermore, even the most nutrient-packed foods lose vitamins in a variety of ways. For example, so-called fresh fruit and vegetables begin losing their nutrients the moment they're picked. By the time "fresh" produce reaches your home, it was probably shipped and stored for several days or longer, further depleting its natural nutrient level—and then you cook it and expose it to heat and/or water, thus decreasing its vitamin content even more. All of which is why vitamin supplements are a smart idea.

VITAMIN CHART

This chart explains the functions, focusing on this stage of your life, and suggested amounts for key vitamins. You will notice that there are two recommended levels of intake, "conventional" and "alternative," both in the chart that follows and in the mineral chart. The amount given for the "conventional" recommendation corresponds, for the most part, to the RDAs. The amount under the "alternative" recommendations is an average; some "alternative" practitioners suggest larger amounts, others smaller amounts.

Keep in mind that certain medications (such as antibiotics), foods (including sugar, alcohol, and caffeine) and lifestyle habits (such as smoking) can interfere with vitamin (and mineral) absorption and thus effectiveness. Also keep in mind that certain vitamins (and minerals) may interfere with medication you may be taking.

VITAMIN A
(ALSO KNOWN AS PREFORMED VITAMIN A)

Function
- aids in growth and repair of body tissue
- helps maintain healthy skin, hair, and eyes (prevents night blindness)
- keeps tissues of the uterus, cervix, vagina, urinary tract, and other mucous membranes lubricated and increases resistance to infections in these areas
- helps maintain the intestinal walls so nutrients, especially calcium, can be absorbed
- has been shown in some cases to protect against cancer

Found In
- liver
- fish liver oil (from cod, halibut, and salmon)
- egg yolks
- cheese and fortified milk products
- spinach, collard greens, turnips, beet greens, and other dark green leafy vegetables

Most-Absorbable Forms
vitamin A palmitate or vitamin A acetate

Recommended Daily Dosage
    Conventional: 4000 IU
    Alternative: 10,000 IU

BETA-CAROTENE (ALSO KNOWN AS PRO-VITAMIN A)

Function
  • when converted by the body into vitamin A, acts as an antioxidant and may help prevent heart disease and some types of cancers.

Found In
  • oranges, apricots, papayas, cantaloupe, and other deep yellow fruits
  • sweet potatoes
  • carrots
  • dark green vegetables such as spinach, broccoli, romaine lettuce

Most-Absorbable Form
    beta-carotene

Recommended Daily Dosage
    Conventional: 6 mg
    Alternative: 30–50 mg

A Word about Vitamin A and Beta-Carotene

There's been a lot of controversy recently about the pros and cons of supplemental antioxidants, which include vitamin A, beta-carotene, vitamin E, and selenium. One recent Finnish study *seemed* to disprove years of evidence that antioxidant supplementation (specifically vitamin E and beta-carotene), when taken in amounts larger than the RDA, help prevent chronic disease. The study was considered by many experts to be questionable, and so the many benefits that have been attributed to antioxidant supplementation should not be disregarded.

Is it best to take vitamin A or beta-carotene? You should try to get as much of your vitamin A in the form of beta-carotene as possible because it is water-soluble, and any excess is not stored in the body. Also, because excess beta-carotene is quickly excreted from the body, you need to take it regularly.

You may want to take additional beta-carotene the days during, before, and after having a mammogram, which some experts believe might protect you against the free radicals from X ray exposure.

B VITAMINS

Function

- help maintain a healthy nervous system that can ward off moodiness, irritability, and fatigue resulting from the body's hormonal fluctuations during menopause.
- increase energy levels, since B vitamins are involved in the proper metabolism of protein, carbohydrates, and fat.
- keep the liver functioning properly
- help in the proper functioning of the adrenal glands, the main supplier of the hormone androstenedione, which is converted into estrone, the form of estrogen available during menopause.
- help strengthen the body's resistance to disease and infection
- keep vaginal membranes lubricated during and after menopause

A Word about B Vitamins

Because B vitamins work closely together, it's not a good idea to increase your intake of one B vitamin without increasing your intake of all the others. Keeping a good balance of B vitamins will help maximize absorption by the body.

As with other water-soluble vitamins, B vitamins can be destroyed in cooking liquids. So, to cut down on nutrient loss, cook in small quantities of liquids, steam vegetables instead of boiling them, etc.

Continuous emotional and/or physical stress may increase your B vitamin requirements.

In addition to the benefits previously mentioned, each B vitamin has its own unique benefits:

THIAMIN (B₁)

Function
- keeps membranes, including the vaginal lining, moist
- keeps skin, nails, and hair healthy

Found In
- brewer's yeast
- whole grains, including brown rice and whole-grain breads
- enriched flours and cereals
- meat (especially pork), poultry, and fish
- organ meats, especially liver
- egg yolks
- cooked dried beans and peas
- peanuts

Most-Absorbable Forms
thiamin pyrophosphate, mononitrate, or thiamin hydrochloride

Recommended Daily Dosage
Conventional: 1 mg
Alternative: 10–50 mg

RIBOFLAVIN (B₂)

Function
- may prevent cataracts
- may, in combination with B₆, be useful in treating carpal tunnel syndrome
- deficiency may increase susceptibility to carcinogenic effects of other substances

Found In
- milk, cheese, and other dairy products
- egg yolks
- enriched or whole-grain products
- cooked dried beans, peas, and lentils
- green vegetables including broccoli, turnip greens, asparagus, and spinach

Most-Absorbable Forms
riboflavin or riboflavin-5-phosphate

Recommended Daily Dosage
Conventional: 1.2 mg
Alternative: 10–50 mg

A Word about Riboflavin
Riboflavin is destroyed by light, so be sure to buy milk in opaque containers rather than clear glass or plastic bottles, and store enriched breads and cereals in containers that keep light out.

Estrogens in ERT/HRT can interfere with riboflavin absorption, so supplementation is especially important if you're taking ERT/HRT.

NIACIN (B₃)

FUNCTION
- dilates blood vessels, which can often relieve headache.
- may help reduce cholesterol and triglyceride levels

Found In
- meat, poultry, and fish (especially the white meat of turkey and tuna)
- enriched or whole-grain products
- milk and eggs

Most-Absorbable Forms
niacin or niacinamide

Recommended Daily Dosage
    Conventional: 13 mg
    Alternative: 10–50 mg

A Word about Niacin
    When taking niacin supplements, be sure it's in the form of niacin or niacinamide. Other forms of niacin dilate the blood vessels, which may help to relieve headaches but might make your hot flashes worse.

B$_6$ (PYRIDOXINE)

Function
- helps alleviate bloating and water retention
- when combined with vitamin C, helps promote restful sleep, calmness, and relief of tension headaches
- boosts the immune system
- aids in decreasing the risk of heart disease

Found In
- meats, including organ meats, and the white meat of turkey and tuna
- whole-grain products
- wheat germ
- dried cooked beans, peas, and lentils
- nuts

Most-Absorbable Form
    pyridoxine-5-phosphate or pyridoxine hydrochloride

Recommended Daily Dosage
    Conventional: 1.6 mg
    Alternative: 10–50 mg

A Word about B$_6$
    Estrogens in ERT/HRT can interfere with B$_6$ absorption, so supplementation is especially important if you're taking ERT/HRT.

Magnesium and riboflavin enhance B_6 absorption, so be sure to take these nutrients so that your B_6 is properly absorbed.

FOLIC ACID

Function
- helps the body manufacture and use estrogen
- believed to help prevent cervical dysplasia, a precursor to cervical cancer
- promotes the formation of healthy red blood cells, which helps to prevent anemia
- is an anticarcinogen and aids in decreasing the risk of heart disease.
- involved in the development of all tissue

Found In
- brewer's yeast
- beef and chicken liver
- spinach, collard greens, romaine, broccoli, and other dark green leafy vegetables
- dried cooked beans, peas, chickpeas, cowpeas, and soybeans

Most-Absorbable Form
folic acid

Recommended Daily Dosage
Conventional: 180 mcg
Alternative: 400 mcg

CHOLINE

Function
- helps maintain the health of the liver, which, in turn, helps convert estradiol—in excess a potentially harmful type of estrogen available during your pre- and perimenopausal years—into a less carcinogenic form
- strengthens weak capillary walls, which may reduce high blood pressure

- may decrease blood cholesterol levels and protect against heart disease

Found In
- brewer's yeast
- egg yolks
- organ meats
- wheat germ
- fish
- dried cooked beans, soybeans, peas, and lentils
- cauliflower and lettuce

Most-Absorbable Form
lecithin

Recommended Daily Dosage
Conventional: 400–900 mg
Alternative: 1000 mg

A Word about Choline
Choline is not considered a vitamin by the Food and Nutrition Board, but is included here because it is an important "non-vitamin."

INOSITOL

Function
- aids in fat metabolism and thus can help lower cholesterol levels
- vital for hair growth and may prevent thinning and baldness

Found In
- whole grains
- brewer's yeast
- citrus fruits
- meat

- milk
- vegetables

Most-Absorbable Form
    inositol

Recommended Daily Dosage
    Conventional: 400–900 mg
    Alternative: 1000 mg

A Word about Inositol
    Inositol is not considered a vitamin by the Food and Nutrition Board, but is included here because it is an important "nonvitamin."

PABA (PARA-AMINOBENZOIC ACID)

Function
- important for maintaining healthy skin, hair pigmentation, and intestinal health
- acts as a sunscreen
- helps in the metabolism of protein

Found In
- organ meats
- wheat germ
- yogurt
- leafy green vegetables

Most-Absorbable Form
    para-aminobenzoic acid

Recommended Daily Dosage
    Conventional: none established
    Alternative: none established

A Word about PABA
    PABA is not considered a vitamin by the Food and Nutrition

Board, but is included here because it is an important "nonvitamin."

PANTOTHENIC ACID

Function
- needed for the synthesis of hormones
- may lower blood levels of cholesterol and triglycerides, which, in turn, helps reduce risk of heart disease
- keeps adrenal glands functioning properly

Found In
- brewer's yeast
- egg yolks
- cooked dried beans, peas, and lentils
- lean meats
- wheat germ

Most-Absorbable Forms
pantothenic acid or calcium pantothenate

Recommended Daily Dosage
Conventional: 4–7 mg
Alternative: 10–50 mg

B_{12}

Function
- keeps cells, blood, and nervous system healthy (a deficiency can cause pernicious anemia)
- a B_{12} deficiency may be linked to Alzheimer-like dementia
- helps lower risk of heart disease

Found In
- meat and fish
- dairy products
- eggs

Most-Absorbable Form
  hydroxycobalamin

Recommended Daily Dosage
  Conventional: 2 mcg
  Alternative: 10–50 mcg

A WORD ABOUT B₁₂

Estrogens in ERT/HRT may interfere with B_{12} absorption, so supplementation is especially important if you're taking ERT/HRT.

BIOTIN

Function
  • essential for the absorption of vitamin C
  • keeps skin healthy
  • thinning deficiency may lead to hair loss and thin, splitting nails.

Found In
  • whole grains
  • egg yolks
  • liver
  • brewer's yeast
  • saltwater fish, including sardines
  • dried cooked beans, peas, and lentils

Most-Absorbable Form
  d-biotin

Recommended Daily Dosage
  Conventional: 30–100 mcg
  Alternative: 30–100 mcg

A Word about Biotin
  Estrogen interferes with biotin absorption, so if you are taking ERT/HRT, keep this in mind.

BIOFLAVONOIDS

Function
- antioxidants, they are believed to help ward off certain cancers and strengthen the immune system
- help to control hot flashes since they have a chemical activity similar to that of estrogen
- strengthen and maintain capillary walls and, as a result, may relieve heavy menstrual flow
- decrease the rate of LDL oxidation and so can decrease the risk of heart disease
- strengthen and maintain collagen, which helps the skin to maintain its elasticity and smoothness and may decrease wrinkling

Found In
- citrus fruits
- black currants

Most-Absorbable Form
bioflavonoid hesperiden

Recommended Daily Dosage
Conventional: none established
Alternative: 1000 mg

A word about Bioflavonoids
Bioflavonoids are not considered vitamins by the Food and Nutrition Board, but are included here because they are an important "nonvitamin."

VITAMIN C

Function
- as an antioxidant, vitamin C may help ward off certain cancers including cervical dysplasia, the precursor to cervical cancer
- decreases the rate of LDL oxidation and so may reduce the risk of heart disease

- helps fight infection and heal wounds
- aids in the absorption of iron
- promotes healthy teeth and gums
- helps form collagen, the protein vital to keeping skin, blood vessels, muscles, and bones intact, and in so doing may help prevent osteoporosis and keep skin from sagging
- helps maintain the health of the adrenal glands, which produce the hormone androstenedione, which is converted into estrogen and is the main source of estrogen during menopause
- may reduce the growth of bacteria in the intestinal tract and therefore help prevent/treat vaginal and bladder infections
- may help keep vaginal tissues lubricated during and after menopause
- protects against cataracts
- may reduce blood pressure
- when combined with vitamin B_6, helps promote restful sleep, calmness, and relief of tension headaches

Found In
- oranges, grapefruit, and other citrus fruit
- strawberries, cantaloupe, and honeydew
- vegetables including broccoli, red and green peppers, tomatoes, asparagus, and Brussels sprouts
- dark green and yellow leafy vegetables, including spinach
- potatoes

Most-Absorbable Forms
calcium ascorbate (nonacidic) or ascorbic acid

Recommended Daily Dosage
Conventional: 60 mg (100 for smokers)
Alternative: 500–2000 mg

A Word about Vitamin C

Vitamin C is easily destroyed by cooking, as well as by exposure to light, air, and water. When preparing vitamin C-rich fruits and vegetables, cook them as quickly as possible, using as little liquid as possible—e.g., steam them instead of boiling.

You may want to take the highest-recommended doses of vitamin C if you are undergoing surgery or taking ERT/HRT, experience high levels of stress, or smoke cigarettes (or are regularly exposed to passive smoke).

Vitamin C supplements in large doses may cause diarrhea, excessive urination, dry nose, and/or skin rashes. If you're experiencing such unpleasant side effects, reduce the dosage.

VITAMIN D

Function
- promotes healthy bones by improving the way calcium and phosphorus are absorbed and used by the body
- may help prevent certain types of cancer

Found In
- fatty fish, such as salmon, sardines, and herring
- fortified milk and milk products
- some fortified cereals
- egg yolks

Most-Absorbable Forms
  D_2, D_3, or calciferol

Recommended Daily Dosage
  Conventional: 200 IU
  Alternative: 400 IU

A Word about Vitamin D

Vitamin D is often called the "sunshine vitamin" because it can be made within your skin if you're exposed to sunlight for at least 20 minutes a day. However, skin is less effective at synthesizing vitamin D as you age, so eating foods high in vitamin D is vital, along with supplementation. Also, sunscreens may interfere with the body's ability to synthesize vitamin D.

VITAMIN E

Function
- as an antioxidant, vitamin E helps keep other nutrients from being destroyed by oxidation and, in so doing, might prevent heart disease and certain types of cancer
- slows the effects of aging by preventing oxidation and the resulting deterioration of body cells and skin
- helps in the production of sex hormones, which may explain why vitamin E may relieve hot flashes and certain cases of vaginitis
- relieves dry, itchy skin and vaginal dryness
- may help relieve headaches and migraines

Found In
- cold-pressed vegetable oils, including corn, cottonseed, and safflower
- eggs
- wheat germ
- organ meats
- whole grains
- nuts, including almonds, peanuts, and walnuts

Most-Absorbable Forms
d-alpha tocopherol acetate or dl-alpha tocopherol acetate

Recommended Daily Dosage
Conventional: 8 IU
Alternative: 100–800 IU

A Word about Vitamin E
Vitamin E supplementation may not be recommended for women with diabetes, rheumatic heart disease, high blood pressure, or those who take blood-thinning medication or aspirin regularly without a doctor's okay.

Note that the recommended dosage varies depending on which menopausal symptoms you're treating. (Refer to Chapter 4 for specific dosages.)

Vitamin E is available in pills taken orally, in suppository form, and in capsules that are opened and applied directly to vaginal tissues. Try different forms to see which you prefer and which works best for you.

Estrogen may interfere with the absorption of vitamin E, so if you're taking ERT/HRT, you may need to increase your intake of vitamin E.

VITAMIN K

Function
- helps the blood clot properly
- protects against osteoporosis by aiding in calcium absorption and retention

Found In
- dark green leafy vegetables, including spinach and green cabbage
- cauliflower
- egg yolks
- cooked dried beans, especially soybeans
- liver

Most-Absorbable Forms
  K_1 or K_2

Recommended Daily Dosage
  Conventional: 65 mcg
  Alternative: 70–140 mcg

A Word about Vitamin K
Although vitamin K can be created by the bacteria in your intestines, long-term antibiotic use can interfere with this process. Hormonal changes and changes in bone metabolism during menopause seem to indicate the need for extra vitamin K through diet and supplementation.

If you are taking aspirin or medication to "thin" your blood, check with your doctor before taking vitamin K.

MINERALS

Minerals are substances necessary for regulating various body processes. They are contained in the tissues and internal fluids of the body as well as in bones, teeth, soft tissue, muscle, blood, and nerve cells. Minerals are necessary for maintaining skeletal structures; keeping the heart, brain, and muscle systems working properly; and for the production of hormones.

The minerals essential for good health fall into two categories: major minerals (macrominerals) and trace minerals (microminerals). Major minerals, which include calcium, phosphorus, chloride, sodium, potassium, sulfur, and magnesium, are found in the body in amounts greater than five grams and are measured in milligrams (mg). The remaining minerals include, for example, copper, chromium, iodine, iron, molybdenum, nickel, manganese, fluorine, selenium, and zinc. They are found in the body in amounts of fewer than five grams, and are measured in micrograms (mcg).

Minerals function interdependently, so it's important to maintain a delicate balance between and among them. For example, calcium and magnesium, in the proper amounts, work together in regulating bone formation, muscle contraction, and nerve function. But when there's too much calcium in your body, it can impair the absorption of magnesium. So achieving balance is critical, and the following chart will tell you how.

MINERAL CHART

BORON

Function
- prevents bone loss and may enhance bone density
- may raise blood levels of estrogen of post-menopausal women not on ERT/HRT to levels comparable to those of women who are

Found In
- apples, pears, and other fruits
- broccoli, carrots, and other green and dark yellow vegetables
- almonds and hazelnuts

Most-Absorbable Form
boron

Recommended Daily Dosage
Conventional: 1–2 mg
Alternative: 3–6 mg

A Word about Boron
Boron is not considered a mineral by the Food and Nutrition Board, but is included here because it is an important "nonmineral."

CALCIUM

Function
- helps prevent osteoporosis by aiding in the development and maintenance of strong bones and teeth
- helps the blood clot properly
- helps wounds heal faster
- essential for proper functioning of the heart
- may lower blood pressure
- may help prevent colon and rectal cancer (provided your vitamin D intake is adequate)
- helps regulate muscle contractions
- necessary for nerve transmissions
- gives strength and structure to all body cells

Found In
- nonfat or low-fat milk, yogurt, and dairy products
- canned sardines and salmon (with bones)
- collard greens, mustard greens, broccoli, and other dark green leafy vegetables
- calcium-fortified cereals and juices
- tofu made with calcium sulfate

Most-Absorbable Forms
calcium citrate, calcium carbonate, or calcium hydroxyapatic

Recommended Daily Dosage
Conventional: 1000–1500 mg
Alternative: 1500 mg

A Word about Calcium

You need more calcium now than you did, for example, in your late thirties or early forties because, as you age, your body is only able to absorb about 20–40 percent of the calcium you take in, whereas children can absorb around 75 percent. And because estrogen aids in calcium absorption, the loss of estrogen you're experiencing during menopause can compound the problem. Calcium absorption is decreased by a number of factors, including drinking excessive amounts of alcohol; consuming too many caffeinated foods and beverages, such as chocolate and coffee; eating/drinking too many foods high in phosphorus, such as carbonated soda; eating too much animal protein, dairy products, or foods high in phytate, a phosphorus-like substance found in whole-grain breads; eating too many foods high in oxalic acid such as spinach, asparagus, and chocolate; and using excessive amounts of sodium (salt) bicarbonate and sugar. In addition to excesses, a lack of critical nutrients can also decrease calcium absorption. For example, calcium requires vitamin D for absorption, so a deficiency of vitamin D can result in decreased calcium absorption.

If you experience bloating, gas, or diarrhea soon after having milk or foods containing milk, you may be lactose intolerant. This means that you may be deficient in—or lack—the enzyme lactase, which aids in milk digestion. As you age, the body's supply of lactase, the enzyme that helps you digest milk, generally decreases. If you feel that you are lactose intolerant, try drinking a smaller portion of milk at a given time, for example ½ cup rather than one cup, to see if reducing the quantity alleviates the problem. Or try eating yogurt with active cultures (which is another way of saying live bacteria, since they provide their own lactose-digesting enzymes and continue to digest the yogurt's lactose even further, once inside your digestive tract). Or, in place of drinking milk you may want to try reduced-lactose low-fat milk, sold under names like Lactaid and Dairy Ease, or droplets you can add to your milk.

Avoid calcium supplements made of bone meal, dolomite, and oyster shells, as they may be contaminated with lead. Also try to stay away from antacids, as they may contain toxic metals, such as aluminum, and can also neutralize the stomach acid that is needed for calcium absorption.

If you've been experiencing gassiness and you normally take your calcium citrate before bedtime, try dividing up the dose, taking some with each meal. Otherwise, switch to another form of calcium, such as calcium carbonate. This form, unlike calcium citrate, should be taken with meals.

CHLORINE

Function
- helps regulate the body's acid-base balance
- stimulates the production of hydrochloric acid, which is necessary for digestion and calcium absorption, which typically decreases with age.

Found In
- table salt
- seafood
- meats
- ripe olives

Most-Absorbable Form
chlorine

Recommended Daily Dosage
Conventional: 0 (adequate amounts derived from food)
Alternative: 0 (adequate amounts derived from food)

CHROMIUM

Function
- helps in the metabolism of carbohydrates and fats, as well as in the synthesis of protein

- helps insulin transport sugar from the blood to the body cells and, in so doing, keeps glucose levels normal
- helps prevent heart disease by keeping levels of LDL ("bad") cholesterol low and HDL ("good") cholesterol high

Found In
- whole-grain products
- brewer's yeast
- meat
- liver

Most-Absorbable Form
chromium piccolinate

Recommended Daily Dosage
Conventional: 50–200 mcg
Alternative: 200–600 mcg

A Word about Chromium
You may be hearing a lot about the value of chromium piccolinate supplementation—the positive impact it has on building muscle, reducing body fat, changing body composition, decreasing weight, or increasing strength. Yet the latest study reported April 29, 1994, by the U.S. Department of Agriculture Human Nutrition Reseach Center, did not support these findings.

However, the general value of chromium is not being questioned. Stick to whole-grain foods as much as possible, since refined grain foods—white bread, refined cereals, and sugar—are actually low in chromium. These same foods actually *require* chromium in order to be used by the body. If these types of foods are eaten regularly, they may over time deplete the body's chromium stores and create a chromium deficiency.

COPPER

Function
- maintains the health of blood vessels, nerves, and the immune system

- necessary for healthy bone development and maintenance
- protects against cardiovascular disease by decreasing total cholesterol, reducing "bad" LDLs, and increasing "good" HDLs
- helps wounds heal
- aids in the absorption of iron which, in turn, aids the formation of hemoglobin in red blood cells

Found In
- oysters and other shellfish
- nuts, especially almonds
- dried cooked beans, peas, and lentils
- organ meats, especially liver
- whole-grain products

Most-Absorbable Form
copper gluconate

Recommended Daily Dosage
Conventional: 0 (adequate amounts derived from food)
Alternative: 0 (adequate amounts derived from food)

A Work about Copper
Try to cook your food in copper cookware. Small amounts of copper will actually seep into your food and boost your body's copper supply.

FLUORIDE

Function
- helps prevent tooth decay and gum disease
- believed to help in the formation and maintenance of bones and teeth

Found In
- fluoridated water
- seafood
- tea
- fluoridated dental rinses

Most-Absorbable Form
fluoride

Recommended Daily Dosage
Conventional: 0 (adequate amounts derived from food/water)
Alternative: 0 (adequate amounts derived from food/water)

IODINE

Function
- aids in the proper functioning of the thyroid gland, which regulates the metabolic rate and in so doing helps burn calories efficiently and sustains energy levels
- keeps hair, nails, teeth, and skin healthy

Found In
- iodized salt
- seafood
- seaweed

Most-Absorbable Form
sea kelp (tablets or concentrated drops)

Recommended Daily Dosage
Conventional: 0 (adequate amounts derived from food)
Alternative: 0 (adequate amounts derived from food)

IRON

Function
Helps deliver oxygen to body tissues and in so doing prevents iron-deficiency anemia, which can lead to excessive bruising, stress, extreme fatigue, and increased susceptibility to illness

Found In
- poultry, meat, and fish
- iron-enriched cereals and breads
- liver

- dried fruits, especially prunes
- green leafy vegetables

Most-Absorbable Form
iron fumerate or iron glycinate

Recommended Daily Dosage
Conventional: 0 (adequate amounts derived from food)
Alternative: 0 (adequate amounts derived from food)

A Word about Iron
Iron deficiencies are more prevalant among premenopausal women, who lose blood every month through menstruation, than among menopausal women. If your monthly periods are over or nearly over, it is easier to get adequate amounts of iron through the food you eat, providing you eat healthfully. If you're trying to lose weight by decreasing your food intake, you may also be cutting out some iron-rich foods. Over time, this can increase your susceptibility to iron deficiency. However, since recent studies suggest that excess iron in the blood may lead to cancer and heart disease if your LDL cholesterol level is high, iron supplementation is *not* generally recommended for menopausal women, who do not have regular menstrual cycles, and for post-menopausal women. You should be able to get adequate amounts of iron from your diet if you plan well, since your iron needs are lower as a postmenopausal woman. Keep in mind that iron absorption from animal sources is better than from plant sources.

To enhance your body's absorption of iron, cook acidic food like tomatoes in iron pots (some of the minerals from the cookware will seep into the food), and combine iron-rich foods with foods high in vitamin C.

Magnesium

Function
- essential for building and maintaining bones and so helps prevent osteoporosis

- helps regulate nerve and muscle function and so helps promote muscle relaxation
- aids in the conversion of blood sugar, stored in the liver as glycogen, into energy
- promotes the absorption and metabolism of calcium, phosphorus, sodium, vitamins C and E, and other nutrients
- protects against heart disease and blood clots, and may increase the survival rate after heart attack if given in very large doses immediately following the attack

Found In
- whole-grain products
- dark green leafy vegetables
- dried cooked beans, especially soybeans
- nuts, especially almonds
- meat, fish, and seafood
- milk and dairy products

Most-Absorbable Forms
magnesium citrate, magnesium glycinate, magnesium aspartate

Recommended Daily Dosage
Conventional: 280 mg
Alternative: 400–600 mg

MANGANESE

Function
- necessary for bone growth and maintenance and so helps prevent osteoporosis
- keeps adrenal glands healthy by helping the body use vitamins B and C
- aids in the production of sex hormones
- helps regulate insulin and therefore contributes to a healthy blood sugar balance
- may act as an antioxidant, thus playing a role in preventing cancer and heart disease

Found In
- nuts
- spinach and other green leafy vegetables
- whole-grain products
- egg yolks

Most-Absorbable Forms
manganese piccolinate or manganese gluconate

Recommended Daily Dosage
    Conventional: 2–5 mg
    Alternative: 2–5 mg

MOLYBDENUM

Function
- activates the body's enzymes so that iron is mobilized from liver stores and can be used by the body, and so that fat can be burned
- maintains normal growth and development

Found In
- whole-grain products
- dried cooked beans and peas
- dark green leafy vegetables
- liver

Most-Absorbable Form
    molybdenum

Recommended Daily Dosage
    Conventional: 75–250 mcg
    Alternative: 75–250 mcg

PHOSPHORUS

Function
- works hand in hand with calcium to build strong bones and teeth and thus ward off osteoporosis

- vital for energy production
- stimulates muscle contraction

Found In
- poultry, meat, and fish
- dairy products
- eggs
- dried cooked beans and peas
- nuts
- carbonated soft drinks (limit intake)

Most-Absorbable Form
phosphorus

Recommended Daily Dosage
Conventional: 0 (adequate amounts derived from food)
Alternative: 0 (adequate amounts derived from food)

POTASSIUM

Function
- helps regulate the activity of the heart, thyroid gland, muscles, nerves, and kidneys
- along with sodium, helps regulate water balance in the body and so prevents water retention and bloating
- low levels may be associated with high blood pressure, stroke, and heart disease

Found In
- fresh and dried fruits
- whole-grain products
- dried cooked beans, peas, and lentils
- tomatoes and potatoes

Most-Absorbable Form
potassium (liquid or tablet)

Recommended Daily Dosage
    Conventional: 0 (adequate amounts derived from food)
    Alternative: 0 (adequate amounts derived from food)

SELENIUM

Function
- as an antioxoidant, selenium enhances the body's immune system and helps protect against cancer and heart disease
- preserves the elasticity of tissues, including those of the vagina and urinary tract
- may help alleviate hot flashes

Found In
- fish and shellfish
- whole-grain products
- red meat/organ meats

Most-Absorbable Forms
selenomethionine or sodium selenite

Recommended Daily Dosage
    Conventional: 55 mcg
    Alternative: 100–200 mcg

SODIUM

Function
- helps the thyroid gland function properly
- helps maintain water balance in the body

Found In
- table salt
- baking powder and baking soda
- pickles and other products packed in brine
- smoked foods
- processed/prepared convenience foods

Most-Absorbable Form
sodium

Recommended Daily Dosage
Conventional: 0 (adequate amounts derived from food)
Alternative: 0 (adequate amounts derived from food)

A Word about Sodium
Salt-sensitive people can retain excess sodium in their tissues, which leads to fluid retention and may cause high blood pressure. If you're one of these people, be particularly cautious about the amount of sodium in your diet, and read food labels carefully.

ZINC

Function
- aids in digestion and absorption of nutrients
- as an antioxidant, zinc helps boost the body's immune system and protects against cancer and heart disease
- reduces total cholesterol and raises "good" HDL cholesterol, thereby preventing heart disease
- speeds the healing of wounds
- helps insulin deliver sugar from the blood to the cells

Found In
- meat and poultry, especially dark meat
- oysters and other seafood
- liver
- eggs
- dried cooked beans and peas
- whole-grain products

Most-Absorbable Forms
zinc piccolinate, zinc gluconate

Recommended Daily Dosage
Conventional: 12 mg
Alternative: 15–25 mg

A SAMPLE DAY'S VITAMIN AND MINERAL
SUPPLEMENTATION CHART

Vitamin/Mineral	Conventional	Alternative
Vitamin A	4000 IU	10,000 IU
Beta-carotene	6 mg	30–50 mg
Thiamin (B₁)	1 mg	10–50 mg
Riboflavin (B₂)	1.2 mg	10–50 mg
Niacin (B₃)	13 mg	10–50 mg
B₆ (Pyridoxine)	1.6 mg	10–50 mg
Folic acid	180 mcg	400 mcg
Choline	400–900 mg	1000 mg
Inositol	400–900 mg	1000 mg
Pantothenic acid	4–7 mg	10–50 mg
Para-aminobenzoic acid	*	*
B₁₂	2 mcg	10–50 mcg
Biotin	30–100 mcg	30–100 mcg
Bioflavonoids	none established	1000 mg
Vitamin C	60 mg	500–2000 mg
Vitamin D	200 IU	400 IU
Vitamin E	8 IU	100–800 IU
Vitamin K	65 mcg	70–140 mcg
Boron	1–2 mg	3–6 mg
Calcium	1000–1500 mg	1500 mg
Chloride	*	*
Chromium	50–200 mcg	200–600 mcg
Copper	*	*
Fluoride	*	*
Iodine	*	*
Iron	*	*
Magnesium	280 mg	400–600 mg
Manganese	2–5 mg	2–5 mg
Molybdenum	75–250 mcg	75–250 mcg
Phosphorus	*	*
Potassium	*	*
Selenium	55 mcg	100–200 mcg
Sodium	*	*
Zinc	12 mg	15–25 mg

*Adequate amounts derived from food.

If you find it too difficult to put together your own vitamin/mineral formula, you may find it easier—and just as effective—to choose a single multivitamin/mineral tablet available from such manufacturers as Schiff, Solgar, Wellness By Design, or Twin Labs. Read the labels carefully. If the product you buy is low in one particular vitamin or mineral, you might want to buy that specific supplement separately as well.

THE DIETARY SUPPLEMENT HEALTH AND EDUCATION ACT

The Dietary Supplement Health and Education Act requires a label on dietary supplements to show how much of the RDA is contained in the product. This is consistent with the terminology on the food label. (See Appendix B for more information).

This bill is an attempt to improve the safety of dietary supplements, including vitamins, minerals, herbs, botanicals, amino acids, concentrates, and extracts. Some of the major provisions include: the substantiation of health or nutrition claims made on the label about curing or preventing a disease; increasing consumer information by displaying scientific literature at the point of purchase; printing expiration dates on all supplements; establishing the National Institutes of Health Office of Dietary Supplements to encourage research on the health benefits of supplements; and setting up a Presidential Commission on Dietary Supplements to make recommendations about label claims on dietary supplements. The commission will report to the FDA.

Unlike new drugs and food additives, dietary supplements currently on the market require no FDA scrutiny. Rather, the FDA bears the burden of proving dietary supplements unsafe before it can pull them off the shelf. New ingredients will require FDA approval for safety, but not effectiveness before they can be put on the store shelf. Yet there are some unanswered questions, not addressed in the bill, including: What doses are effective? What dose is considered an excess or toxic? This is, nevertheless, a good beginning.

4

Treating the Symptoms, Cutting the Risk

Whatever your stage of menopause right now—whether you're just in the earliest phases or your last menstrual period was a year ago—your body's been going through some remarkable changes for which no one could have fully prepared you. To think you might be untouched by all these changes is a bit unrealistic. After all, some *three hundred different kinds of tissues* in a woman's body—the vagina, breasts, bones, hair, heart, and skin, to name just a few—are affected by estrogen. And progesterone is a key player too—it affects your adrenal glands' hormone production, as well as your bone, vaginal, skin, and hair health—just to mention a few. So as your estrogen and progesterone levels drop, you're bound to experience some sort of variation on the ways you typically look and even the way you think about yourself.

But perhaps you are one of the lucky women *not* experiencing any symptoms. Although it may be hard to believe, in light of the tremendous role these hormones play in the body, a symptom-free menopause may indeed happen, so don't go looking for symptoms if you don't have them! Also, keep in mind that your body's reactions to menopause and the way you handle it may vary depending on such factors as your genetic makeup, culture, body build, coping abilities, and attitude about menopause—and, as you'll learn in the chapters to come, the foods you eat, the vitamins and minerals you take, how much and what type of exercise you do, and the way you manage your response to stress.

You'll also learn in this chapter about synthetic and natural estrogen replacement therapy (ERT) and hormone replacement therapy (HRT)—the risks and benefits.

If you've started your journey through menopause, you may have tried some old family "remedy" for hot flashes, or a neighbor's sure-fire "cure" for those mood swings that have made your significant other think you've lost your mind. Perhaps these remedies have worked—but the odds are they haven't done the whole job, and you're ready to try almost *anything* to feel better. Luckily, most of the treatments I'll suggest—which have worked wonders for many of my menopausal clients—are simply a matter of eating a bit differently from the way you usually do, or adding some exercise to your life. Or you may experience tremendous relief by adding vitamins and minerals or upping your daily intake. Or, estrogen replacement therapy (ERT)/hormone replacement therapy (HRT) may be the answer for you. You may be pleasantly surprised at how little it takes for you to get back on track and ease some of the obvious signs of menopause, as well as cut your risk for potential long-term health problems like heart disease, osteoporosis, and cancer, which might not make their presence known until years from now, if at all.

As you'll see, I'll discuss many menopausal symptoms, but the list is not all-inclusive. The symptoms have been divided into two categories: the physical and the emotional. These are followed by diseases for which menopause may put us at greater risk, such as osteoporosis and heart disease. Keep in mind, as you review the remedies, that what works for some women may not work as well for you, and that you may have to try a number of different remedies—singly or in combination—until you find the best one for your particular situation. Wherever vitamins and minerals are suggested and amounts are not stated, refer to Chapter 3 for recommended dosages. Also, consult the Selected Glossary at the back of the book for definitions of terms with which you may be unfamiliar.

One common recommendation during this life phase, no matter what your symptoms, is to eat foods high in *phytoestrogens* as a means of relieving menopausal symptoms. These hormonelike substances are derived from plant foods and mimic the action of estrogen in the body, although they are about 1/400 as potent as the estrogen produced by the body. Some rich sources include alfalfa, apples, barley, carrots, cherries, chickpeas, coffee, garlic, green beans, miso, oats, peas, potatoes, rice, rye, soybeans, tofu, yams and yeast.

As always, check with your doctor before beginning any course of treatment.

PHYSICAL SYMPTOMS

(IRREGULAR MENSTRUAL) BLEEDING

The Situation: As the body's hormone levels decrease, so may the regularity of menstrual periods. During this time, some women find that their flow is lighter. Others experience a lighter flow but have more frequent periods. Yet others experience just the opposite—fewer periods, but with heavier bleeding, which may be prolonged and excessive. Some will alternate between these two patterns. Still other women report that although they maintain their usual periods, there's some spotting or bleeding during the cycle.

Why do some women experience heavier and more profuse bleeding? As your body's hormone levels fluctuate and decrease, so may the regularity of your menstrual periods, until they stop altogether. In Chapter 1, I explained that this generally occurs because as you approach menopause, the estrogen levels in the first two weeks of the cycle get lower and lower, so fewer egg follicles are stimulated to grow. In addition, you are less likely to ovulate since the supply of eggs is running out.

Without ovulation, there is no corpus luteum to produce progesterone. So estrogen stimulates the growth of the uterus lining during the first two weeks of your cycle, which is no longer opposed by progesterone during the remaining two weeks. Without progesterone, the endometrium becomes thicker and thicker, which can result in later, heavier, and prolonged bleeding.

What to Do Immediately: If your usual bleeding has become heavier or more frequent and/or occurs for prolonged periods of time, check with your gynecologist immediately to rule out the possibility of endometrial hyperplasia (the overthickening of the lining of the uterus), uterine or cervical cancer, fibroid tumors, or other potential health problems. Let your doctor know what medications you may already be taking, including aspirin, which can interfere with the blood's ability to clot and, therefore, may be affecting your menstrual bleeding. Besides a clinical exam, your doctor may decide to perform an endometrial biopsy and a progesterone challenge test to determine what is causing the problem. In an endometrial biopsy, tissue is collected from the endometrial lining to determine whether you have hyperplasia or cancer. In the progesterone challenge test, the doctor generally prescribes ten milligrams of progestin (synthetic progesterone) a day for seven days. If your periods become regular in both flow and timing, you are probably okay. If not, and you haven't already had an endometrial biopsy, your doctor may request this test to develop a diagnosis.

If this bleeding has been occurring for a while, have your doctor check your blood for iron-deficiency anemia, a condition that can result from large, frequent losses of blood. You may be urged to take an iron supplement.

What to Do Next: If menstrual irregularities have just recently started, begin keeping a record of the changes in your periods. (Use the Menstrual Flow Chart in Chapter 1). If your pattern has become very irregular or it concerns you in some way, see your gynecologist to discuss what's going on and what the next step, if any, should be.

Other Treatments That May Help:

- Eliminate alcohol from your diet, since it can interfere with blood clotting and thus cause heavier menstrual flow.
- If you smoke, stop.
- Engage in consistent, moderately strenuous exercise, as it may increase the length of your menstrual cycle, thus decreasing the number of menstrual cycles you have annually. Also, practice stress-reduction techniques, as outlined in Chapter 10.
- Avoid hot baths and showers during heavy bleeding, since this can increase blood flow.

- Avoid aspirin.
- Discuss the possibility of taking progesterone with your gynecologist. Once irregular bleeding has stopped, it is thought that very little estrogen is being produced by the ovaries. At this time, if you are experiencing other menopausal symptoms, your doctor may suggest HRT. Or, if you are still menstruating, he/she may advise low-dose birth control pills.
- "Alternative" therapies include the herb Vitex agnus castus, available in health food stores. Follow label instructions for dosage. Also, take vitamin C, vitamin K, bioflavonoids, and calcium. Refer to Chapter 3 for recommended amounts.

BLOATING/WATER RETENTION

The Situation: You may feel abdominal bloating, which can be caused by food allergies or enzyme deficiencies that prevent your body from properly processing certain foods (for example, an allergy to milk, referred to as lactose intolerance, is the result of a deficiency of the enzyme lactase; without it you can't process milk products well, or at all).

Or, you may feel like you are retaining water now—your ankles may be swollen, or perhaps you can't wear your rings because your fingers are swollen. This could be a result of hormone imbalance—specifically an excess production of estrogen, since estrogen binds sodium, and sodium attracts water—a side effect of *synthetic* ERT/HRT, and/or the result of eating a lot of salty foods.

What to Do Immediately: For abdominal bloating: If you don't know what you're allergic to, you may wish to go to an allergist. If you know you can't tolerate particular foods, such as milk products, you may want to try an elimination diet yourself, by keeping these "irritating" foods out of your diet, or by trying them on a rotational basis—eliminating them for two weeks, then gradually reintroducing them into your diet on a four-day rotational basis in small quantities, to see how your body tolerates them. If you have a milk (lactose) intolerance, try getting your calcium—vital for bone health—in the form of lactose-free milk, or other high-calcium foods such as sardines, kale, and calcium-fortified soy milk as well as from calcium supplements.

For fluid retention: To be sure that your fluid retention isn't diet-related, use the Lifestyle Journal found in Chapter 11 to keep an accurate record of everything you eat and drink for the next seven days. You want to make sure you're not taking in a lot of high-sodium foods (pickles, soy sauce, salty snacks, etc.), which can cause water retention.

What to Do Next: For fluid retention try vitamin/mineral supplementation such as vitamin B_6 (a natural mild diuretic), taken with magnesium, or an herbal tea such as parsley tea or dandelion leaf tea, available in health food stores.

For abdominal bloating and fluid retention talk with your gynecologist about the possibility of synthetic ERT/HRT causing your bloatedness or fluid retention. If it is, perhaps your dosage needs to be adjusted, or if you are taking synthetic forms, you may discuss switching to the natural forms, which is certainly the healthier alternative.

HAIR: LOSS, THINNING, OR FACIAL HAIR

The Situation: Additional and/or more-noticeable facial hair may grow above your upper lip, chin, or cheeks as your body's production of female and male hormones shifts. Be aware that certain drugs, including hypertension medications, tranquilizers, antidepressants, and diuretics—may encourage facial hair growth. Alternatively, you might find that your hair is thinning or falling out. Rapid hair loss is sometimes the result of a thyroid problem, iron deficiency, or insufficient protein in your diet for a prolonged period of time, or can result from rapid weight loss if you've been following an unbalanced, unhealthy eating plan for any length of time.

What to Do Immediately: Nourish your body (and hair) with a low-fat, protein-rich diet. (See the Protein-Packed Plan—an eating plan described in Chapter 8.) If weight loss is your goal, eat a healthy, balanced diet and take a multivitamin and mineral supplement. Aim for a weight loss of up to two pounds a week. Avoid alcohol, sugar, and caffeine.

Other Treatments That May Help:

For Excess Hair Growth
- Try electrolysis, waxing, or bleaching.
- HRT, which elevates the level of female hormones, may help slow or eliminate facial hair growth.

For Thinning Hair/Hair Loss
- Try vitamin/mineral supplements: vitamins A, B-complex, and vitamin C; biotin, inositol, manganese, selenium, zinc. Also, don't forget your essential fatty acids (Omega-3 and -6 unsaturated fats). They lubricate the hair and may prevent hair loss.
- Drink plenty of water.
- Learn to identify techniques to use so you manage your response to stress, such as meditation, yoga, exercise, or any other methods that work for you.
- Check with your doctor about minoxidil, a hair-restoration product sold under the trade name Rogaine, which has a 30–40 percent effectiveness rate. It generally takes about eight months of daily application to determine its effectiveness.
- Ask your gynecologist about HRT, which may help slow or eliminate hair thinning.

HEADACHES/MIGRAINES

The Situation: Twice as many women as men suffer regularly from headaches, although the frequency of headaches usually decreases with age. The tapering off of estrogen during menopause usually has some impact on headaches—for the better in many women, but in other cases for the worse. Synthetic ERT/HRT is usually discouraged for women with migraines.

What to Do Immediately: If your headaches or migraines are more severe than usual or have increased in frequency, check with your doctor to rule out the possibility of food allergies/intolerances, anemia, or hypothyroidism.

What to Do Next: Watch your diet. Because certain substances in foods trigger headaches and migraines by affecting blood vessels, avoid alcohol and eating very cold foods, cured foods, the food additive MSG, beans, pork, and yogurt. Also, the compound tyramine—found in herring, organ meats, aged cheeses, peanuts and peanut butter, and other foods—has been known to produce migraines. Other foods associated with headaches or migraines include milk, wheat, grapes, raisins, and shellfish.

Other Preventive Strategies/Treatments That May Help:

- Vitamin/mineral supplements: vitamins C, B_6, and E, magnesium.

- Avoid chewing gum, which may exacerbate the pounding in your head.

- Exercise and practice relaxation techniques, to help you deal better with stress and thus prevent the development of tension headache.

- For simple headaches, try the herbs skullcap or passionflower, both available in health food stores in powder and capsule form, or you can prepare them as an herbal tea.

- For migraines, the most effective therapy is to lie down immediately in a quiet, darkened room. Other preventive measures are splashing cold water on your face or taking a steamy hot shower to dilate the blood vessels in your head and then gradually switching to cold water, to contract the vessels. You may also want to try feverfew, an herb available in health food stores in powder or capsule form. Also, Omega-3 fatty acids in the form of EPA (eicosapentaenuic acid), available in capsule form, relax blood vessels and may relieve migraines.

- The standard drug for migraine sufferers is ibuprofen (Advil, Motrin, etc.). If your migraines occur more frequently—two to three times a month—ask your doctor about preventive prescription drugs, for example, Propranolol, sold under the trade name Inderal. Keep in mind that this drug can have side effects—it may cause restless or fitful sleep. If you have bronchial asthma, Inderal should not be taken. Keep in mind that if you just treat the symptom with prescription medication, rather than finding and eliminating the cause, headaches and migraines are likely to continue.

HOT FLASHES/NIGHT SWEATS

The Situation: Hot flashes, or flushes, are the result of blood vessels dilating and constricting in an irregular, unpredictable pattern due to changing estrogen levels. Often the first sign of menopause, hot flashes affect some 70 percent of menopausal women, with each flash usually lasting from just a few seconds to several minutes. They generally start in the face and neck and work down to the chest, sometimes also affecting the back and entire body. When they occur at night they're called night sweats, and they may wake you out of a sound sleep. Those women who tend to report more intense and frequent symptoms include small, thin women; women who've experienced surgical or chemical menopause; and smokers. Hot flashes typically stop one to two years after your final menstrual period but may linger as long as five to ten years.

What to Do Immediately: As soon as you experience your first flash, start keeping a diary for a week or two to record the incidence of hot flashes and what factors—such as stress or eating spicy foods such as Chinese (particulary Szechwan) or Mexican dishes—may have triggered them. Use the Lifestyle Journal in Chapter 11 to track this. You might want to see your gynecologist to talk about how to relieve them.

What to Do Next: Vitamin E is a frequently used treatment for hot flashes; ask your gynecologist if it's right for you. (Note: Women with conditions such as high blood pressure, diabetes, or rheumatic heart disease, or those taking the heart medication digitalis may be discouraged from taking vitamin E.) Many women get fairly quick relief (anywhere from a week to a month) after they start taking vitamin E. Most of my clients start with 400 IU a day, and if they don't get relief within four weeks, they may need to step up the amount to 800 IU a day; others require a daily dosage of up to 1200 IU. Because vitamin E is fat-soluble, it should be taken with a meal that includes some fat to aid in its absorption.

Other Treatments That May Help:

- Avoid such common "trigger foods" as alcohol (particularly red wine, which can cause the body's thermostat to be reset and can trigger a flash), caffeine (found in coffee, tea, chocolate, colas, etc.), spicy foods, sugar, aged cheeses, and very hot drinks. Keep track of and avoid any other foods that you suspect may set off your hot flashes.

- Do eat foods containing phytoestrogens such as tofu, soybeans, alfalfa, and miso.

- Drink cool beverages (especially water) throughout the day.

- Eat several smaller meals, rather than two or three larger meals, throughout the day. Eat slowly.

- Engage in moderate aerobic exercise on a regular basis.

- Keep the house cool.

- Practice relaxation techniques. Some studies show that muscle relaxation and deep-breathing exercises decrease hot flashes by half.

- Dress in layers, in cottons and other fabrics that "breathe." Avoid tight-fitting clothes. Use lightweight blankets.

- Lose weight if you need to—excess weight may cause more hot flashes.

- Natural or herbal remedies that have proven effective for some women include gamma linolenic acid (GLA) or evening primrose oil, a botanical source of GLA; black cohosh; ginseng; the botanical extract gamma oryzanol, which is a naturally occurring component of rice bran oil; or dong quai, a Chinese herb containing plant sterols that have estrogen-like effects. (All are available in tablet form. In all cases, follow the recommended dosage on the bottle.)

- Other vitamin and minerals to pay particular attention to are vitamin C, bioflavonoids, niacin, magnesium, and selenium.

- Your gynecologist may prescribe natural progesterone, in cream form, or ERT/HRT, which gives many women tremendous relief. Because hot flashes, unlike other menopausal symptoms, generally abate on their own, the dosage of any hormones you take specifically to treat hot flashes will probably need to be adjusted over time.

If you can't tolerate ERT/HRT, your doctor may prescribe a drug called clonidine, a hypertension medication that has proven effective in reducing the frequency, duration, and intensity of hot flashes. A few women report relief with doses of 50 mg per day, but most require higher doses (200–400 mg), which may produce such side effects as low blood pressure, headaches, dizziness, insomnia, and/or irritability.

AMY'S STORY

Amy was very sensitive to the onset of a hot flash, and found that a change in her eating habits alleviated her situation:

I know exactly when I'm about to have a hot flash. First, I get a feeling like a pinprick, about a half-inch above my right eyebrow. I wait a little while, and then the flash comes on, full-blown. What's interesting is my body goes from full heat to cold. I break out in beads of perspiration all over my body, feeling intense heat, and then I feel very clammy and the chills.

I have definite patterns. I usually get a flash just before I get out of bed in the morning. Then, about two hours later, right after I have my cup of coffee at work, I flash again. Sometimes I get a flash between breakfast and lunch when I'm really hungry. A couple of hours after I eat lunch, I flash. And then I usually have one final flash at night, just as I'm laying my head down on the bed.

A change in my eating has helped, though. If I reduce my fat and oils to two to three teaspoons a day, I have fewer hot flashes—strangely enough, when I eat too much fat, I flash more. The same with sugar. I also find I'm more water-retentive now than I used to be, so I take B_6—100 mg a day. (Note: whenever you take a B vitamin, always take B complex as well. B vitamins work synergistically.) Also, it's better for me not to eat too many calories at once. By eating small, frequent meals, rather than three large meals, and by taking vitamin E supplementation (400 IU per day), I can better control my flashes.

In general, I think the best way to handle these flashes is to have a sense of humor about it. This is just another phase of life, and laughing about it is a good coping mechanism.

SEXUAL DIFFICULTIES/LOSS OF SEX DRIVE

The Situation: Vaginal dryness and/or weakened vaginal muscles, which can result from decreased estrogen levels, may make intercourse unpleasant or even painful. Some women also report a loss of sex drive or responsiveness, which may be the result of a decrease in both female hormones. That's because the chain of sensations leading to orgasm is involved in a series of estrogen-sensitive cells. With declining amounts of estrogen, the sensation may not be strong. Sometimes, these symptoms may be emotionally and/or psychologically based and have little if any physiological connection.

Interestingly, the testosterone:estrogen ratio changes drastically after menopause because of the marked decline in estrogen. Since testosterone is related to sex drive, it *would appear* that women's sex drive would increase at this time of life, or at least remain the same. Yet, this often does not happen.

What to Do: Learn how to do Kegel exercises, which can enhance vaginal elasticity and sexual pleasure, as well as improve bladder control (explained later in this chapter). These simple exercises strengthen the pubococcygeus (PC) muscles, the band of muscle tissue that extends from the pubic bone in the front of your body to the coccyx bone in the back. To locate your PC muscles, deliberately start and stop the flow of urine repeatedly the next time you have to urinate. The contraction you feel comes from these muscles. (See following box.)

Other Treatments That May Help: To provide relief from vaginal dryness:

- Talk to your doctor about vaginal lubricants such as K-Y jelly, Lubafax, Astro-Glide, Replens, or a vitamin E suppository, which may provide relief from dryness.
- Regular sex and/or masturbation can encourage vaginal lubrication.

Kegel How-tos

Kegel exercises can be done anywhere—sitting, standing, or lying down. Try to do them three times a day. While sitting or standing, contract your PC muscles. Hold for three seconds, then relax for three seconds. Gradually build up to ten seconds of holding and relaxing. Then, aim to contract and release the PC muscles as quickly as you can. Start with twenty times and work your way up to two hundred. You may prefer doing the exercises lying flat on your back on the floor, knees bent, feet flat on floor. Raise your pelvis until you feel a pull. Hold that position, then begin contracting and relaxing your PC muscles as just described.

To restore sex drive:
- Remain sexually active (with a partner or through masturbation) to help maintain vaginal resiliency.
- Certain herbs, including jilen ginseng, mimic some of the properties of estrogen and may help restore sex drive.
- Also, ask about intravaginal ERT/HRT therapy, which has been helpful to some women in increasing low-level libido. ERT/HRT may improve the situation within two to three months. Also, discuss with your doctor testosterone therapy, which may help to increase low-level libido but may promote the growth of facial and/or other body hair because testosterone is no longer "opposed," that is, kept in balance, by estrogen.

SKIN CHANGES

The Situation: The skin is the largest organ in the body, and the most visible. As you age your skin changes, but these changes seem to happen more rapidly during menopause. As estrogen production decreases, collagen, a protein responsible for keeping skin elastic, diminishes too. When that happens, the skin secretes

---

Skin Cancer: The Risk Is Real

We've all heard that exposure to the sun's UV rays can lead to damage of the skin's DNA, which may, in the very worst case, lead to malignant melanoma—skin cancer. While this is a risk throughout your life, your risk increases as you get older, so you need to be particularly careful. First, if you normally like to lie in the sun, especially between 10:00 A.M. and 2:00 P.M. standard time, when UV rays are their strongest, stop. If you *must* tan, wear sunblock and limit your exposure to the sun to other hours of the day as well as the time spent tanning yourself. *Never go out without wearing some sort of sunblock* (for longer than twenty minutes, the amount of time necessary for vitamin D to be synthesized from your skin)—the fairer and more delicate your skin, the higher the number. And avoid tanning lamps and tanning booths, which, despite their safety claims, still expose your skin and eyes to dangerous rays.

---

less oil and becomes drier and thinner, loses its natural "plumpness," and may start to wrinkle and sag. You may also develop dark spots, known as liver spots even though they have nothing to do with your liver, on the backs of your hands, your arms, or on your face.

What to Do Immediately: If you smoke, stop, and limit your exposure to passive smoke—both can cause wrinkling. Avoid prolonged exposure to the sun, or use sunscreen when you are outdoors, to protect your skin. Start drinking six to eight glasses of water a day to help replenish your skin's moisture. Consider seeing a dermatologist about any skin changes that concern you.

What to Do Next:

- Vitamin/mineral supplementation: vitamins A, riboflavin, biotin, vitamins B$_6$, C, and E; PABA, copper, and zinc. Also, don't forget about your essential fatty acids (Omega-3 and -6 unsaturated fats), as they lubricate the skin.
- Avoid alcohol, which can dehydrate the skin, as can abrasive soaps that have a lot of perfume and detergent. Dermatologists generally recommend products that contain lanolin. Use an alcohol-free, emollient-rich facial cleanser and moisturizer.
- Aerobic exercise, which increases circulation and nutrient flow to the skin.

Other Treatments That May Help:

- You may want to see your gynecologist to discuss ERT/HRT, which has been shown in a number of studies to slow the loss of collagen. Or you might consider natural progesterone cream, which many women say maintains skin moisture and decreases wrinkling.
- Or, you may want to talk to your doctor about tretinoin cream, sold under the brand name Retin-A, which may also help prevent the formation of new wrinkles after several months of use or help liver spots to fade within a few weeks.

SLEEP DISTURBANCES/INSOMNIA/FATIGUE

The Situation: As you move into menopause, your customary sleep patterns may be disturbed for a number of reasons: hot flashes and night sweats, stress, or simply getting older, which often leads to shifts in sleep patterns. You may also have a decrease in dream-rich sleep, which is the deep sleep called rapid eye movement (REM), as estrogen levels drop. As a result of all of this, you may find yourself more tired and/or irritable during the day and have greater difficulty concentrating.

What to Do Immediately: Eliminate nicotine and caffeine, both stimulants, and alcohol, a depressant, which may help you fall asleep quickly but won't result in a deep, sound sleep and will only increase your feeling of lethargy. Start (or step up) a program of regular exercise, which improves sleep for many people. Some women find exercise just before bedtime helpful; others report that it only makes them feel more alert—so find the time that's best for you. Practice relaxation exercises to reduce stress. Some find a warm bath just before bedtime soothing.

What to Do Next: Be sure your diet includes foods rich in tryptophan, an amino acid that is converted in the body to serotonin, a neurotransmitter or nerve chemical that has a calming effect and helps promote sleep. Complex carbs like bread and cereal also have this effect. (The Carbohydrate-Packed Eating Plan (CPP), outlined in Chapter 8, is a good one to follow here.)

Other Treatments That May Help:

- Vitamin/mineral supplementation: vitamin B_6 and magnesium.
- Herbs such as hops, passionflower, skullcap, and Chinese or American ginseng can help alleviate insomnia. (Follow dosages on the label.)
- Some women find that HRT helps reduce insomnia.

STRESS INCONTINENCE/ URGE INCONTINENCE

The Situation: Because the urinary system is dependent on estrogen, changes do occur during menopause. Since the bladder and urethra are less toned without estrogen, maintaining continence can be a problem. Stress incontinence may result in leaking of urine during exercise, coughing, laughing, sneezing, or lifting heavy objects—anything that causes extra pressure or "stress" on the bladder. With urge incontinence, you're unable to hold back the urine when you feel the need—or urge—to urinate.

What to Do: Kegel exercises strengthen the muscles around the vagina that help support the bladder. (See how-tos under the heading Sexual Difficulties on page 93.)

Other Treatments That May Help:

- Train yourself to make frequent trips to the bathroom, so you void regularly.
- Avoid alcohol and caffeine.
- If you're eating citrus fruits and/or spicy foods, try eliminating them from your diet—they may be aggravating your condition.
- Bring your weight down to a reasonable level. Overweight women are more prone to incontinence problems.
- Review with your doctor any prescription or over-the-counter medications you are taking, to make sure none of them is causing or aggravating your bladder problems. Also ask about whether hormone replacement therapy may help you.
- If these symptoms are very debilitating, discuss a more rigorous treatment plan with a urologist; some prescription medications may be recommended. If there are structural problems, such as an abnormality in the position of your bladder, surgery may help.

THYROID DYSFUNCTION

The Situation: The thyroid gland—a butterfly-shaped gland located in the neck that regulates metabolism—can undergo changes during mid-life. Hyperthyroidism (an overproduction of thyroid hormones by the thyroid gland) can result in hot flashes, heart palpitations, nervousness, irritability, hair and weight loss, intolerance to heat, insomnia, and bone loss. Hypothyroidism, an underproduction of thyroid hormones, can result in lethargy, depression, muscle weakness, stiffness or cramping, poor memory, cold intolerance, dry and flaky skin, inability to concentrate, hair loss, and weight gain.

What to Do Immediately: Take your basal body temperature (the temperature of the body at rest) before arising in the morning for four consecutive days. For the most accurate reading, keep the thermometer next to the bed so you don't have to get out of bed before taking your temperature. Place the thermometer in your armpit and keep it secure for ten minutes. If you are still menstruating, it's best to take your temperature the week of your period. If it reads 97.4 or lower and you have some of the symptoms listed above, then you might have hypothyroidism.

What to Do Next: See your doctor and ask to have T3, T4, T7, TSH, and T.B.G. blood tests, although indications of thyroid dysfunction don't always show up in test results.

Other Treatments That May Help:

• Zinc, vitamins A, E, thiamin, and riboflavin, and GLA.
• Eat foods high in protein, including lean meat, chicken, fish, and low-fat or nonfat cheese, and rich in iodine (salt-water fish or seaweed).
• Check with your doctor about medication. Although doctors typically recommend Synthroid for hypothyroidism, talk to your doctor about taking Armour thyroid, a natural thyroid hormone. Since prolonged use of excessively large doses of thyroid hormone can cause osteoporosis, you may wish to discuss the impact of your thyroid medication on your bones with your doctor. Some doctors recommend ERT/HRT along with thyroid medication, which may remedy this situation.

URINARY TRACT PROBLEMS

The Situation: During menopause, the decline in estrogen levels affects the urethra (the tube that carries urine from the bladder to outside the body), the bladder (the sac that holds the urine), and the lining of the urinary tract. Your urethra may become thinner, and, if coupled with loss of pelvic strength, it may prolapse, or collapse slightly, making bladder control more difficult. Frequent urination or the sensation of a full bladder when it is actually empty is also common. Urinary tract infections may be recurrent.

What to Do Immediately: See your doctor to rule out the possibility of bladder infection. If you do have an infection, he or she may prescribe antibiotics. Repeated use of antibiotics not only destroys the "bad" bacteria but also destroys the "friendly" bacteria in your body. If you take antibiotics, combine them with acidophilus and bifidus tablets, taken at different times of the day than the antibiotics.

What to Do Next: Step up your daily intake of water to eight glasses throughout the day. Unsweetened cranberry juice (about ten ounces a day) and blueberries also help prevent the development of urinary tract infections as well as speed your recovery. Cranberry extracts are also available in tablet form.

Other Treatments That May Help:

- Avoid alcohol and caffeine, as well as citrus fruits and spicy foods, which can irritate the urinary tract. Vitamin D may also irritate the urinary tract.
- Avoid using a diaphragm, which may increase the risk of bladder inflammation and may cause a burning sensation upon urination.
- Empty your bladder before and after sexual intercourse.
- Vitamin/mineral supplementation: vitamins A and C; selenium.
- Keep your weight at a reasonable level to avoid placing extra pressure on the bladder and urethra.
- Avoid using bubble bath and bath salts.
- Wear cotton underpants.
- Talk to your gynecologist about vaginal estrogen cream, which has been known to help prevent urinary tract infection, or HRT.

VAGINAL DRYNESS/IRRITATION/ ITCHINESS/INFECTION

The Situation: Vaginal tissue, more than any other part of the body, is dependent on estrogen. As estrogen levels fall, the vagina becomes thinner and smaller and its walls less elastic, all of which may cause irritation and itchiness. The vagina also becomes drier (because of the decline in vaginal secretions) and less acidic, leading to greater risk of infection. In addition you may develop more yeast infections now because of the lack of acidity in the vagina plus the presence of unopposed estrogen, which may stimulate an overgrowth of Candida albicans, the yeast found naturally in the body's mucous lining.

What to Do Immediately: Step up your intake of water to eight glasses a day. Drink unsweetened cranberry juice, which is effective in preventing as well as clearing up, vaginal infections, or take cranberry extract, in tablet form.

What to Do Next: Watch your diet. Avoid alcohol and caffeine, which may further dehydrate the vaginal area. Eat heart-healthy fats, including olive and canola oils, to help maintain vaginal moisture. Limit sugar, which decreases the acidity of the vagina and can lead to further dryness and yeast infections. Eat yogurt containing a "live" culture to increase the presence of the "friendly" bacteria, acidophilus, in the vagina. You can also get acidophilus in tablet form. Also take the "friendly" bacteria, bifidus, as well as the fuel that feeds the "friendly" bacteria, Fructo-Oligosaccharida (FOS). If you have a yeast infection, avoid eating foods that feed the "yeast" such as cheese, vinegar, mushrooms, wine, beer, dried fruit, milk, and fermented foods such as tempeh and sugar, and limit your fruit intake.

Other Treatments That May Help:

- Vitamin/mineral supplementation: vitamins A, B, C, and E; selenium. Try a vitamin E suppository once nightly for about six weeks, then about once a week thereafter.
- Wash the vaginal area regularly and pat dry. Wear only cotton underwear and avoid tight-fitting clothes against the crotch.
- Avoid strongly scented bubble bath, vaginal sprays, and deodorant tampons. Avoid douching.

- Avoid over-the-counter antihistamines and diuretics, which can promote vaginal dryness.

- Perform Kegel exercises to keep the vagina well toned and elastic. (See the how-tos under the heading Sexual Difficulties, page 93.)

- Remain sexually active (with a partner or through masturbation) to help you retain vaginal acidity, resiliency, and moisture. Studies show that vaginal dryness and pain are eased when women have intercourse and/or achieve orgasm three or more times a month.

- Talk to your doctor about ERT/HRT or about an over-the-counter vaginal lubricant, such as Astro-Glide, or intravaginal estrogen and/or progesterone creams, which provide some women tremendous relief from vaginal dryness.

WEIGHT GAIN

The Situation: Weight gain—whether you're experiencing it for the first time in your life now or whether it's a problem that seems more difficult than ever with the onset of menopause—affects so many menopausal women that most of the remainder of *Trouble-Free Menopause* will be devoted to this issue.

DISEASES FOR WHICH A WOMAN'S RISK INCREASE DURING MENOPAUSE

BREAST CANCER

The Situation: Today, according to the National Cancer Institute, one in eight women will develop breast cancer during her lifetime (this assumes a 95-year life expectancy). The causes of the disease are still unclear, but current known risk factors include aging (three-quarters of all breast cancers occur in women over 50), a history of or existing breast cancer affecting a first-degree relative such as a mother or sister, late (over 55) menopause, having no children, having a first pregnancy after 30, and possibly a high-fat diet. Your doctor will probably tell you to avoid ERT/HRT if you or a first-degree relative has had breast cancer, or you have benign breast disease, although researchers are unsure about the relationship between ERT/HRT and breast cancer.

What to Do Immediately: Do a monthly breast self-examination—85 percent of lumps are found by women themselves. (Your gynecologist should have a brochure demonstrating the proper method, or order a free copy from the American Cancer Society.) The best time to do BSE is after your period or, if you're no longer menstruating, on some easy-to-remember day, such as the first of the month.

What to Do Next: Have a mammogram if you haven't had one in the past year; if you're over 50, continue getting mammograms annually; if you're 40–50, have a mammogram every two years. To ensure safe and accurate services, as of October 1, 1994, all facilities must be accredited by the Department of Health and Human Services. As added insurance you might want to check to see if the facility is also certified by the American College of Radiology (ACR). Some cities have facilities that provide low-cost, high-quality mammograms; check with your local chapter of the American Cancer Society.

Other Prevention Strategies That May Help:

- Stick to a low-fat diet, such as one of those outlined in this book, and limit sugar intake since sugar, when eaten in large quantities over a long period of time, may be linked to breast cancer. Fill up on cruciferous vegetables such as broccoli, cabbage, and Brussels sprouts, as they are high in phytochemicals (cancer-preventing plant chemicals), as are soybeans, tomatoes, fruits, and other high-fiber foods. Limit your intake of salt-cured, smoked, charbroiled, and nitrate-cured foods.
- Vitamin/mineral supplementation: vitamins A, riboflavin, B_6, folic acid, C, D, E, and beta-carotene; bioflavonoids; calcium, manganese, selenium, zinc.
- Maintain a schedule of moderate, regular exercise.
- Learn to relax, using the stress-management techniques out-

lined in Chapter 10. High-stress lives lead to decreased or compromised immune systems, so your body is less equipped to fight disease and toxins.

- Maintain a reasonable weight.
- If you smoke, stop.
- Limit alcohol consumption to no more than one drink per day.
- "Alternative" therapies include taking garlic tablets, Omega-3 fatty acid (fish oils), and gamma linolenic acid (GLA), all available in tablet form in your health food store.
- Your clinician may recommend tamoxifen (Nolvadex), an estrogen-blocker drug for the breast tissue, often prescribed to women who are breast cancer-prone and to those who've had breast cancer to prevent its recurrence. This drug is believed to have a protective effect on your heart and bones. The downside: it may produce hot flashes and stimulate endometrial growth.

CARDIOVASCULAR (HEART) DISEASE

The Situation: More women in this country die of heart and vascular disease (about 500,000 women a year) than any other illness, including the combined death rate from breast cancer, which takes about 46,000 lives a year, and lung cancer, claiming about 62,000 women's lives annually. Although we seem to hear about far more men suffering from heart disease and dying of heart attacks than women, over the years following menopause the numbers for men and women pretty much even out. Your falling level of estrogen appears to make you more susceptible to heart disease—as estrogen drops, your body's levels of LDL cholesterol (the "bad" cholesterol) may rise. You are considered at particular risk if your LDL cholesterol is over 130 mg/dl, your HDL cholesterol is below 35 mg/dl (levels at 35 mg/dl decrease your risk, while numbers over 60 add heart protection), your triglycerides exceed 150 mg/dl, and/or your lipoprotein (a) level is above 0.3 grams per liter. Other risk factors for heart disease include a family history of heart disease (father and/or brother before age 55; mother and/or sister before age 65), diabetes, cigarette smoking, high blood pressure (140/90 mm Hg or higher), obesity (especially if you're apple-shaped), and high stress levels. Postmenopausal women who are not taking HRT may be at greater risk as well.

What to Do Immediately:

• If you smoke, stop.

• Improve your diet by reducing your salt (sodium) intake. If you have high blood pressure and are salt-sensitive, this can help you decrease your high blood pressure, and hypertension is a risk factor in heart disease.

• Cut down on your total fat consumption and be sure to select small amounts of heart-healthy polyunsaturated fats such as Omega-3 fats (from fatty fish) and Omega-6 fats (from vegetable oils) as well as monounsaturated fats in place of saturated fats. Keep dietary cholesterol consumption to under 300 mg daily.

• Increase your intake of soluble fiber (such as dried beans and peas, fresh fruit and vegetables, oat bran, etc.) and eat foods high in bioflavonoids such as onions and apples.

• Although alcohol has been shown to raise HDL, you want to limit your alcohol intake to no more than one glass a day.

• Limit sugar.

• Bring your weight down to a reasonable level and keep it there.

What to Do Next: See your doctor for a blood pressure check—high blood pressure is a risk factor in heart disease and you may not even be aware that you have it. Also, have a blood lipid profile to check your cholesterol and triglyceride levels. If your blood pressure reading or cholesterol level is very high and you have not been able to get them down through diet/exercise changes, medication may be necessary. However, you should *not* depend solely on medication to prevent or reverse heart disease; making appropriate dietary and exercise changes may be equally if not more effective in the short and long run. Providing that your hypertension is under control, ERT/HRT may also be recommended—studies show that adding estrogen can improve a woman's blood cholesterol profile, as well as protect arteries from becoming clogged.

Other Prevention Strategies That May Help:

- Vitamin/mineral supplementation: vitamins A, B_2, B_6, folic acid, C, E, and beta-carotene; calcium, copper, chromium, magnesium, manganese, selenium, zinc.
- Exercise. Step up your everyday activity, as well as aiming for a minimum of three (with a goal of five) thirty-minute sessions of aerobics each week.
- Practice relaxation exercises so you can learn to manage your reaction to stress.
- Some studies show that taking aspirin daily or every other day helps prevent cardiac infarction. Check with your doctor about whether or not it's right for you.
- "Alternative" therapies include taking garlic, which is believed to lower cholesterol and prevent plaque formation in the arteries. Add at least one-half to one clove of fresh garlic each day to the foods you eat, or take it in pill form. There's also L-carnitine, an amino acid that may be helpful, as well as CoEnzyme Q 10.
- Women who aren't candidates for ERT/HRT might ask their doctor about taking tamoxifen, a drug sold under the trade name Nolvadex, which mimics some of the effects of estrogen in the body and may produce the same beneficial lipid changes as ERT/HRT. If you are taking tamoxifen, your gynecologist may recommend that you have an endometrial or intrauterine biopsy to detect uterine hyperplasia, since this drug stimulates endometrial growth.

ENDOMETRIAL CANCER

The Situation: Endometrial cancer (cancer of the lining of the uterus) is believed to occur because, during menopause, your body's production of estrogen is unopposed by progesterone. Without the presence of progesterone, an overgrowth of the uterine lining may lead to a condition called hyperplasia, which can be a precursor to cancer. Risk factors include a history of menstrual irregularities, late menopause (over age 55), never having had children, taking tamoxifen to prevent recurrence or the onset of breast cancer, having diabetes, and obesity. Women who are overweight—especially those who are apple-shaped, carrying their extra weight in their abdominal area—are at particular risk. Depending on the dosage and duration of use of ERT, women taking ERT have a four to eight times greater risk of developing endometrial cancer than nonusers. That's why a combination of ERT and HRT is generally recommended.

What to Do Immediately: Bring your weight down to a reasonable level through a low-fat diet—fats should comprise no more than 20–25 percent of your total daily calorie intake. The closer you keep your fat intake to around 20 percent, the more you may buck the odds of developing cancer. Keep your consumption of saturated fat and cured, smoked and charbroiled foods to a minimum.

Step up your intake of fruits and vegetables, particularly those high in the antioxidant vitamins A, C, E, and beta-carotene, and selenium, as well as high-fiber whole-grain carbohydrates and yogurt with a "live" culture, rich in "friendly" bacteria that may inhibit the effects of certain carcinogens.

Other Prevention Strategies That May Help:

- Stop smoking, and try to avoid the presence of smokers whenever possible so you're not exposed to secondhand smoke.

- Learn to manage your reaction to stress, which, in some studies of the mind-body connection, has been linked to the development of cancer.

- Exercise regularly.

- If your gynecologist feels that HRT is right for you, a combination of estrogen and progesterone will protect you from developing endometrial cancer caused by unopposed estrogen.

- "Alternative" therapies include taking garlic tablets, Omega-3 fatty acid (fish oils), and gamma linolenic acid (GLA), all available in your health food store.

OSTEOPOROSIS

The Situation: "Osteoporosis" means brittle or porous bones. It's the cause of 1.3 million fractures per year, mostly of the back, hip, and wrist, and affects 25 million Americans each year, approximately 80 percent of them women. Osteoporosis can be the result of aging, physical inactivity, unhealthy diet, and decreased levels of estrogen and progesterone during menopause. Until around age 35, bone is regularly broken down and rebuilt, and this rebuilding process occurs rapidly. However, after 35 you begin to lose bone more quickly than you rebuild it, leading to a steady decline of bone mass—unless you take lifestyle measures to prevent this decline. After menopause, the rate of bone loss is approximately 1–2 percent per year, with the greatest loss often occurring during the first 3–5 years following menopause.

Those considered at greater-than-average risk for osteoporosis include women who:

- have a calcium- and nutrient-deficient diet
- are Asian or fair-haired and fair-skinned Caucasians
- are small-boned
- are thin (with low body fat and low levels of lean body mass), so have less-dense bones as well as less body fat. Since estrogen is produced in the fatty tissues and muscles of the body from the hormone androstenedione, secreted by the adrenal glands, less estrogen may be available in thinner, less muscular people during the menopausal years, so they can be at higher risk for developing osteoporosis.
- smoke
- have a family history of osteoporosis
- go through menopause early or prematurely (for example, due to the surgical removal of their ovaries or chemotherapy)
- have never been pregnant
- are physically inactive
- have undergone long-term treatment with certain medications, such as corticosteroids, high doses of thyroid-replacement drugs for a slugglish thyroid, and some anticoagulants
- have an overactive thyroid and have not been treated for it

Without taking appropriate measures toward osteoporosis prevention, one-third of Caucasian American women can expect to suffer a hip fracture, and half of these women may only survive for one year following. The good news is that you can take vigorous and effective steps to preserve your present bone health and prevent further deterioration.

What to Do Immediately: Have a test to determine your current level of bone health. One of the following tests will probably be recommended to you:

- the single-photon absorptiometry (SPA), which determines bone density in the hand and wrist bone but can't measure bone density in the hip or spine, the areas most affected by osteoporosis
- the dual-photon absorptiometry (DPA) and the dual energy X-ray absorptiometry (DEXA), both of which measure bone density in all areas of the body, including the hip and spine, involve minimal radiation, and are very accurate. DEXA is faster and the most frequently used
- the CAT scan, which has the advantage of being the most accurate and able to measure either the total bone (the outer bone called the cortical bone, as well as the inner, spongy bone, called the trabecular bone), or, just the inner, spongy trabecular bone. This testing technique may expose you to higher levels of radiation than the other tests and is a lot more expensive

After an initial baseline test, you may want to follow up with annual tests. Also, check with your doctor to make sure that none of the prescription or over-the-counter medications you are taking are contributing to osteoporosis.

What to Do Next: Eat an osteoporosis-fighting diet. Focus on foods rich in calcium; vitamin D (needed to absorb calcium and which young women are readily able to get through exposure to sunlight; however, this ability greatly decreases as you age); magnesium, a nutrient critical to bone health; vitamins K,

B_6, and folic acid; manganese; silicon; copper; fluoride; and boron.

Equally important now is avoiding those foods that may rob you of these nutrients and/or block their absorption. These nutrient-robbers, when taken in large amounts and on a regular basis, include:

- phosphorus (found in carbonated beverages, meats, cheese, and highly processed foods)
- salt (the sodium component)
- caffeine (in coffee, tea, etc.)
- oxalic acid (in chocolate and spinach)
- alcohol
- *any* diet that is much too high in fat, protein, or carbohydrate

What to Do After That:

- Exercise. Like muscles, bones need to be exercised to grow and maintain their strength. Do low-impact weight-bearing exercises like walking, jogging, and aerobics as well as strength training on a regular basis.
- Stop smoking.
- Maintain a reasonable body weight, neither too heavy nor too thin.
- Talk to your doctor about natural progesterone cream. It can be rubbed onto your face, neck, breasts, or abdomen and has been shown to increase bone density when used regularly.
- Ask your doctor to check your blood levels of the hormone dehydroepiandrosterone (DHEA). If your own blood levels are too low, small doses of DHEA may improve your bone health.

Other Prevention Strategies That May Help: Ask your doctor whether you could benefit from ERT/HRT, which a lot of the research has shown to be extremely effective in reducing bone loss, as well as fractures in the spine, hip, and arm. (There is continuing debate about how long you must take ERT/HRT to maintain its benefit; some research has shown that bone loss will occur once it's discontinued.) But ERT/HRT alone won't remedy the situation—calcium supplementation along with other vitamin/mineral supplementation (listed above) is just as vital.

If your doctor says that you would benefit from ERT/HRT but can't take it for other health reasons, ask about taking one of the following drugs, some of which are still experimental:

- *Calcitonin* (sold under the name Calcimar), halts bone loss. It's expensive and given by injection, although a cheaper nasal-spray form of the drug has recently been developed.

- *Etidronate*, a biphosphonate (sold under the name Didronel), has been shown to effectively prevent and treat osteoporosis.

- *Sodium fluoride*, which promotes new bone formation, although the bone is structurally different from normal bone and may not be able to withstand the same stress. This treatment may have several serious side effects, including arthritis and anemia.

- *Calcitrol*, which increases calcium absorption and stimulates the creation of bone-building cells.

- Alendronate sodium (sold under the name Fosamax) shifts the bone-remodeling balance in favor of bone formation. Several side effects reported include mild abdominal pain, stomach upset, heartburn, muscle aches, and/or esophageal irritation.

EMOTIONAL SYMPTOMS

ANXIETY/DEPRESSION/ MOODINESS/IRRITABILITY

The Situation: It would be unreasonable to think that the physical changes that occur during menopause—caused mainly by fluctuating estrogen and progesterone levels—would *not* impact on your emotional health as well. Research shows that a woman may feel more anxious when estrogen levels are high, whereas she may become depressed or sad when progesterone dominates. Hormonal shifts can also bring on episodes of increased irritability and/or moodiness. However, the twelve-year-long Massachusetts Women's Health Study of some twenty-five thousand women, during which time they entered menopause, revealed that, contrary to popular belief, depression is *not* a typical symptom of menopausal women—they are no more or less depressed than the general population. Although it's true that you may have a lot to deal with during the menopausal years—everything from wrinkling, hot flashes, and other physical signs of aging, to the death of a spouse or other loved ones, from the chronic illness of a parent to the empty-nest syndrome—it's been shown repeatedly that a positive attitude and optimism about this new phase of life make it much easier to cope with the changes.

What to Do Immediately: Learn to handle the stresses in your life through a program of relaxation exercises. (See Chapter 10.) If emotional problems are severe, you may want to see a counselor or therapist or join a support group. If hot flashes are disrupting your sleep, you may find lack of sleep the main cause of irritability. Follow the guidelines under Hot Flashes (pages 90–93) to help relieve them.

What to Do Next: Start (or step up) your exercise program. A good aerobic workout as often as you can comfortably manage should reduce anxiety and depression and help you better put your problems in perspective. After about 20–30 minutes of continuous exercise, your brain will start releasing mood-improving endorphins. But *any* exercise will benefit you emotionally.

Other Treatments That May Help:

- Don't reach for food as a solution to your emotional problems. Overeating will not make emotional problems better but it will make you feel worse—you'll feel bad about how you "abused" yourself, the excess weight you put on, etc.
- Eat a nutrient-rich, balanced diet, such as one of those described in Chapter 8. Avoid junk food and other empty calories, as well as alcohol, which is a depressant. Focus on foods that have a calming effect. (See suggestions under the heading Sleep Disturbances, pages 96–97.)

- A number of herbs, including St. John's wort, valerian root, chamomile, skullcap, passionflower, and hawthorne berry, as well as ginseng (which may increase your energy level and combat fatigue and mild depression, but may also increase anxiety) may help. All are available as tinctures, teas, or in capsule form. (Follow dosages recommended on the label.)

- Have massages on a regular basis, which many women find to be excellent for tension relief.

- Some women report that their outlook improved considerably after beginning on ERT/HRT, although it's uncertain whether the hormones produced an actual mood elevation or simply that the women were just more comfortable and, therefore, in better spirits, since the ERT/HRT reduced menopausal symptoms like hot flashes. Ask your doctor if ERT/HRT might help your emotional symptoms.

SYMPTOM-TRIGGER FOODS: A MUST TO AVOID

Throughout Chapter 4 you've seen warnings to limit four key items—alcohol, caffeine, sodium, and sugar—in order to relieve or eliminate some of the menopausal symptoms as well as maintain good health. As I've said again and again, the way you eat dramatically affects the way you feel, especially at this time in your life. And this quartet in particular tends to do the most harm in terms of robbing your body of needed nutrients and feelings of well-being . . . not to mention possibly triggering menopausal symptoms. What makes these four so troublesome?

ALCOHOL

You've surely read about the so-called French paradox—that is, how the French eat higher-fat foods and drink more red wine than we do here in the United States and yet their incidence of heart disease is much lower. In fact, although the French eat foods that are higher in fat, they eat only small quantities of them. With regard to their alcohol consumption, we *do* know that drinking alcohol is associated with raising levels of "good" HDL cholesterol. Yes, up to one drink daily may be beneficial to you, especially as you age. But as you'll see in Chapter 9, there are other ways to raise your HDL levels, including regular, aerobic exercise, so if you're not already a drinker, this is definitely *not* the time to start. After all, there are also quite a few health risks linked to alcohol for the more-than-casual drinker, including liver disease and breast cancer, and when intake is excessive, heart disease, too. Furthermore, drinking is a source of empty calories and a depressant and, as such, can exacerbate the blues.

CAFFEINE

Caffeine is a stimulant found in black tea, coffee, chocolate, colas and other soft drinks, and certain over-the-counter drugs. When taken in excess, caffeine can increase anxiety, irritability, and mood swings and may even increase the number of hot flashes you experience. It stresses the adrenal glands, which means that it can interfere with hormone production. It also acts as a diuretic, leading to a loss of potassium, magnesium, zinc, vitamins B and C, and water. Further, it interferes with the absorption of iron as well as calcium. However, with regard to calcium loss, recent research indicates that drinking one glass of milk daily appeared to offset the calcium-draining effect of two cups of caffeinated coffee.

On the other hand, most of us like coffee, tea, and chocolate, and think that life would lose some of its zing without them. What's the solution? You're fairly safe from caffeine-related health problems if you confine your daily caffeine intake to no more than two cups of coffee or the equivalent—about 150 mg per day.

CAFFEINE CONTENT OF FOODS, BEVERAGES, AND OVER-THE-COUNTER DRUGS

(Keep in mind that caffeine counts will be higher the stronger the brew)

Item	Approximate Amount of Caffeine (in mg)
FOODS AND BEVERAGES	
Coffee, 5 fluid oz. (drip)	120–150
(percolated)	80–110

Item	Approximate Amount of Caffeine (in mg)
Decaffeinated coffee, 5 fluid oz.	1–5
Instant coffee, 5 fluid oz.	30–120
Brewed tea (black)	
5 fluid oz. (steeped 3 minutes)	20–50
5 fluid oz. (steeped 5 minutes)	40–100
Brewed tea (green), 5 fluid oz.	30–40
Iced tea, 5 fluid oz.	65–75
Instant tea, 5 fluid oz.	25–50
Hot cocoa, 5 fluid oz.	5–20
Chocolate milk, 8 fluid oz.	10–15
Semisweet chocolate, 1 oz.	35
Cola, 12 fluid oz.	35–45
OVER-THE-COUNTER DRUGS	
Anacin or Midol (1)	35
Dexatrim (1)	200
Excedrin (1)	65
No Doz (1)	100

If you decide to cut back from your present caffeine level, be sure to do so gradually—a sudden withdrawal may cause headaches and increased irritability. If you're a coffee drinker, you can slowly reduce the number of cups of coffee you drink a day—say, go from four cups the first week to three cups the next, to two, and then to one—or you can mix your regular-brewed coffee with some decaf. Herbal teas without caffeine are widely available, and many cola products are sold in caffeine-free versions. You might also want to try a caffeine-free, grain-based coffee-like beverage like Postum, Cafix, or Pero, each tasty and under twelve calories per serving.

SODIUM

Menopausal women need to take special pains to avoid added salt—more specifically, the sodium component of table salt, or sodium chloride. The reason? Your kidneys' ability to rid themselves of or release sodium declines as you age, so generally more of it remains in your body. This, in turn, can cause too much water to be retained, which puts stress on the heart and circulatory system and can lead to high blood pressure. And high blood pressure may lead to conditions such as kidney failure, stroke, and heart disease. Excess sodium intake can also enhance your risk of osteoporosis, because the more sodium you excrete, the more calcium you lose. If you consume one teaspoon of salt (about 2300 mg of sodium) a day, you could lose through your urine enough calcium to cause your skeleton to dissolve by approximately ten percent per decade. Reducing sodium intake to about 1600 mg a day would lessen the calcium excreted by one-third. Another good reason to limit sodium: taken in excess, it may trigger hot flashes.

If you tend to retain sodium, you can solve the problem by avoiding sodium in your diet as much as possible. Of course, that's easier said than done—we Americans love our sodium. We take in about fifteen percent of it from the salt shaker, ten percent more from salt occurring naturally in foods, and the rest from processed foods, including soups, ketchup, salad dressing, and frozen entrées. If you experiment with fresh and dried herbs and spices, you'll find lots of tasty, sodium-free ways to add zip to your cooking. (See Appendix A for suggestions.) Vitamin B_6, a natural diuretic, also helps. (For more vitamin information, see Chapter 3.) Also, if you find that you're retaining water, drink water. It helps to flush excess sodium out of your system.

SUGAR

Sugar is everywhere and by far one of the most widely used additives. You probably already know that too much sugar in your diet can make you put on pounds and feel sluggish. After menopause, the number of reasons to avoid—or at a minimum, decrease—your intake of sugar soars.

Like caffeine, sugar stresses the adrenal glands, critical producers of hormones all your life but especially during your menopause years. Sugar can raise your triglyceride levels, and it may speed osteoporosis because it depletes your body's store of phosphorus—which, in turn, can interfere with your calcium absorption. Plus, unlike other foods you eat, which contribute calories *and* vital nutrients, sugar provides no nutrients to speak of. And in order to be metabolized, it *uses* vital nutrients like calcium, magnesium, manganese, and others. Thus a regular diet high in sugar can cause a nutrient imbalance in your body—and possibly lead to mood changes, irritability, and anxiety resulting from depletion of B vitamins. Too much sugar can also aggravate heart disease and osteoporosis.

Eating sugar further exacerbates existing blood sugar imbalances. The impact is much greater when you eat sugar alone, rather than as part of a meal. When you have a chocolate bar as a snack, for instance, or a donut as your breakfast, blood sugar levels rise rapidly, signaling the pancreas to produce insulin so that sugar from the blood is transferred to the cells. A rapid rise in blood sugar may cause the pancreas to overreact and produce more insulin than needed, which results in a dramatic fall in blood sugar, since insulin transports some sugar from the blood to the cells. Repeated stress on the pancreas can cause pancreatic cells to become exhausted and eventually one of two things may happen: the pancreas may stop producing insulin or produce only an insufficient amount, or the cells' uptake of sugar is minimized, leaving more of it behind in the blood. In both these cases the result is the same: high blood sugar. Also, a diet high in sugar can exacerbate the genetic tendency toward adult-onset diabetes.

On the other hand, if you suffer from low blood sugar, eating sugar can only make it lower, causing the body to remove even more sugar from the blood and transfer it to the cells. The result may be feelings of shakiness, fatigue, moodiness, faintness, headache, or lethargy. Again the impact will be much greater if you eat sugar alone, rather than as part of a meal.

Another problem with excess sugar intake is that it may affect the body's acid-base balance. During menopause, vaginal secretions are more alkaline than before, and eating sugar boosts these alkaline levels even higher. As a result you become more susceptible to vaginal infections and excess candida albicurs, causing a yeast infection.

And as if all this weren't enough, sugar can make you fat, because excess calories, no matter what the source, is stored in the body as fat. Sugar intake, as I mentioned earlier, leads to the release of insulin, which in turn encourages fat storage, particularly when large amounts of sugar are eaten between meals, with no other food.

Keeping sugar out of your diet is admittedly a tough task—after all, sugar can be found in everything from peanut butter to aspirin, not to mention the obvious sources like candy bars and cake. To get an idea of just how prevalent sugar is, check out the following:

Hidden Sources of Sugar	Number of Teaspoons of Sugar (approximate)
Chewing gum, 1 stick	.5
Ketchup, 1 tablespoon	1
Marshmallow, 1	1.5
Beets, pickled, ½ cup	2
Granola bar, 1 oz.	2
Ice milk, vanilla, ½ cup	3
Low-fat frozen yogurt, ½ cup	7
Cranberry sauce, ¼ cup	3
Low-fat fruit yogurt, 1 cup	13

What's more, there are more than a dozen varieties of sugar, including sucrose, glucose, fructose, raw sugar, honey, molasses, maple syrup, lactose, dextrose, corn syrup, high-fructose corn syrup, brown syrup, and the three sugar alcohols known as sorbitol, mannitol, and xylitol. To get ahead of the game, become an avid reader of food package labels, and keep an eye out for those "ose" and "itol" words. Make sensible food swaps—oatmeal cookies sweetened with fruit juice instead of the chocolate chip kind, fresh fruit or a frozen fruit bar instead of ice cream for dessert, and spices like ginger, nutmeg, cinnamon, and vanilla instead of sugar. And fruit-flavored vinegars like raspberry and blueberry can add a sweet touch to salads.

HORMONE REPLACEMENT THERAPY
WHAT IS IT? IS IT FOR YOU?

If you're just starting to experience some of the symptoms of menopause, then you've probably been thinking about some things you've never thought about before . . . like hormones. You may be wondering about how those menopausal symptoms you're experiencing relate to diminished hormone levels—and about the possibility of restoring some of these hormones in the form of natural or synthetic estrogen replacement therapy (ERT) or hormone replacement therapy (HRT) to help you feel more like your old self again. Some of your friends may be on hormone replacement and raving about the good results they've gotten. Still, you've read and heard *other* things about these treatments that worry you. What should you do?

First, the facts.

WHAT'S ERT/HRT?

For many women, ERT/HRT allows the body to function much as it had prior to "the Change." ERT/HRT helps alleviate many of the unpleasant early symptoms of menopause such as hot flashes and vaginal dryness, as well as delaying or preventing some long-term health problems including osteoporosis and heart disease.

What's the difference between estrogen replacement therapy and hormone replacement therapy? The treatment is called ERT when the supplement contains estrogen only, and HRT when the supplement contains either estrogen with progestin (the synthetic form of progesterone) or estrogen with natural progesterone.

In general, ERT is prescribed only for those women who've had a hysterectomy who don't need the addition of progesterone to counteract the effects of estrogen on their uterine lining, since they don't have a uterus. No treatment is without its side effects, and the problem with ERT is that it can greatly increase a woman's risk of cancer of the endometrium (lining of the uterus). As a result, the vast majority of women who opt for hormone replacement therapy take the combination found in HRT. However, some doctors think that even women who've had their uterus removed can still benefit from HRT because progesterone may help them delay the onset or halt the progression of osteoporosis as well as alleviate many menopausal symptoms. So chances are, if you and your doctor agree that hormones are right for you, you'll be given a prescription for HRT.

In making the decision to take hormone replacement therapy or not, you'll also need to decide whether to take it in natural or synthetic form. What's a "natural" hormone? You may have thought "natural" meant a natural source, but it does not. It is a hormone that matches the type of circulating hormone that your body produces.

What are the sources of hormones? As for estrogen, there are currently three forms of estrogen. One is made from the urine of pregnant mares (one brand is Premarin). Another form is estradiol; one brand is Estrace. And a third form, estriol, is frequently prescribed for women who normally can't tolerate estrogen. This form of estrogen has been available in Europe for many years but is not licensed for use in the U.S. Since it is a weak form of estrogen, it must be taken in larger-than-usual quantities to be effective. It is believed that unlike all the other estrogens, estriol does not increase a woman's risk of endometrial hyperplasia (overthickening of the lining of the uterus). Other brands of synthetic forms of estrogen include Estinyl, Estrovis, Estratas, and Ogon.

As I noted above, there are three members of the estrogen family: estradiol, estrone, and estriol. Typically, human estrogen is composed of 10–20% estradiol, 10–20% estrone, and 60–80% estriol. Synthetic estrogen, for example, sold under the name Premarin, is roughly composed of 5–19% estradiol and other types of estrogen, 75–80% estrone, and 6–15% equilin (a form of estrogen found exclusively in horses). Other synthetic estrogens, including the estrogen patch (Estraderm) and estrogen cream (Estrace), are 100% estradiol. Estradiol is the most powerful form of estrogen, which is found in substantially smaller amounts (10–20%) of circulating human hormone.

Why is estriol omitted from synthetic estrogen? Many physicians view estriol as a weak and unimportant estrogen. Yet the European medical community has been using estriol for years, and has found it particularly helpful in eliminating vaginal thinning, painful sexual intercourse, urinary incontinence, and recurrent urinary tract infections.

Alternative physicians question whether the primary cancer danger is not due to estrogen that is unopposed by progesterone or progestin, but rather from estradiol and estrone, and that is not opposed by estriol, which is known to oppose the growth of cancer as it antagonizes the proliferative activities of other estrogens.

Alternative practitioners frequently use "triple estrogen" or "Tri-Est," which contains 10–20% estradiol, 10–20% estrone, and 60–80% estriol. This estrogen combination mimics the body's but does not increase the risk of endometrial cancer as synthetic estrogens do.

Progesterone is found in the roots of the wild yam and in soybeans, and then made into a progesterone cream or oil you can rub into the skin or as a tablet you can take orally. Natural progesterone is identical to the progesterone produced by the ovaries, while synthetic progesterone, progestin, does not match the body's chemistry exactly and can produce many side effects.

However, for the time being, most traditional doctors recommend the natural forms of estrogen and synthetic forms of progesterone. Why the synthetic form of progesterone? As Dr. Leon Speroff, of the Department of Obstetrics and Gynecology at the Oregon Health Science University in Portland, says, "The natural progesterone out there has no quality control. Who knows what's in there? How often does one milligram really contain one milligram?"

Yet there are many doctors who believe that natural progesterone is the only way to go. I suggest that, whenever possible, my clients use the natural form because it usually produces fewer side effects. For example, synthetic progesterone has been associated with depression, anxiety, irritability, bloating, fluid retention, weight gain, and breast tenderness, and it may negate or reduce the positive effects estrogen has on the heart. On the other hand, natural progesterone has not been shown to have these effects.

You'll also be able to choose the *way* you take your ERT/HRT. It's available as estrogen skin patches, estrogen vaginal suppository creams, estrogen pellets, estrogen injections, estrogen tablets, progesterone-coated pills, progesterone oils (taken orally), progesterone creams, progesterone nasal sprays and suppositories, and estrogen/progesterone combination tablets.

ERT/HRT can be taken cyclically (estrogen is taken days 1–25, and progesterone is added from days 16–25. After day 25, when both hormones are not being taken, vaginal bleeding occurs. Or, it can be taken continuously . . . estrogen is taken every day and progesterone is taken days 16–25. Vaginal bleeding then occurs. Or, the combined continuous therapy may be used, where you take estrogen and progesterone every day. Ideally this should eliminate bleeding entirely. Some women may experience episodes of spotting or bleeding when they first start taking this, but it generally stops after about six months.

Of course, you'll want to discuss any questions you might have with your gynecologist, including whether you should consider taking HRT and why, what is the best type of hormone treatment for you, and how frequently you should have follow-up appointments so that you're properly monitored.

BENEFITS OF ERT/HRT

The benefits of ERT/HRT are many. They include:

Stronger, healthier bones. One of the most important benefits of HRT is in preventing osteoporosis, a progressive and debilitating disease. HRT seems to be one of the most effective ways to prevent bone loss and reduce fractures caused by osteoporosis. The estrogen reduces the rate of bone loss, while the progesterone helps to build the bone.

To be effective in fighting osteoporosis, it's best to take HRT as soon as possible after the onset of menopause. Some researchers say that ERT/HRT must continue for 5–10 years after menopause to best protect bones, while others believe that women should continue with ERT/HRT for life. Taking ERT/HRT along with 1000 mg of calcium per day and several other vitamins and minerals listed in Chapter 3, as well as doing weight-bearing exercise such as walking, stair-climbing, or strength training, can help preserve bones even more.

A healthier cardiovascular system. Research indicates that ERT significantly reduces the risk of coronary heart disease, by raising the level of high-density lipoproteins (HDL), or "good" cholesterol, and lowering the level of low-density lipoproteins (LDL), or "bad" cholesterol. As for HRT, the most recent study, known as the Postmenopause Estrogen/Progestin Interventions (PEPI) Trial, found that *both* ERT and HRT reduced the risk of heart disease.

Specifically, the impact hormone replacement protocols had on HDL was studied in 875 healthy postmenopausal women aged 45 to 64 years for three years. The following results were obtained:

- placebo resulted in a small increase in HDL
- synthetic estrogen alone (unopposed) resulted in a large increase in HDL

- synthetic estrogen plus progestin (Provera) resulted in a small increase in HDL
- synthetic estrogen plus natural (micronized, oral) progesterone resulted in a large increase in HDL.

Alzheimer's disease. Research shows that women taking estrogen have a lower risk of developing this disease compared to other post-menopausal women.

Decrease in hot flashes. ERT/HRT has been shown to decrease the number and severity of hot flashes and, in certain cases, to stop them altogether.

Increased vaginal lubrication. Treating the vagina with estrogen or natural progesterone helps replenish vaginal moisture. Vaginal dryness is not only uncomfortable in and of itself but can also cause painful intercourse and soreness.

Fewer infections. ERT/HRT has been shown to reduce the number of vaginal, bladder, and urinary tract infections.

Overall improved feelings. Many menopausal women report fewer mood swings while on ERT/HRT. That's because the return of estrogen and progesterone to the system helps stabilize the activity of the hypothalamus, which controls our emotions. It also frequently leads to a better outlook on life, because of the link between estrogen, progesterone, and endorphins (pain-blocking chemicals secreted from our central nervous system and associated with the "runner's high" athletes experience). What's more, many women say that their once-dormant sex drive awakens when they begin hormone treatment.

Improvement in shape. When levels of estrogen and progesterone are low or absent, menopausal women's body shape frequently changes. The body shape changes can result from loss of muscle and ligament strength, changes caused by osteoporosis, and a change in body fat distribution—a thickening of the waist and abdomen. HRT may help prevent some of these changes.

Keep in mind that, as good as estrogen and progesterone may be, they are *not* miracle cures for aging or poor health. These treatments will not relieve clinical depression, prevent wrinkles, make you slim, or keep your breasts firm.

RISKS OF ERT/HRT

For all the benefits of ERT/HRT, it is not without certain risks, some of which have already been mentioned.

Breast cancer. Some research indicates a link between synthetic estrogen and breast cancer, which has increased in recent years. According to the National Cancer Institute, one in eight women today will suffer from breast cancer (which assumes a 95-year life expectancy). Several studies have shown that the higher the dosage of estrogen and the longer it is taken, the greater the risk—although no one now knows whether estrogen might promote existing growths or cause new growths.

In terms of natural ERT, research suggests that estriol has less breast-cancer-causing potential than synthetic estrogen and may even inhibit the activities of these other estrogens.

Some experts believe that supplementing estrogen with progesterone helps minimize the risk.

Endometrial cancer. The incidence of endometrial cancer (cancer of the mucous membrane lining of the uterus) increases from 5–14 times with synthetic estrogen replacement therapy. Studies indicate that the risk for getting this type of cancer becomes significant after 2–4 years of estrogen therapy. However, if this cancer is detected in the early stages, the cure rate is high—about 90 percent. Also, when progesterone is added to the estrogen treatment for a minimum of 10 days each month, endometrial cancer may be prevented.

In terms of natural estrogen, when estriol is given in reasonable doses and in a pattern that mimics the menstrual cycle (noncontinuous or cyclic doses), it does not appear to be a precursor of endometrial cancer. Actually it may antagonize the proliferation activities of the other estrogens.

Gallbladder disease. Located beneath your liver is the gallbladder, a sac that stores the bile produced by the liver. Bile, which is composed of cholesterol and other substances, is essential to help digest fatty substances after they enter the small intestine. Unfortunately, it's been found that estrogen can increase the amount of cholesterol in the bile. This can result in gallstone formation, which can be painful because stones can cause infection and irritation in the gallbladder. Women taking synthetic ERT [as premarin] ERT have up to two and one half times as many gallbladder operations as other women.

Enlarged fibroids. ERT may increase the size of existing fibroids in the uterus for as long as you're on the treatment. Progesterone therapy, alone, tends to decrease fibroids.

Other possible side effects from synthetic ERT/HRT. Women on *synthetic* ERT/HRT have complained about other symptoms, including:

- breast tenderness caused by fluid retention
- swollen legs and feet caused by fluid retention
- weight gain often caused by fluid retention
- overall bloatedness (estrogen decreases the amount of sodium and water excreted by the kidneys)
- decrease of vitamin B_6 stores, which may cause symptoms including fatigue, depression, irritability, insomnia, and the inability to concentrate (estrogen interferes with the metabolism of B_6)
- nausea, which may occur during the first 2–3 months of ERT/HRT
- migraines
- insomnia
- "withdrawal bleeding" for those taking the cyclic or continuous type of hormone treatment (you bleed each month after day 25, when you stop taking one or both hormones for that month). The bleeding often becomes lighter over the years. In time, you may have no bleeding at all, even if you stay on the hormones.
- "breakthrough bleeding" for those taking the combined con-

tinuous type of hormone treatment—you may experience irregular bleeding at the beginning of treatment. Generally, after six months, the bleeding stops.

Other symptoms, listed below, result from the *way* HRT is taken.

ERT/HRT: SHOULD YOU OR SHOULDN'T YOU?

Because of all you've read and heard on the subject, you might be under the impression that most menopausal American women are receiving some sort of hormone replacement therapy. But you'd be wrong—the number is a mere fifteen to twenty-four percent of women in this country. Why so few? For one thing, ERT/HRT is not recommended for women with certain medical conditions (although special conditions may override them): breast cancer, endometrial cancer, stroke, a history of abnormal blood clotting, uncontrolled hypertension, gallbladder disease, diabetes, thrombophlebitis, liver dysfunction, and undiagnosed abnormal genital bleeding. So if you suffer from any of these, ERT/HRT is generally not recommended.

In addition, another large group of women—which includes those with sickle-cell disease, migraine headaches, uterine fibroids, fibrocystic disease or fibroadenoma of the breast, benign breast disease, endometriosis, seizure disease, a family history of breast cancer, and smokers—are discouraged from taking ERT/HRT.

If you have any of these conditions, don't despair. You can still get relief from menopausal symptoms using nonhormonal treatments, as described in the symptom/treatment section earlier on.

When you go to your gynecologist to discuss the possibility of ERT/HRT, make sure you review your medical history and have a complete exam to rule out any of these conditions. This baseline testing will probably include a breast and pelvic exam, a blood pressure check, a pap smear, a urinalysis, a blood chemistry profile including a lipid profile, a mammogram (if you haven't had one in the last year), a baseline proctosigmoidoscopic (which should be done once every three years after age fifty), and perhaps an endometrial biopsy. You should also ask about getting a bone density assessment.

The question of ERT/HRT comes down to a personal decision for all menopausal women. Some feel that it's unnatural to add hormones to the body, while others see hormone replacement as a way to restore some essential substances to the body, much as a diabetic restores needed insulin through medication.

I usually recommend to my clients who are undecided about taking ERT/HRT for relief of menopausal symptoms that if their doctor is in agreement, they try it only *after* trying the kind of program of diet/exercise/vitamins and minerals outlined in this book, *provided* they do not have immediate health risks that ERT/HRT can relieve. And I recommend *natural* HRT. If those changes fail to relieve their menopausal symptoms, then they might revisit the hormone issue. The choice is ultimately theirs.

5

Is Menopause Making You Fat?

"I'm getting fat—help!"

"I'm eating the same as I always do and I weigh the same, but I can't fit into my clothes anymore. What's happening?"

"I'm eating less, I exercise five times a week, yet the pounds keep creeping up—and I can't shake them loose. It's like they're glued onto me. What can I do?"

Many of my menopausal clients come to see me for advice on how to relieve menopausal symptoms such as hot flashes and fatigue through a change in food and lifestyle. The majority of them, though, are looking for the solution to one problem in particular: weight gain. Because this is such a big issue for so many women, I'm devoting much of the remainder of this book to the subject of weight—why it's happening now and what specifically you can do about it.

Some women entering menopause have struggled with extra pounds all their lives. Other normally thin women never knew the meaning of "watching your weight"—till now. But regardless of your weight history, it's easy to become upset and frustrated—and to blame your problem on menopause.

IS IT MENOPAUSE . . . OR SOMETHING ELSE?

Some research shows that there is indeed a tendency for women at menopause to get heavier. Research scientist Judith Wurtman,

128

Ph.D., of the Massachusetts Institute of Technology's Office of Nutrition and Behavior Studies, did a study, questionioning 490 postmenopausal women about their weight. She discovered that about 65 percent of those who had been of normal weight prior to menopause got heavier during menopause, usually adding 10 or 15 pounds, whether the menopause was surgical or natural. And a whopping 96 percent of overweight or obese women entering menopause eventually gained even more—as many as 23 additional pounds. The length of time over which this weight was gained is not known. The results were more or less the same for those taking hormones as for those who weren't. The logical assumption might be that some of these women just started *eating* more, but that didn't appear to be the case. A mere 22 percent of the women studied reported increasing their food intake. Of course, research also indicates that people often underestimate the amount they eat, so a much larger percentage of women may in fact have been eating more than they had realized (and reported).

However, there are other equally compelling findings on menopause and weight gain that suggest there's no direct link between the two. In 1984 Rena Wing, Ph.D., and Karen Matthews, Ph.D., of the University of Pittsburgh studied 485 pre-menopausal women between the ages of 42 and 50, then re-evaluated them in 1987. By the end of the study, the subjects had gained an average of five pounds, and no significant difference was seen between the weight gain of those who began menopause during that three-year period and those who didn't, nor between those who started at a healthy weight and those who were overweight or obese. The extra pounds, the researchers concluded, were probably the result of the normal slowing down of the metabolism due to aging.

It's certainly possible that aging can be responsible for your weight gain now. But the role that menopause plays is not as clear. The reason the answers seem so fuzzy is that it's hard to separate the natural consequences of aging from those that are a result of menopause. Science has not yet provided us with that information since most health research that's been done in recent years has been limited to white, middle-class *men*. That situation is slowly changing, and new findings relevant to women's health are beginning to emerge. But for now the experts believe that—apart from obvious factors like genetics, overeating, or underactive thyroid—menopausal weight gain may be attributed to one or more of the following:

Loss of muscle mass. As you age, you gradually lose muscle mass, so your resting metabolism slows down. When that happens, the calories you eat aren't being burned as efficiently as before. The metabolism slows down by about 2–3 percent every decade, which means that even if you continue to eat and exercise the same as always, you'll probably gain weight.

A history of yo-yo dieting may further complicate matters. Whenever you lose weight, you lose mostly fat and some lean muscle mass. When you gain the weight back, some researchers believe that you add it back mostly as fat. So every time you lose weight and put it back on, you may be changing your fat-to-lean ratio—for the worse. If you've been a yo-yo dieter, you could be starting out menopause with a disadvantage.

The solution? Strength training, which can help you rebuild some of the lost muscle and help you sustain it. And if you decide to decrease your caloric intake, think *lifelong* healthy eating style changes.

Inactivity. If you're doing more resting than running around these days, you're going to gain weight. Again, there's an easy answer to the problem: exercise. Even if you've never been a big exerciser before, you can drop extra pounds, lose body fat, build up your bones and muscles, and feel better with regular aerobic activity and strength training. More on that in Chapter 9.

Powerful food cravings. By definition menopause is a time when there's no clear hormonal pattern; as a result you may experience food cravings until your hormones start stabilizing. These cravings, if left uncontrolled, can lead to overeating and possible weight gain. With proper planning you can fuel your system at regular, frequent intervals (e.g., six mini-meals rather than three meals with no snacks) and control those cravings.

Loss of the calorie-burning effect of menstruation. Some studies show that a woman's metabolism varies throughout the menstrual cycle, with stepped-up metabolic activity during the second half of the cycle. It's possible that your body burns additional calories during those fourteen-odd days, and obviously, that benefit is lost once you enter menopause.

Increased insulin stores. Insulin is a hormone that, besides regulating blood sugar, favors fat storage and inhibits fat breakdown. Some experts believe that as you age your insulin production increases. Some believe that insulin production rises because you have a genetic tendency toward this, while others believe it's linked to being overweight; still others say it's tied in with diminished estrogen levels. Until the experts reach agreement, what you can do to avoid excess insulin production is to limit your intake of refined sugars, step up your intake of low-fat sources of protein, eat whole grains, watch your portion size, exercise, and maintain a healthy body weight.

Increased fluid in the body. During menopause, some women retain more fluid in their bodies. But unlike normal water weight, which usually is short-lived, this tendency towards fluid retention may remain until your hormonal fluctuations stop. Experts don't quite understand the reason for this phenomenon, but they agree that it can often cause frustrating weight problems for menopausal women.

Brown fat. There are actually *two* types of fat cells in the body: white fat, the insulating fat layer stored under the skin, and brown fat, found along the backbone, the adrenal glands, the kidneys, and the aorta of the heart. Brown fat actually *burns* excess calories as heat rather than storing them the way white fat does. Although some studies conducted indicate that you lose your brown fat very early in life, other studies conducted on animals show that adults do in fact retain brown fat, but the number of brown fat cells gradually decreases with age, which may be one of the reasons you're gaining weight now. But it may be possible to boost your level of brown fat through exercise and by taking gamma linolenic acid, an Omega-6 fatty acid found in vegetable oils, or evening primrose oil and borage oil (all available in health food stores). For more on this, see Chapter 2.

THE SHAPE OF THINGS TO COME

Besides any weight gain you may be experiencing now, you have probably also noticed a chance in your body's *shape*. To get a better idea of why your body build is changing, let's look back at how your body first began to take the shape it did.

Think back to when you were a young girl—say age ten or eleven. Chances are that your body pretty much resembled those of the other girls—and boys—your age: straight up and down. Then came the "P" word: puberty, the time of raging hormones and all sorts of physical changes. That's when your body, and those of other adolescent girls, started to assume the basic female shape, with your breasts, hips, and buttocks generally curving out and your waist curving in. As for those guys you knew, their bodies were starting to change, too. While the basic up-and-down shape stayed pretty much the same, the baby fat gradually disappeared and they developed more muscle mass, usually in the chest and shoulders.

The reasons for these different shapes? Those hormones I mentioned earlier. Although both sexes carry male and female hormones, they are in dramatically different amounts. A man's dominant hormone, testosterone, enhances muscle mass, not fat. If there *is* any excess fat to be stored, testosterone directs it to the male abdomen. Meanwhile, the primary female hormones that kick in during puberty are estrogen and progesterone. Estrogen distributes female fat to the breasts, thighs, and hips. This explains why overweight men tend to develop an apple shape, with the extra weight centered on their middle, while overweight women are usually pear-shaped, with *their* additional pounds concentrated in the hips and thighs. While you may not love your lower-body bulges, they *do* give you an added health advantage over a chubby, apple-shaped man (or woman). Research shows that lower-body fat doesn't stress the body as much as upper-body fat does, and so you're at less risk for cardiovascular disease, diabetes, hypertension, and certain types of cancer.

THE MENOPAUSE FACTOR:
HOW IT MODIFIES BODY SHAPE

Your body continues to change as you age and go through menopause. Now, your body manufactures smaller and smaller amounts of the female hormones estrogen and progesterone. Suddenly, the ratio of female-to-male hormones changes, with testosterone possibly becoming a more dominant hormone. Consequently, your once-curvy body starts to square off or, as one gynecologist puts it, "It changes from an hourglass to a cereal box." Now you may see your body fat shifting to your belly—the spot where men typically store *their* extra fat. The scale may show that you weigh the same as ever, but suddenly you may have a hard time fastening the waistband on your skirt or slacks. What's more, you now become more susceptible to the kinds of health risks associated with the apple-shaped body.

Is there anything that can be done to prevent or reverse this shift in body fat? Some experts believe ERT/HRT can delay this redistribution of fat, although the findings have been inconsistent. Exercise, to keep your muscle, ligament, and bone strength can help, too, since loss of strength in these areas can all contribute to a changed body shape. If you're very concerned about the potential health risks, measure your own waist-to-hip ratio (see the formula that follows). If it's high, you might want to discuss this with your doctor.

ARE YOU REALLY OVERWEIGHT?

You may indeed have put on a few pounds since entering menopause, and your body may not look quite the way it used to, but are you *truly* overweight—is it causing your health to be at risk? It's entirely possible that you'll need to pay more attention to proper eating, exercise, and nutritional supplements to ease many of your menopausal symptoms, though you *may* not need to worry about dealing with excess weight.

How can you tell? Below are three ways, which you can use singly or in combination.

Method 1: Waist-to-Hip Ratio. Before deciding that you have to lose weight, let's look at *where* your fat is located. This waist-to-hip ratio will tell you whether you're predominantly apple-shaped or pear-shaped and thus at how much risk you are for certain diseases. As I said earlier, apple-shaped folks are at greater risk for developing such conditions as diabetes, hypertension, heart disease, gallbladder disease, and certain types of cancer when compared to pear-shaped people.

To see how you fare, you'll need a calculator, pencil and paper, and a tape measure.

1. Stand in a relaxed position, with your legs slightly apart. Measure your waist at the smallest part *without holding your stomach in*. Record that number.
2. Take your hip measurement, around the widest part of your buttocks. Record that number.
3. Divide your waist measurement by your hip measurement:
   $$\frac{\text{WAIST}}{\text{HIP}} = \underline{\hspace{1cm}} \text{ inches}$$
4. The number you end up with is your waist-to-hip ratio.

The magic number here is 0.80, which means that your waist measurement is 80 percent of your hip measurement. If your number is lower than 0.80, you do not carry the majority of your fat in your upper body and so you are probably not at medical risk. If your number is higher, you are at greater health risk.

Method 2: Body Mass Index (BMI). With this formula, you'll determine the *amount* of fat you have and whether that places you at an increased health risk. To calculate your BMI, you'll need a calculator, pencil, and paper.

1. Multiply your current weight by the number 705.
2. Divide that number by your height, in inches.
3. Divide once again by your height, in inches.
4. The number you end up with is your BMI.

Let's say Joanne is a 5'4" woman who weighs 140 pounds. Multiply 140 by 705, to get 98,700. Then divide that number by

64 inches, and you get 1542 (rounded off to the nearest whole number). Divide 1542 by 64, and you get 24 (rounded off to the nearest whole number).

The "ideal" BMI numbers range from 20–25, so Joanne's weight is just fine and she is within the range designated as producing the lowest health risk. If your number is higher than 25, you're considered overweight, and if it's above 30, you're medically obese—and if it's below 20, you're considered too thin.

If you fall into the overweight or obese category, you may be at increased risk for heart disease, certain cancers, and diabetes mellitus.

Method 3: Suggested "Healthy" Weights for Adults. Next, determine what's considered a "healthy" weight for your height and frame. Although the Metropolitan Life Insurance tables have long been considered the standard, I prefer using the chart that follows. Made available by the U.S Departments of Agriculture and Health and Human Services, it recognizes the fact that "healthy" weight does change with age. The "healthy" weight range provided below is for women 35 years and older.

You'll notice that weights given are for both men and women, but as a woman you might want to refer to the middle to lower end of the range because women are generally smaller than men and have less muscle and less-dense bones.

SHOULD YOU TRY TO LOSE WEIGHT?

Now that you've evaluated your waist-to-hip ratio, BMI, and "healthy" weight, you can decide whether your excess weight is increasing your health risk. If it is, you may consider dropping a few pounds to remedy this situation by following the guidelines to one of the weight-loss plans in Chapter 8. Or perhaps your weight is not causing a health problem, but getting rid of some excess weight might make you feel better about yourself.

Whether or not you decide to lose weight is ultimately up to you. That's your choice.

Suggested "Healthy" Weights for Adults (35 years and older)	
Height (without shoes)	Weight in Pounds (without clothes)
5'0"	108–138
5'1"	111–143
5'2"	115–148
5'3"	119–152
5'4"	122–157
5'5"	126–162
5'6"	130–167
5'7"	134–172
5'8"	138–178
5'9"	142–183
5'10"	146–188
5'11"	151–194
6'0"	155–199
6'1"	159–205
6'2"	164–210
6'3"	168–216
6'4"	173–222
6'5"	177–228
Source: Derived from National Research Council, 1989.	

6

Your Lifestyle Inventory— Starting Your Trim-Down/ Shape-Up Journey

You've seen it happening for weeks or even months . . . and so have your family and friends. You know the change in your body shape and that extra weight that's crept on. Before, it always seemed so *easy* to knock off a few pounds whenever you needed to, or maybe you didn't even bother to lose weight and made peace with your weight and the way you look. But things have changed. Now you're definitely *not* happy. You may not be able to do much—short of costly plastic surgery—about your sagging breasts, or about those laugh lines that are nothing to laugh about. But understand this: *how much you eat, whether you exercise, and how much you succumb to stress each day are things you have control over*.

While you can't regulate many of the changes you're now going through, your lifestyle is definitely one area where *you* call the shots. Sure, you can always sit back and bemoan the loss of your once-girlish figure—and keep eating that coffee cake. *Or* you can take control so you can look and feel your best, for all the years ahead of you. And statistics show that there are *plenty* of them. If you're fifty, you can plan on living about *thirty more years*—and probably even longer if you take care of yourself.

The question is: What are you going to do about it?

Presumably, you're going to get into gear and start eating right and exercising, regularly even if modestly. After all, isn't that why you're reading this book? And help is here! So, let's get started!

GET A CLEAN BILL OF HEALTH

Before beginning any weight-loss or shape-up plan, it's a good idea to get a physical exam and a doctor's go-ahead for your program. My clients have found it helpful to have their blood pressure taken and have laboratory tests of urine and blood (including a lipid profile) to provide baseline information on their nutritional status, blood cholesterol, and other important data. Later on, as they follow the weight-loss guidelines outlined in Chapter 8, they have their blood rechecked and see substantial health improvements, which makes them all the more motivated to keep going.

Along with lab work, some clients who use an alternative health practitioner may have a mineral-tissue analysis, also called a hair analysis because pieces of hair very close to the scalp are clipped and examined at a special lab. Admittedly, this is a very controversial test. Yet some health professionals find it a helpful guide in revealing the level of any toxic metals present in the patient's body, such as lead, aluminum, and cadmium. Whatever baseline tests you undergo is up to you and your doctor.

LIFESTYLE INVENTORY

No slim-down/shape-up program, no matter how good, will be effective until you've established your own personal starting point and set reasonable, doable goals for yourself. Remember, your goal *isn't* to end up looking like Julia Roberts, who's about a head and a half taller than most women and won't be worrying about menopause for another few decades. No, you're striving to be your own personal best, trying to ward off any potential health problems and meet, head-on, any obstacles you encounter along the way to your goal. So let's see where you are right now. Answer all of the following questions True or False.

MY HEALTH

I am making some diet, exercise, and
   lifestyle changes since my doctor told
   me my weight was aggravating or the
   cause of my high blood pressure,
   cholesterol, diabetes, heart disease, etc. __True __False

I do not smoke cigarettes. __True __False

I do not use "recreational" drugs. __True __False

I usually get seven or more hours of
   sleep a night. __True __False

TOTAL: True____ False____

MY WEIGHT LOSS HISTORY

I've been a yo-yo dieter—no sooner
   do I slim down than I regain the
   weight (and sometimes more)—but
   now I'm determined to break that
   pattern. __True __False

In the past I've been able to lose
   weight and keep it off for at least a
   year. __True __False

When I've decided to lose weight in
   the past, I did it by eating a sensible,
   balanced diet and by exercising. __True __False

My current weight is not the cause
   of any of my health problems. __True __False

I resist fad diets. __True __False

TOTAL: True____ False____

MY EATING HABITS

Every day I eat a variety of foods
   from the six basic food groups:
   fruits, vegetables, proteins, breads/
   cereal, low-fat dairy products (skim
   milk, nonfat yogurt, etc.) and heart-
   healthy fats (canola and olive oils, etc.). __True __False

I rarely eat fried foods.	__True	__False
I usually bake, broil, or steam foods.	__True	__False
I eat whole-grain breads rather than white breads.	__True	__False
I try to get as much fiber as possible into my daily diet by eating plenty of fresh fruits and vegetables.	__True	__False
I limit the number of egg yolks I eat to four or fewer per week.	__True	__False
I eat little or no cake, candy, cookies, or other sweets.	__True	__False
I limit my intake of heart-healthy fats to about one tablespoon per day.	__True	__False
I limit my saturated fat intake by removing the skin from chicken and visible fat from meats, and by rarely, if ever, eating high-fat meats such as pork sausages, luncheon meats, and bologna.	__True	__False
I generally don't add salt to my foods.	__True	__False
I generally don't add sugar to my foods or beverages.	__True	__False
I limit my caffeinated coffee- or tea-drinking to two or fewer cups a day.	__True	__False
I drink six to eight glasses of water daily.	__True	__False
I limit my alcohol intake to one drink a day.	__True	__False
I take a multivitamin/mineral tablet daily.	__True	__False
I eat regularly throughout the day (two to three meals, plus healthy snacks).	__True	__False

TOTAL: True___ False___

MY EXERCISE HABITS

I try to fit in exercise whenever I can. __True __False

I do aerobic exercise (walking, jogging,
aerobic classes, etc.) three to five times
a week for *thirty or more* minutes per
session. __True __False

When there is a choice of stairs or an
elevator, I usually opt for the stairs. __True __False

When given a choice between walking
or driving, I will usually walk. __True __False

When I'm away from home on business or vacation, I still squeeze some
exercise into my routine. __True __False

I do strength training two or three
times a week for twenty to forty-five
minutes per session. __True __False

TOTAL: True__ False__

MY STRESS LEVEL

I am not under a great deal of stress
right now and I'm able to concentrate
on a slim-down/shape-up program. __True __False

When something stressful in my life
happens, I'm able to let go of it and
accomplish what I set out to do. __True __False

When I'm under a lot of stress, I use
exercise or relaxation techniques to
help relieve the stress. __True __False

I don't find it difficult to lose weight,
even when I'm under a lot of stress. __True __False

I've learned how to remain calm even
in the most stressful situations. __True __False

TOTAL: True__ False__

MY MOTIVATION LEVEL

I am now determined to stick to a
slim-down/shape-up plan.   __True __False

I have clearly identified the reasons I
want to lose weight now.   __True __False

During my weight-loss journey, when
the going gets rough I will remind
myself of the reasons I want to lose
weight, rather than respond by eating.   __True __False

Compared to my previous attempts
to slim down, I am now extremely
motivated.   __True __False

I recognize that losing weight takes
time and I have the patience to
persevere.   __True __False

I have learned how to focus on my
feelings, rather than feed my negative
feelings.   __True __False

If I eat a high-fat or high-calorie food
I didn't plan on having, I can let go of
it rather than telling myself I blew it
and start bingeing.   __True __False

I am in touch with my physical hunger.   __True __False

I do not have trouble controlling how
much I eat because I realize that if I
don't have a particular food today, I
can always have it tomorrow.   __True __False

I recognize that, to lose weight and
maintain it, I have to develop other
pleasures in life besides eating.   __True __False

I do not need instant weight-loss gratification; I can stay motivated even if weight
loss is slow and takes a long time.   __True __False

Once I start a weight-loss program
and I find it isn't working for me, I
will change what doesn't work, rather
than giving up.   __True __False

I feel extremely confident that I will
   keep the weight off once I lose it.   __True   __False

                                      TOTAL: True___   False__

   Yes, there are a *lot* of questions, but they're all here for a reason. The best way to know where you're going is to know where
you *are*, and this self-test will give you insight into your current
habits and attitudes, so you know exactly how to proceed. Count
up the number of True and False responses so you can see how
you fare in each category. Each True represents a positive attitude
or eating and exercise habit, as well as reveals good news about
your health and weight history. There is no one "right" number of
True answers—your aim is simply to have as many Trues as possible, now and as you follow your new eating-exercise-and-stress-
management program.
   Take a look for a moment at your False responses—they will
help you figure out where you should focus your attention. For
example, perhaps you responded False to the statement "Compared to my previous attempts to slim down, I am now extremely
motivated." Maybe you are, in fact, *not* motivated now because
what you're doing is remembering your dieting failures, and so
you're somewhat skeptical about your current chances for success. But your past need not repeat itself, providing you find—
and break—the weak link in the chain. Maybe in the past you
tended to follow the latest fad diet, or you latched onto weight-
loss gimmicks that you couldn't sustain long-term; if so, no wonder your results were short-lived. In this book you're going to
learn new approaches to weight loss and exercise and experience
how different foods and levels of activity affect your weight-loss
efforts and your state of well-being *for life*.

GET READY FOR SUCCESS!

   While there's not much you can do about certain aspects of
your health or your weight-loss history, most of the situations
detailed here involve changes that are indeed under your control—and that will, if you work on them, help you achieve your
health, fitness, and weight-loss goals. Don't overwhelm yourself

by attempting to change too many things at once. If you want to see success, focus on small, manageable changes and keep practicing them until they become habits.

Start now by choosing one of the questions that you do, in fact, have some control over and that you answered with False. Figure out what steps you can take to turn this around. For the next couple of weeks, work on this goal. Then in two more weeks, take some time to review the questions and choose a second attitude or habit you would like to change and tackle that one. Whatever you work on will need continual practice, even after you shift your attention to new goals. As you keep practicing, your new behaviors and attitudes will become habit.

7

Getting Psyched to Trim Down
and Shape Up

No goal you set for yourself—whether it's to land a better job, find a significant other, lose weight, or shape up—will ever be reached unless one thing happens first: you are properly motivated. You can talk all you want about how much you want something . . . to lose weight, reclaim your waistline, be more active, cut down on some of the junk you are eating . . . but talk is cheap. Only *action* brings change, and only *internal motivation* drives a person to act and to keep going until the goal has been met, and beyond.

What do I mean by internal motivation? It's the strong desire to do something because *it's very important to you.* It's internal motivation that propels you to lose weight once and for all when you catch yourself saying or thinking things like:

"I want to lose weight because it's holding me back from doing the things I want to do."

"I want to lose weight because it's important to me that I fit into my clothes better."

"I want to change my eating habits because I will be healthier."

"I want to slim down because it will make me happier with the way I look in the mirror."

Get the idea? All of these statements express a feeling on the part of the speaker—"I" statements. If you look carefully, you'll notice that there are *no* statements like:

"Steve won't go near me sexually until I lose some weight. So I'd better lose some weight quickly because I wouldn't want him turning to other women to satisfy his sexual needs."

"My son's wedding is coming up this summer. I'd better do something about my weight fast."

"My sister told me my weight is getting out of hand. Maybe she's right."

In my experience as a nutritionist and health consultant for twenty-one years, I've witnessed one pattern time and time again: when someone is internally driven to lose weight, the weight usually comes off and *stays* off. But when the motivation comes from an external source—an upcoming event like a class reunion or bathing suit season, or the desire to please another person—the weight may be lost initially but is often eventually regained. That's because, after the event has passed, or the person you're trying to please loses interest in your weight (or you), there's no real reason left to keep up the eating-and-exercise plan. You have to want to lose the weight *for yourself*—because you want it, because it's important to you. And if you do, *and are persistent*, chances are excellent that you'll reach your weight-loss finish line.

The good news is that external motivation can actually be transformed into internal motivation. For instance, let's say you decide that, in order to look terrific in your mother-of-the-groom gown this July, you're going to start to exercise, for the first time in your life. Someone suggested you take up race-walking—for a half hour a day, a few days a week, around your neighborhood park. And you do. As you slowly get into the groove of tying up the laces of your walking shoes every Saturday, Monday, and Wednesday morning, zipping around the park and seeing good results—the waistband on your skirt is finally comfortable or your weight has dropped—something unexpected happens: you suddenly find that you're *enjoying* the exercise for its own sake—wedding or no wedding! You *like* the way you feel working up a slight sweat and getting your pulse going a bit and knowing as you take your post-workout shower that you've just done something very good and very healthy for yourself. You feel more energetic, more in control of your life—and, yes, you're going to look better in that dress at your son's wedding. But there's more. To your surprise, you find yourself making a vow to continue race-walking . . . long after the kids are back from their honeymoon.

That's the way external motivation can become internalized. But let's say your motivation needs a bit of stoking right now. You *know* you want to slim down, but you can't get yourself sufficiently fired up to make the necessary commitment. Spend a few minutes right now focusing on exactly *why* you want to lose weight.

On the lines below, finish this statement:

I want to lose weight NOW because_____

_____

_____

_____

Next, get in touch with the benefits you'll receive from losing weight—anything from hearing compliments to fitting more comfortably into an airplane seat to liking yourself more to enjoying the sense and feeling of empowerment you get from taking control. Also, focus on those things you may have to give up—after all, there's some trade-off for anything that's worthwhile. Fill in the following lines:

The benefits of losing weight are:

_____

_____

_____

_____

_____

The trade-offs of losing weight are:

_____

_____

_____

Obviously, your list should reflect your belief that the benefits will outweigh the costs. If they don't, you may want to reconsider why you're attempting a weight-loss program. Permanently changing your eating and exercise routine takes time and effort; there's no point in starting if you're not going to see it through. Long-term weight loss and shape-up depend on a total commitment to a brand new life-style—and the deep-seated belief that you will benefit in many ways besides wearing a smaller size dress.

AFFIRMATIONS/VISUALIZATIONS

Affirmations are positive statements in the present tense. When repeated—silently, spoken aloud, or written down—they can help you replace negative mind chatter with more positive ideas, attitudes, and expectations, become more motivated, and reach your desired goal. Here are some examples of relevant affirmations:

- "I have the power to manage my moods without turning to food."
- "I am eating healthy foods and exercising today."
- "I am feeling better every day thanks to my improved diet."
- "Taking a daily walk is enjoyable."
- "Exercising when I don't particularly feel like it reinforces my commitment to my weight-loss program."

Whenever you feel yourself slipping back into some undesirable eating behavior or resisting your exercise program, try repeating an affirmation such as those above. Rather than let a motivational slump sneak up on you and cause you to sabotage your efforts, head it off at the pass with a powerful affirmation that you believe in. It's a surprisingly effective technique. Better yet, follow your affirmations with a visualization. Visualize yourself in a potentially dangerous food situation— imagine that it's a rainy Sunday morning, you've just had breakfast, and are going out to get the morning paper. Yet you remember the great pastries they have in the bakery across the street from the newsstand. What do you do to keep yourself from this detour since you know that if you buy it you will eat it—and then feel awful about yourself. Mentally see yourself handling the situation positively—for example, you go to the newsstand, purchase the paper, and immediately walk back to your car without even looking in the bakery window. Or . . . you get the paper and come home and make yourself a freshly brewed cup of decaffeinated coffee to sip while you're reading the paper. If you don't *see yourself in your mind's eye* successfully handling this situation, then change your action plan. Go to a different newsstand. You don't *have* to give in to temptation, and the more you mentally "see" yourself handling your food challenges, the more you'll be able to do it in real life.

GETTING THE SUPPORT YOU NEED

Are you the kind of person who enjoys doing things alone? Do you usually keep to yourself—and like it? Or do you prefer the company of others as often as possible, whether it's a relative, friend, or an entire *kaffee klatsch*? Your answer to these questions will help you decide whether you would benefit from getting some outside support as you go through the stages of menopause and work on slimming down and shaping up.

Of course you know that when it comes to your eating habits and your exercise routine, *you're* responsible. *You* must do the work to see the results you desire; simply showing up at support group meetings doesn't change any of that. Still, being part of a caring, comforting environment—whether it's over a hot cup of tea in a friend's living room or in the church basement where a

weight-loss group meets weekly—can make dealing with menopause, shedding pounds, and getting back in shape that much easier. Remember that asking for the help you need isn't a sign of
weakness but rather one of strength.

Follow these tips for getting the support you may need:

Identify the type of support you want. If you feel that you can
benefit most from working one-on-one with a person sympa-
thetic to your situation, locate an appropriate friend, family
member, or coworker. If it's someone who is menopausal her-
self and/or has successfully lost weight and kept it off, so much
the better. The person you select might be a health professional
rather than a personal friend—a nutritionist, perhaps, or a psychologist who works with menopausal women. Whomever you
choose, be certain that it's someone who is essentially empa-
thetic, with a positive attitude about life. Avoid those who will
try to make you feel bad when you deviate from your plan of
action, or who will pity you when times get tough, or who is in
her own bind and just wants to commiserate with you about her
weight or health woes. None of these types of people will help
you reach your goals.

Alternatively, you might decide to enroll in a commercial
weight-loss program, such as Weight Watchers or Jenny Craig;
you can find them listed in your yellow pages. Keep in mind that
you will be expected to follow their eating programs and, possibly, to buy and eat their foods, which may or may not suit you.
In addition, your local YWHA or YWCA might also have classes
on health, nutrition, or fitness for menopausal women or even
informal discussion groups on these topics. Or, if you're ambi-
tious, you may want to try to form your own group of like-
minded women by asking your doctor or nutritionist to pass your
name and phone number to his or her other menopausal clients.

Specify the kind of feedback you want. Once you've identified the person who will be your "buddy," let her know the type
of interaction you expect. How frequent do you want the conversations or get-togethers to be? A brief phone call every morning, to touch base? Or do you simply want her to be available on
an as-needed basis, when a crisis or weak moment occurs?

Also, spell out whether you want direct or indirect feedback. Direct feedback might mean a word of praise and recognition for your accomplishments, such as after you've completed a full two weeks of regular aerobic exercise. On the other hand, you may simply prefer indirect encouragement, such as when your buddy suggests that you two get together for a movie instead of dinner at a favorite all-you-can-eat restaurant. In order for her support to be most helpful, you have to let her know at the outset what's best for you.

Praise your partner. Support works both ways. Periodically tell your buddy what a good job *she's* doing in helping motivate you. Ask her if the routine is still comfortable for her and, if not, work out an alternative plan of action. Showing consideration for your supportive person increases the likelihood that the support will continue for as long as you need it.

Review your need for support. Every month or two, step back and take a fresh look at your current support system, and determine whether it's still working for you. Perhaps you could use a new buddy—or maybe your needs have changed and you want to do it solo, without regular feedback from anyone but yourself. If something about your support system isn't as effective for you as you'd like, don't be afraid to change it.

PREPARE FOR WAR IN TIME OF PEACE

There's no easier time to get geared up for a new eating-and-exercise program than at the beginning, when you're convinced that your fondness for broccoli will see you through your chocolate cravings month after month after month. But the truth is that there *will* be times when the thought of putting another vegetable in your mouth could send you scurrying straight to Dunkin' Donuts.

However, you need not succumb to those trying times—if you prepare for them *now* while your motivation is high. Here are

Beware the Saboteurs!

The "evil twin" of the friend or relative who's eager and willing to give support—without a hidden agenda or neediness of her own that must be addressed—is the weight-loss saboteur. She may have a friendly face and claim to have your best interests at heart, but beware! How often have you heard comments like these from so-called loved ones?

- "Oh, come *on!* I spent all day making this meal for you. You can't do this to me!"
- "Have the piece of cake—just this once. What's the harm?"
- "You? Going to the gym at *your* age? Don't you feel embarrassed with all those young people around?"

Why in the world would people say such things when they know you are trying to lose weight and it's important to you? Maybe they feel uncomfortable with the changes you've been making and are unsure how to deal with the "new you." Maybe they don't know how to show you their love in any other way than with food. Maybe they're envious of your new figure and your extra energy.

Whatever the explanation, try to understand the origin of their remarks. If it bothers you enough, you may want to have a heart-to-heart with the person, especially if it's someone you live with or see often—he or she may not even be aware of what's going on. In any case, don't let this saboteur be an excuse to stray from your goals. Stay calm and focused on what you want to achieve.

some tips to help you stay on track in the weeks and months to come:

Shatter the myth of all-or-nothing. Don't expect perfection from yourself. In fact, you don't need to be perfect to be successful. If you miss a day of walking, don't berate yourself; just make sure you squeeze it in the next. If you happen to overdo the fatty foods or eat a bit more than you'd planned at the party, be extra careful with your meals the next couple of days. Remember, doing something positive most of the time is better than nothing.

Challenge your excuses. There'll be days when you simply don't feel like exercising, or want to chuck your sensible eating plan out the window. When those days arrive, ask yourself: what's going on? Find ways to challenge your negative self-talk . . . and talk back!

Don't let a lapse turn into a relapse. What if you start getting sloppy with the foods you eat or your exercise routine? Look at it as a temporary lapse—a simple slip-up—and a warning sign to evaluate what's getting in the way. Then, either continue the program you established for yourself or make necessary adjustments. If you pay attention to your actions and keep focused on your goals, you can stay on top of the situation and avoid a total relapse.

Don't let yourself get bored. If you find you *always* have broiled fish on Monday nights, and you *always* race-walk around the park at 8:30 A.M., it won't be long before you start rebelling against your routine—and maybe throw all your good work away by sliding back into bad habits. Deliberately vary your menus and your workouts so you stay interested. Keep in mind that you're going to be eating and exercising for the rest of your life, so you can't afford not to be creative about both.

Focus on the big picture. What you're doing now is developing behaviors that will last you a lifetime; weight loss is simply a nice by-product. You'll be able to maintain the momentum if you constantly remind yourself of *all* the health and emotional benefits you're deriving from your program.

Set realistic goals. You're not going to turn into an athlete overnight if you've been a couch potato for the last twenty years. If you haven't been exercising, start with five- or ten-minute sessions and slowly build up to more. If you haven't been cooking low-fat meals all along, try introducing one or two new low-fat recipes into your menu each week. You'll reach your overall goal if you set small, manageable goals for yourself each week . . . and if you're persistent. Refer to the assessment you completed earlier in Chapter 6 to identify goals to set.

DETERMINING YOUR NATURAL "HEALTHY" WEIGHT

You've made the decision to lose weight now, once and for all, and your commitment is strong. Great. Now's the time to determine just how much weight—or body fat—you intend to lose.

There are many things people consider when selecting a desirable weight they would like to achieve and maintain. You may be thinking about dropping enough weight to get back down to the size you were at your high school prom or on your wedding day. Or maybe you fantasize about being as slim as one of your slender friends or a favorite movie star. Admit it: You probably have some "magic" number in your head, the number you hope you'll see on the scale one of these days.

So what *should* you be aiming for? If you're looking for some guru to reveal the "perfect" weight for you, surprise! You're *not* going to find her here—or, for that matter, on any table of "ideal" or "healthy" weights or body fat percentages. Remember that the Suggested "Healthy" Weight table is just that—it is suggested. It gives you an idea. But it is not a definitive answer. Not even your trusted doctor or nutritionist is necessarily the best judge of what you should weigh. But . . . *you* are. When all is said and done, the "right" weight is a very personal matter, based on what weight best suits you—your health, your lifestyle, the way you want to look and feel—and a weight that you feel you can sustain for the long term.

If you're unsure at the moment, take a minute to review the information in Chapter 5 on whether or not you truly need to lose weight. Then answer the following questions. Your responses will help you zero in on what your goals should be:

- What weight have you been healthiest at? Keep in mind that, for some people, losing as little as five or ten pounds can have a very positive effect on their blood pressure and cholesterol levels.
- What weight makes you feel attractive and confident? Think in terms of a size that's desirable to you *now*, rather than a silhouette you coveted in your twenties or thirties.
- What weight have you comfortably maintained for a year or more? If a particular weight is a struggle to maintain, it's bound to be short-lived.

Also, keep in mind that you should ideally be aiming for a weight *range*, not a single number. After all, numbers on the scale may fluctuate for reasons that have nothing to do with the way you've been eating or exercising, so you can avoid driving yourself crazy by targeting a three-to-five-pound weight range to stay within. The key here is to set yourself up for weight-loss success, not failure. And the way to do that is by selecting a "healthy" weight for yourself that's doable, comfortable . . . and can be maintained for life.

HOW WILL YOU KEEP TRACK?

In order to get where you want to go weight-wise, you've got to know where you are right now. There are several methods you can use to gather vital baseline information and keep track of your weight/fat loss and body measurements. Choose one method or several—it's up to you. Use the Journals in Chapter 11 to track your progress.

THE SCALE

Whether you view your bathroom scale as a friend or foe, it's the most common—though not necessarily the most accurate—way to track your weight. If you don't already have a super-accurate scale, toss your old clunker out and get yourself a brand-new one, ideally a digital model.

To get an initial reading before you launch your program, you could hop on the scale and jot down the number in the Weight/Fat Loss and Body Measurement Chart in Chapter 11, which you can use to record your progress for the first few weeks you're sticking to the eating plan guidelines in Chapter 8. Plan on weighing yourself no more than once a week. And do keep in mind that your weight on the scale measures fat, muscle, and water weight—and you want to focus on losing that fat. So if, for instance, you had a terrific week in terms of eating mindfully and exercising, yet the scale shows that you've stayed at the same weight, it could be because you're holding on to more water for some reason—and that could be awfully frustrating after all your hard work. If you keep in mind that the scale lies occasionally, you'll be able to keep things in perspective.

Perhaps you'd prefer to keep track of your waist-to-hip ratio or BMI in place of, or in addition to, the scale. If you choose to use these measures, do so once a month.

BODY FAT ANALYSIS

Since the scale measures fat, water, and muscle weight, a more accurate measure is body fat. Body fat can be measured by a trained professional using calipers, bioelectric measurements, underwater weighing, or other methods. Have your body fat measured every 4–6 weeks.

BODY MEASUREMENTS

Another good way to measure body changes is with a tape measure. Now, and again every four weeks or so, jot down the following measurements:

- around your shoulders (about an inch from top of shoulders)
- chest (wear a bra and measure under your armpits and around the largest part of your breast)
- upper arm (about four inches below the armpit)
- waist (around the narrowest part). Try not to hold in your stomach
- hips (around the largest part of your buttocks)
- thighs (around the very top)

It's very exciting to see these numbers get smaller and smaller, and they can help keep you motivated because, as many of my clients report, their measurements keep getting smaller even when the scale reflects little or no change. A combined loss of ten inches usually means a drop in one dress size. You can record these successes on the Body Measurement Chart in Chapter 11.

CLOTHING

Since one of your goals, no doubt, is to look better in your clothes, why not use a particular garment to help you keep track of your progress? Some of my clients like to use a favorite pair of slacks as their measuring tool, and they try them on every couple of weeks or so to get a sense of how their lower-body shape is improving. It may seem impossible now, but if you stick with the plan, those slightly snug pants will eventually be loose. Another option: use a favorite belt as your measuring tool.

PHOTOS

Even if it seems dreadful to you now, take a picture of yourself. Put the photo away. When you've reached your "healthy" weight, you might want to compare the before and after. That will be rewarding.

LAB VALUES/HEALTH PROFILE

Keep in mind that you're not only going to be slimming down but also feeling better and healthier. What better way of keeping tabs on your improved state of health than by tracking the changes in your cholesterol, triglycerides, blood pressure, and the like from one doctor's visit to the next? Refer to the Blood Pressure/Cholesterol Tracking Journal in Chapter 11, to monitor your results.

8

The Trim-Down/Shape-Up Eating Plan

You've heard about—and maybe even tried—dozens of diets over the years. If you have, chances are they haven't worked long-term, if at all. So now you may be a bit discouraged about *ever* being able to lose the weight you've put on as you have gotten older and started going through menopause. But you *can*—with the *Trouble-Free Menopause* eating plans. What makes the plans so effective? The eating plans—along with the exercise program that will be explained in Chapter 9—are based on information I've personally gathered while working with women like you over the last twenty-one years, as well as my own experiences with overweight, exercise, and menopause. (I began going through the earliest stages of menopause at forty-two.) After talking with and helping literally thousands of menopausal women with weight problems and health concerns, I've come to two key conclusions:

1. A one-size-fits-all approach to weight loss doesn't work— least of all during menopause, where so many other factors enter into the equation.

2. In order to learn what style of eating is best for you, you need to *live with* several eating plans to see exactly how they affect your mind and body. Then you can select elements from all of them to create your own plan.

Let's explore these ideas a bit further. I've already discussed some of the ways menopause is changing your body both inside and out, what may be *causing* your weight gain, and what may also be *inhibiting* any weight-loss efforts. Since you're going through a stage in your life very different from anything you've experienced before, it would be foolish to think you can just pick up any diet book or women's magazine eating plan and expect it to do the trick for you. Yes, it may . . . but more likely, it won't. As a menopausal woman, your body isn't going to react as it once did, and a weight-loss plan that might have worked when you were in your thirties may flop now. You've got to take your current metabolism and lifestyle into consideration before launching any weight-loss program and then test *different* eating plans to see which works best for you.

Trying all three eating plans outlined on the next few pages is recommended and is a technique that's proven effective for many of my clients trying to lose weight. Sticking to each plan for a full two weeks gave them the time to really experience how the food they were eating affected their mind and body. Given the myriad physical changes you're now undergoing—many of which are throwing your body into untraveled territory—your body may need a new style of eating to keep its calorie-burning mechanism in high gear. Your body is apt to respond with the kind of weight-loss results you desire. That, coupled with the exercise plan outlined in Chapter 9, will give you a trim, strong body—rather than the thin-but-saggy body found on so many menopausal women who don't exercise and drop pounds without paying attention to proper nutrition.

If you are satisfied with your current weight, but want to learn to eat healthier, look over these various plans to get an idea of different eating styles and how different foods affect your mood. You may even wish to take a look at the menus in Appendix A as well. Then proceed to Chapters 9 and 10.

YOU ARE YOUR OWN BEST NUTRITIONIST

In my practice as a nutritionist I've always tried to encourage my clients to learn the nutrition basics so they could become self-empowered when it comes to their weight and eating habits. I feel strongly that no one really knows what's right for you and your body better than you yourself. As a result you'll find a number of guidelines here to help you plan your course of action. In Chapter 7 you already determined whether your weight places you at an increased health risk. You've also determined what a "natural" or "healthy" weight is for you. Now I'll introduce you to three different eating styles or "eating plans." They're intended to allow you the opportunity to experience different ways of eating and see how they impact your weight and overall feeling of well-being. Once you've tried all three, each for two weeks, you'll get a sense of what eating style feels right for you. You'll then be ready to choose a plan that works best for you, or, better yet, take the best from each of the plans and design your own plan. After all, I'm talking about a health style and life style change, not a quick-fix diet, which is why I've strenuously avoided using the word "diet" in this book. Your goal now should be a lifestyle improvement that includes not only healthful eating to help you to feel good and lose weight, but also regular exercise and attaining mastery over your response to daily stress. You aren't simply going on a diet for a few weeks—you're changing your *life* for the better.

And that, more than anything else, means making *choices*, and recognizing, too, that the choices you make have consequences. Start to pay attention to the choices you make every day. Do you really want to eat that cheesecake, or can you choose something better for you? Are you going to remain glued to that easy chair all weekend, or will you plan an outing with some friends or take a pleasant walk by yourself through the park or around the mall? Are you going to let those angry feelings fester after that fight you had last week with your son—or are you going to somehow make peace with yourself about the situation? Maybe that involves picking up the telephone and discussing it with him, or perhaps reflecting on the situation and deciding how you will handle it differently next time and then letting go. These are all choices you can make, so choose wisely. Your health depends on it.

EATING PLANS

So here you are, ready to launch a brand new eating plan! You'll notice, as I've said, that there are actually *three* plans, which are described in detail in the pages that follow. You'll choose one, based on your answers to a short self-assessment. The goal is to live with that plan for two weeks—in fact, it will take a full two weeks for you to determine how you and your body react to it. Then, you'll reevaluate your needs and switch to one of the other two plans. And once you have "lived" all three plans and know what you like best about each, take the best from each, and design your own.

The plans are also created to help minimize the particular menopausal symptoms you may be experiencing now. To help you accomplish this, it's best to spread your food evenly throughout the day—three meals and two snacks, rather than a couple of large meals. Some clients prefer the "grazing" technique—six small meals a day. They feel that fueling their body consistently provides them with a steady and even flow of energy, fewer menopausal symptoms, and the weight-loss results they desire.

All the food included in each plan is meant to work *with* your body and its rapidly changing chemistry. All three eating plans are healthy, meet current U.S. government dietary guidelines, are low in fat, emphasize whole grains and fiber, and consistently fuel your body throughout the day.

Start by reading through all of the plans, and see which one might best fit you:

THE CARBOHYDRATE-PACKED PLAN (CPP)
(high-carbohydrate, low-protein, low-fat)

Highlights of CPP: You're determined to lose weight, but you don't want to sacrifice your favorite high-carb foods—your morning bagel, that sandwich with veggies at lunch, some steaming linguini at dinner, your nighttime snack of popcorn. The CPP is full of tasty carbs—enough to satisfy the most powerful carbohydrate cravings—and will keep you feeling relaxed and satisfied all day long. It worked for Gail.

GAIL'S STORY

I'd say I was about 15 pounds overweight before I started menopause at age 50. Menopause added 15 pounds more, but I guess a lot of it was my fault, because I confess I was eating more than before. I also stopped working out at the gym because my job—I'm the director of public relations for a large corporation—has gotten much busier over the last few years and I've had to put in more hours. So the exercise fell by the wayside.

By the time I started seeing Judy Marshel for my weight problem, I had about 30 pounds to lose. We mutually decided that the CPP program would probably be best for me for several reasons. First, Judy asked me what my favorite foods were (besides ice cream!). When I told her I love bread, pasta, and potatoes, she said I would probably enjoy the foods on the CPP program, and she was right. The plan has enough pasta, potato, and rice dishes, and bread, to keep me happy and feeling satisfied all day. Second, I'm too busy to think about menu planning and what I'm going to eat when, so I decided to use a restaurant-style menu, which spelled everything out for me. (See Appendix A for menu suggestions.) I realized it might not be the best thing to blindly follow a menu plan, but this was helpful in getting me started in learning how to design my own menus. I had been eating a lot of white bread before, but Judy got me to increase my fiber by switching to whole-grain bread, which I now enjoy, and by eating more fresh fruit and vegetables. (I've become a broccoli freak!) Not only do I feel a sense of control but the weight's been coming off me nicely. I lost four pounds in the first two weeks, and another pound or two each week after that. I just have a few more left to lose.

Another wonderful thing about this program is that the foods I've been eating have somehow got me more on an even keel, which really helps in my pressure-packed job! Judy says some of that has to do with cutting out most of the sugar I had been eating before—I would snack on a candy bar or a couple of cookies when I was starving at around four o'clock in the afternoon. Now, instead, I'll have a cup of herbal tea with three graham cracker squares or a couple of apple-cinnamon rice cakes. It's filling and satisfying.

A Typical Day on CPP Might Look Like This:

Breakfast: ½ small whole wheat bagel, 1-oz. slice low-fat Swiss cheese or low-fat soy cheese

Snack: 1 small apple

Lunch: 3 oz. turkey stuffed in 1 large (2-oz.) whole wheat pita, lettuce and tomato; crudités dipped in nonfat salad dressing

Snack: 1 cup nonfat fruit-flavored yogurt

Dinner: 2 cups cooked pasta primavera (with marinara sauce and steamed vegetables); green salad with one tablespoon low-fat salad dressing

Snack: ½ cup reduced-fat chocolate pudding topped with 1 small banana, sliced

THE PROTEIN-PACKED PLAN (PPP)
(protein-rich, moderate carbohydrate, low-fat)

Highlights of PPP: You've been on high-carbohydrate eating plans in the past, but they haven't worked for you. Not only did the breads and starches leave you craving more, but you felt sluggish afterward—so you couldn't maintain this way of eating and the weight you lost eventually returned. Anyway, you enjoy protein foods—lean meats, poultry, fish, and low-fat/nonfat dairy foods—and the alert feeling they leave you with. The PPP is for you.

Elaine never had to worry about her weight until she began menopause. The PPP plan helped her control cravings that she now has to keep in check.

ELAINE'S STORY

Once I started menopause at forty-seven, I saw the way my body was changing and I honestly couldn't believe my eyes. I felt *betrayed*—betrayed by my own body. I had never had a weight problem my whole life. I was always able to eat what I wanted, whenever I wanted, without gaining weight. I've always been a sugar junkie and a carbohydrate-craver. I'd nibble on candy and cookies and, when they weren't available, I'd eat a bagel. No matter what I ate, my body stayed more or less the same. One thing I *did* do was exercise—I'd walk fast, three times a week, for about half an hour each time. I guess that helped.

Then suddenly, over the last three years, I gradually put on twelve pounds. I looked awful and I felt like a bloated pig. It didn't help that I kept eating candy and cookies, but in a way I couldn't control myself. I really feel that I was addicted to these things, like a smoker is addicted to nicotine. They'd call my name . . . and I'd have to answer.

Judy and I talked about my weight problem and my food cravings, and I started the PPP food plan. She said it seemed best for me because eating more protein foods and fewer carbohydrate foods should make my blood sugar fluctuate less, which meant my cravings should decrease and maybe even go away. We also agreed that I was ready for a radical new eating plan. The food choices and quantities offered on PPP were very different from what I had been used to, but I was really ready for a change. And Judy said that by eating these kinds of foods throughout the day—three meals, plus three snacks—my blood sugar would probably remain steady. It all sounded great to me!

I looked at my food choices on the PPP plan, and I wrote down what I planned to eat for a whole week. I stuck to it pretty well and I tried to limit my bread intake to my dinner meal, as Judy suggested, which I found actually helped minimize my cravings. Over time I felt a greater sense of control, with a wonderful byproduct: weight loss. I lost three pounds the first week, two pounds the next week, and about a pound and a half each week after that.

Not only did I lose my extra twelve pounds but I also lost that bloated feeling and felt much more energetic—I experienced a new sense of alertness I never felt before. And somehow I even lost my cravings for sweets. I really don't eat them now. Sure, every once in a while I'll think about having a candy bar or some M&Ms, but it doesn't seem worth it anymore because the way I'm eating now makes me feel so much better.

All my life I heard the expression "You are what you eat," but I guess it never made sense to me before trying this new way of eating. Judy had said that there's a real connection between food and mood and the way my body feels, but nothing brought that home to me as much as following the PPP plan. It's wonderful to eat well and at the same time to have my "uncontrollable" cravings under control.

A Typical Day on the PPP Might Look Like This:

Breakfast: Cheese 'n Chive Scrambler made with 3 egg whites (or 1 whole egg) scrambled, with ¼ cup low-fat cottage cheese and 2 tsp. fresh chopped chives
Snack: 1 cup low-fat (1%) milk or soy milk
Lunch: Chef's salad made with 1 oz. turkey strips, 1 oz. ham strips, 1 oz. low-fat cheddar cheese strips, lettuce and tomato wedges, 1 tbsp. nonfat salad dressing, 1 small pear
Snack: 1 small orange
Dinner: 4 oz. roasted chicken (skinless), steamed broccoli, 1 large baked potato, green salad with 1 tbsp. salad dressing
Snack: Crudités dipped in 1 cup nonfat plain yogurt mixed with fresh dill and garlic

THE INDULGE, IN MODERATION, PLAN (IMP)
(reasonable amounts of carbohydrates and protein, low-fat)

Highlights of IMP: You know what to do, have basically healthy habits—and you want to eat what you *like*. You've *had* it with conforming to rigid eating plans, and you can't be bothered weighing and measuring your food. You may be guilty of having a sweet tooth, but you can eat a spoonful of dessert since you have "trained" yourself to feel perfectly satisfied with a taste—you don't need to devour it all. With the IMP program, you have reasonable-sized servings of many of your favorites—even an occasional sweet—while still keeping on the healthy-eating track.

Jane is one of many clients who lost weight and kept it off with this plan.

I had been overweight all my life. It was hard to believe I was entering a new phase of my life, menopause, and *still* struggling with the weight. I always *knew* what I needed to do to lose weight, but whenever I joined a weight-loss organization—I've been on Weight Watchers and Jenny Craig—I would rebel. I always found the eating plan too regimented. It never seemed to work with my lifestyle, which involved cooking for a family of three active teenage boys and a husband, plus a lot of running around all day long. So I made the decision to live with my excess weight—I knew no other alternative.

When I talked to Judy about my lifestyle and my eating habits, it became clear right away that I understood how to eat healthfully and had a good sense of what moderate portions are. I was never a binger, and although I sometimes craved chocolate or salty things, I could eat one piece and stop, which I realize was a gift, since many of my friends would have difficulty stopping once they got started. Because I could pretty much put the brakes on my eating as I needed to—and because I wouldn't go off and have, say, a donut for breakfast and a couple of Big Macs for dinner—Judy and I agreed I was a good candidate for the IMP plan. It would pretty much let me do what I wanted in terms of food and flexibility, as long as I kept my portions in check and made healthy food choices for the most part.

Sticking to my own way of eating was easy for me. I didn't have to make many major adjustments, but I *did* have to become more aware of my options and be a more *selective* eater. For instance, I learned to ask myself constantly if I was hungry and whether I truly wanted the foods in front of me. Because so many decisions were left up to me, I knew I had to be more responsible and think things through. I couldn't leave too many things to chance.

For the first week, since my portions were so large, I decided to simply cut all my usual portions in half, including desserts. I also kept a diary. I wrote down everything I ate in a little spiral notebook, which helped a lot. Anyway, I lost one pound by the end of the week. That was OK, but I felt I could do better, so I reviewed my diary and decided I was eating too much dessert. So I cut back on that a lot; some nights I'd eat fruit instead of cake. By the end of the second week, I'd lost another three pounds, so I was very pleased. The only problem, if you can call it that, was that instead of feeling *physically full*, as I always had in the past, I would feel *emotionally full*, or satisfied. There were times when I felt that I could keep eating more, but I didn't. Eventually, I got used to the feeling, and when I really felt like I wanted *something* and I had eaten enough, I'd munch on a carrot or drink a glass of ice water. I continued to lose about a pound or two a week pretty consistently until I reached a comfortable weight for myself.

I'll admit the first week on the program was challenging, but overall it's been great. I felt empowered in my weight-loss efforts for the first time ever. The flexibility was very important to me—as I said, I'm not one to follow an eating plan blindly. I have to admit, though, I feel great and I've even been inspired to exercise regularly, something I never did before. It may not sound like a big deal, but to me my fifteen-minute walk every day is a tremendous accomplishment. And I know it's helped me maintain my new weight for the last year.

A Typical Day on IMP Might Look Like This:
Breakfast: ½ toasted bagel with a smear of low-fat cream cheese
Snack: 2 popcorn-flavored rice cakes
Lunch: ½ tuna salad sandwich on a roll, lettuce and tomato, carrot sticks
Snack: 1 cup nonfat fruit-flavored yogurt
Dinner: (at a Chinese restaurant)
   ½ portion stir-fry chicken and vegetables
   ½ portion brown rice, small dish pineapple chunks
Snack: 2 small cookies, 1 cup skim milk or low-fat soy milk

WHICH PLAN SHOULD YOU CHOOSE?

To help you decide which plan you want to follow to launch your weight-loss program, check off the goals below that are especially important to you right now. The eating plan next to each item is the one most likely to help you accomplish that particular goal.

I want:

__To feel full, *satisfied*, and more *relaxed*. (CPP)

__To feel full, *satisfied*, and more *alert*. (PPP)

__To have *fewer food cravings*, particularly for carbohydrate-rich foods. (PPP)

__To eat as many of my *favorite foods* (within reason) as possible. (IMP)

__To make *carbohydrates the centerpiece* of each meal I eat. (CPP)

__To make *protein the centerpiece* of each meal I eat. (PPP)

__To *change my basic lifestyle as little* as possible. (IMP)

__To *avoid weighing and measuring* my food. (IMP)

__To feel free to *grab a sandwich* whenever my schedule precludes a sit-down meal. (CPP)

Now, take a look at how many checks you have next to:

CPP:_____

PPP:_____

IMP:_____

Whichever plan has the most checks is the best one for you to start with for the next two weeks. If two plans have the same high number of checks, go back to the descriptions above and choose the one that sounds more to your liking, and begin with that one.

PUTTING THE PLAN INTO ACTION

WHAT WILL YOU EAT?

You can't be successful with *any* of the plans you choose unless you have a solid foundation in good nutrition and eat healthy foods in the right proportions—and that's exactly what these easy-to-follow lists will give you. Even if you've determined that you don't really need to lose any weight—or maybe just a pound or two—using these eating plans as a guide and choosing from these Food Groups will enable you to nourish your body and help to relieve many of your menopausal symptoms.

There are six basic Food Groups. They are:

- Protein (poultry, meat, fish, beans, peas, lentils, tofu, eggs)
- Starch (bread, cereal, rice, pasta, starchy vegetables)
- Vegetables
- Fruit
- Dairy (milk, yogurt, cheese)
- Fat

To these I've also added a seventh Food Group called Add-Ons. With each plan, you get to "add-on" an additional 100 calories a day. They can be chosen from any of the six Food Groups or any other food for which you know the calorie count. They are designed to help add variety and excitement to your daily eating.

All the Food Groups are important, but as you'll see, you eat different amounts from each Food Group each day for optimal nutrition and weight loss. Within each Food Group, the foods listed are similar in calories and nutritional value in the serving size given. You will also notice that certain foods are included in two different Food Groups because they're good sources of the key nutrients found in both of these Food Groups. For example, milk is listed in both the Protein and Dairy Group; dried beans, peas, and lentils, in the Starch and Protein Group, etc.

Even though you're being provided with a healthy, balanced way of eating in all three eating plans, you will still benefit from the addition of vitamin/mineral supplements. It's difficult to get all your nutrients in, no matter how balanced your eating is, when you're taking in fewer calories. (See Chapter 3 for details.)

HOW MUCH SHOULD YOU EAT?

Now that you've decided which of the three plans—CPP, PPP, or IMP—you'll be following for the next two weeks, look at the chart that follows to see how many servings of each type of food you can have each day on your plan:

Food Group	CPP	PPP	IMP
		(Number of units per day)	
Protein	4–5	8–10	6*[1]
Starch	4–6	2–3	4*
Vegetables		At least 4	
Fruit	2–3	2–3	3*
Dairy	2	2	2*
Fat	2–3	2–3	3*
Add-Ons		Up to 100 calories	

NUTRIENT BREAKDOWN OF THE PLANS[†]

Nutrients (per day) (per day)	CPP	PPP
Calories	1050–1475	1050–1425
Protein** (in grams)	60–80	70–95
Carbohydrates** (in grams)	160–220	130–180
Fat** (in grams)	20–30	25–35
% of calories from:		
Protein	20	25
Carbohydrates	60	50
Fat	20	25

---

*These are average values—with IMP you are designing your own eating plan.

[†]These are averages. **With IMP you are designing your own eating plan so nutrient information will vary.**

**These values are based on a combination of animal and plant sources of protein. If you select more plant sources of protein, rather than animal sources, you will be taking in extra carbohydrates and less protein and fat.

Which End of the Range Should You Choose?

How many servings should you eat? You'll notice that for many of the food groups there's a range of units. Should you be having the lower end or upper end of the range?

Choose the lower end if:

- you're petite
- you're not very active
- you are not losing weight when you are selecting the upper end of the range—so may need fewer calories (plus more exercise!)
- you want to break out of a weight-loss plateau and have been following the upper end of the range.

Choose the higher end if:

- you're a larger and bigger-boned woman
- you're more active than most
- you're in no hurry to see the weight come off
- it's a special occasion (vacation, holiday time, etc.) and you want to eat a bit more now
- you're under a great deal of stress and want to eat a bit more now
- you want to break out of a weight-loss plateau and have been following the lower end of the range. Maybe you were eating too little!

Keep in mind that you can always switch from one end of the range to the other, from meal to meal or day to day, as your needs and desires change. But never sacrifice your health or comfort for a speedier weight loss. If you do, you'll find it much harder to stick with your eating plan and enjoy long-term success.

HOW BIG ARE YOUR SERVING SIZES?

Foods	Unit Sizes
PROTEIN	
(40–85 calories per unit)	
Beans, peas, or lentils	
(dried, cooked)	¼ cup (2 oz.)
Cheese: soft (cottage or ricotta),	
nonfat or low-fat	¼ cup
Cheese: hard (American, Swiss,	
cheddar, etc.), nonfat or lowfat	1 oz.
Cheese: hard, non-dairy (tofu,	
soy or rice) lowfat or nonfat	1 oz.
Eggs (limit to 4 per week)	1
Egg substitutes	¼ cup
Egg whites	3
Fish/shellfish	1 oz.
Meat (beef, pork, ham, lamb, veal):	
(loin, round or leg cut)	1 oz.
Milk, skim or low-fat (1%)	½ cup
Milk, soybean, low-fat	½ cup
Non-dairy "cheese" hard: tofu,	
rice or almond, low-fat	1 oz.
Peanut or almond butter	1 tablespoon
Poultry (turkey, chicken, cornish	
hen, duck) (skinless)	1 oz.
Tofu	2 oz.
Yogurt, nonfat, plain, aspartame or	
fruit juice sweetened	½ cup
STARCH	
(70–120 calories per unit)	
Bagel	½ small (1 oz.)
Beans, peas or lentils (dried, cooked)	¼ cup (2 oz.)
Bread, whole wheat or enriched	1 slice
Bread, reduced-calorie	2 slices
Cereal, cold	1 oz. (about ¾ cup)
Cereal, hot (cooked)	½ cup
Graham crackers, 2" squares	3
Melba toast	4 slices or 6 rounds
Pasta (macaroni, spaghetti,	
noodles, etc.) (cooked)	½ cup
Pretzels	1 oz.
Popcorn, hot air-popped	3 cups
Popcorn, oil-popped	2 cups
Potato, sweet potato, yam	1 small

Rice (cooked)	½ cup
Rice cakes	2 large or 6 mini
Roll or pita	1 small or ½ large
Starchy vegetables (corn, peas, lima beans, water chestnuts, winter squash), (cooked)	½ cup

VEGETABLES
(5–25 calories per unit)

Any vegetable (other than those listed under Starches)	½ cup cooked or 1 cup raw

FRUIT
(50–75 calories per unit)

Apples, oranges, pears, etc.	1 small
Banana	1 small or ½ medium
Berries	¾ cup
Fruit, canned, sweetened in its own juice	½ cup
Fruit, dried	1 oz.
Fruit juice, unsweetened	½ cup
Grapes, cherries	12 large
Melon, cantaloupe, honeydew, watermelon	1 cup (chunks)
Spreadable fruit (all-fruit jam)	1 tablespoon

DAIRY
(80–150 calories per unit)

Cheese: Hard (American, Swiss, cheddar, etc.), nonfat	1½ oz.
Hot cocoa or dairy shake, low-fat or reduced-calorie	1 packet
Milk, skim or low-fat (1%)	1 cup

NON-DAIRY

	1½ oz
Cheese: hard (tofu, rice or almond)	1½ oz.
Milk, skim or low-fat, soy, rice or almond	1 cup
Pudding, reduced-calorie (prepared with skim or low-fat (1%) milk)	½ cup
Yogurt, nonfat, plain, or fruit-juice sweetened	1 cup

FAT
(30–45 calories per unit)

Butter*, mayonnaise*, or margarine* (made from liquid vegetable oil)	1 teaspoon
Non-dairy mayonnaise	1 teaspoon
Reduced-calorie butter*, mayonnaise*, or margarine* (made from liquid vegetable oil)	2 teaspoons
Vegetable oil (safflower, corn, canola, sunflower), flaxseed, olive, peanut oil	1 teaspoon
Salad dressing (regular)	1½ teaspoons (½ tablespoon)
Olives	5

ADD-ONS

Any food of your choice	Up to 100 calories

---

*May be a source of trans fatty acid or saturated fat; limit intake.

Obviously, these lists aren't all-inclusive; you'll have greater flexibility in your menu planning if you learn to read nutrition labels or buy a good calorie counter book. For example, if you'd like some crackers as part of your lunch or snack, and the Nutrition Panel on the label says they contain 90 calories per ounce, you could use one ounce of crackers to substitute for one of your daily Starch servings since one starch serving is typically 70–120. Or you could count it toward your Add-On (up to 100 calories per day) for the day. Refer to Appendix B for more information on nutrition labeling.

HOW CAN I PUT THIS ALL TOGETHER?

To help you get off to an easy start, I've put together some menu suggestions for the CPP and PPP programs. They will help make your menus more interesting. Refer to Appendix A for these menus. Shopping tips as well as a list of kitchen staples to always have on hand are also provided.

SIX WEEKS LATER: ASSESSING THE EATING PLANS

Now that you've tried all three eating plans, this is the perfect time to evaluate your experiences with each one. How did each one make you feel by the end of the two-week period? How much weight did you lose on each plan?

ASSESSMENT #1

The following chart will help you decide what you found to be the best and worst features of each eating plan as well as give you a good indication as to which one (or combination) you should attempt to "model" your eating after from here on in.

Thinking back to your reactions to each of the three plans, check off the results that best apply.

Eating Plan Assessment #1

Benefit	Improved			Same			Worse		
	CPP	PPP	IMP	CPP	PPP	IMP	CPP	PPP	IMP
Energy level									
Satiety level (feeling of fullness)									
Motivation									
Satisfaction with foods eaten									
Mood level									
Alertness									
Calmness									
Menopausal symptoms									
General level of happiness									

ASSESSMENT #2

Now, take a look at the following nine questions. Answer "Agree" or "Disagree" in relation to each of the three eating plans.

Eating Plan Assessment #2

Benefit	CPP Agree/ Disagree	PPP Agree/ Disagree	IMP Agree/ Disagree
I am satisfied with the speed of weight loss.			
It's relatively easy to stick with this style of eating.			
I enjoy the amount of food choice.			
It's easy to eat this way, based on my lifestyle.			
It fits my schedule.			
I feel in control.			
I don't feel like I'm on a diet.			
I have fewer food cravings.			
My menopausal symptoms have been alleviated.			

Tally up your answers. Which plan had the highest numbers?

Assessment #1: Under the "Improved" column:

CPP_____   PPP_____   IMP_____

Assessment #2: Under the "Agree" column:

CPP_____   PPP_____   IMP_____

The plan with the highest number *or* the plan that offers one or two factors that are far more important to you than the others, even if it isn't as highly rated, is the one giving you the greatest overall satisfaction. So you might want to "model" your eating after this plan. For instance, you may have rated the IMP highest of all, but the PPP program eases your food cravings best. If heading off your cravings is your biggest concern at the moment, why not follow the basic guidelines provided for the PPP program? Keep in mind that your needs may change over time. It's a good idea to reevaluate your needs periodically as well as to assess how well you are progressing toward accomplishing the goals you set for yourself.

SOME ADDITIONAL TIPS TO REMEMBER:

- Select a variety of foods from each of the Food Groups. You'll not only avoid boredom, but you'll also get a chance to see how your weight loss as well as menopausal symptoms respond to different foods.
- Pay attention to serving sizes, but don't get too hung up on them. An apple is an apple, and nobody ever gained weight from eating too big an apple.
- If you get the munchies during the day, try some crudités dipped in spicy salsa or nonfat salad dressing, or some sugar-free gelatin, a cup of low-sodium bouillon, or a crunchy rice cake.
- Drink six to eight glasses of water throughout the day to curb your appetite and to help digestion. Try adding a lemon or lime wedge for some zest, or alternate plain water with club soda, seltzer, or herbal tea.

- If you're going to use oil, select expeller-pressed vegetable oils, which are less processed than other types of oils and thus contain more nutrients. The label will indicate if it is expeller-pressed.

- When selecting meat, look for lean cuts, those labeled with the USDA label "Select" Grade. These are lower in fat and calories than either "Choice" or "Prime." The leanest cuts of beef are the loin or round; the leanest cuts of pork, lamb, and veal are the loin and the leg. Before eating, trim any visible fat. Remove skin from chicken, turkey, fish, etc. Bake, broil, or roast meat on a rack. Discard any fat that accumulates.

- Weigh meat, poultry, and fish after cooking. You lose about twenty-five percent during cooking, so one ounce of raw food is equal to about three-quarters of an ounce cooked.

- When selecting fruit-flavored yogurt, go for the nonfat varieties that have no added sugar. Although aspartame-sweetened yogurt contains about 100 calories per cup compared to fruit juice-sweetened yogurt, which contains about 150 calories per cup, they are both good choices.

- Learn to judge serving sizes so you avoid overeating. One ounce of boneless meat, poultry, or fish is approximately the size of a matchbox. A four-ounce serving is roughly the size of a deck of cards or the palm of your hand (thickness and diameter).

- You can learn to enjoy unsalted food if you season your food with herbs and spices instead. Fresh is best, but even packaged flavorings add zip to your cooking, so be adventurous.

- Now that you've learned new eating styles, "call" each style up when you feel it is best suited for you. For example, if you must be exceptionally alert for a presentation you're making, you might want to stick with the protein-packed program (PPP) that day. If you've got a lazy day ahead, relax with the higher-carb foods found in the CPP program. The overall goal is to take the best from all three plans and design your own. Use the calorie information at the top of each Food Group to give you an idea of how many calories your "designer plan" contains.

• If you are varying the amount of carbohydrate you eat, don't be alarmed if you experience slight water retention. Since carbohydrates tend to cause water retention more than protein-packed foods, you might hold more water if you eat more carbs. Try keeping things in perspective. Don't worry about day-to-day water-weight fluctuations, since they do not represent a true fat gain. If you weigh yourself just once a week, or better yet, use a body fat analysis to evaluate your progress, you'll get a true picture of how much *fat* you're losing.

FOOD ALLERGIES, SENSITIVITIES, AND CRAVINGS

Although I urge you to try all three of the eating plans for a minimum of two weeks each, some will work better for you than others. In choosing the plan that's right for you, keep in mind your particular food cravings and sensitivities (for example, the PPP program may help to minimize carbohydrate cravings) because they will not only affect how you feel day to day but also your weight-loss success.

By this time in your life you probably already know which foods, if any, you're allergic or sensitive to and need to limit or avoid. But you may not be aware of the link between your food sensitivities and your weight. For one thing, if you have food sensitivities, you generally crave those foods you're sensitive to. Many of these foods may be carbohydrate-rich (breads and crackers), while others may be high-sugar and -fat (chocolate and candy). Second, food sensitivities and allergies may interfere with the body's natural ability to regulate hunger, which in turn may cause you to continue eating even after a "solid" meal because fullness is not registering! Third, sensitivities as well as food allergies may lead to water retention or bloating, which, although temporary, may get in the way of weight loss.

If you suspect that certain foods are giving you problems, ask your doctor to test you for food allergies. Although this is not as accurate, you can also conduct a test on your own to give you good baseline information. Here's how: Before changing your typical way of eating, jot down in the Lifestyle Journal in Chapter 11 any symptoms you're experiencing that you believe may be linked to the food. Omit that particular food from your diet for fourteen days, and after that rotate *small* amounts of it back into your menu every four days. For example, if you have eliminated bread, you may add one slice a day back into your diet every four days. If you find that your body handles that food well, you can reintroduce it into your diet more frequently and in larger portions, if you like, but do so gradually. Or you may find that your body cannot handle even small amounts of it, so keep the food out of your diet, for now anyway. Then, redo the test with another food until you isolate the one(s) giving you trouble.

Mary used the PPP program to keep her hypoglycemia under control.

MARY'S STORY

I've been a little chunky—around twenty pounds overweight—most of my life. And I've always had cravings for sweets—maybe it's a result of my hypoglycemic problem. I always craved sugar, even as a child. I used to wake up in the middle of the night with sugar cravings and eat cake.

I know what type of foods to eat to feel good and lose weight: a lot of low-fat, protein-rich foods. I've been following the PPP program and I feel better. Once I cut back on the carbohydrates, I stopped feeling the cravings. I know I need to eat regularly and my body tells me when. I also have to make certain I have the right foods in the house. The minute I feel I want to eat, I know I better have something that works for me, which is usually a food with some low-fat protein in it like nonfat yogurt or a piece of low-fat cheese.

I feel that my mood and outlook are directly affected by how much sugar I eat. I am much more optimistic when I'm not junking out on sugar. It's just a matter of getting started . . . and sticking to it.

Hypoglycemia

Hypoglycemia, also known as idiopathic postprandial syndrome (IPS), is the term for low or unstable blood sugar. In the 1970s hypoglycemia became a fad diagnosis, and popular books attributed everything from behavior problems to heart disease to this condition. But although it does occur, many doctors now dismiss hypoglycemia.

If you have it, it's another factor to consider as you determine which eating style is right for you. Hypoglycemia may lead to a midmorning or midafternoon slump; it may also lead to mental dullness, shakiness, weakness, headache, or faintness if you ignore your body's signals that it needs refueling. So it's a good idea to fuel your system regularly throughout the day—plan meals and snacks or many small meals throughout the day (3 meals with 2 snacks or 6 minimeals), including a source of protein or dairy at each meal or snack. Frequent eating as well as including low-fat protein at each meal or snack will help stabilize blood sugar levels. All three plans I've outlined allow for three meals and two snacks, but if you're hypoglycemic, you might do best modeling your eating after the PPP program, which will supply more of the low-fat protein your body needs. Many people with hypoglycemia also report that taking zinc, vitamins C and B complex, chromium piccolinate, and GLA is beneficial. Refer to Chapters 2 and 3 for further information.

Your doctor can tell you through a glucose tolerance test if you have hypoglycemia. However, many people complain of hypoglycemic-like symptoms even when the test results indicate that they fall within the normal range. Bottom line: What's normal for others may not be what is best for you. If you feel any of the symptoms, talk to your doctor. Also, experiment with changing what you eat and when you eat—and you'll probably feel better. Try to avoid overeating in response to blood sugar swings, since this can further aggravate your blood sugar irregularities.

SLIMMING DOWN YOUR MEALS

That meal may *look* harmless, but watch out! Excess calories, fat, sugar, and salt may be creeping into your daily eating despite your best efforts to keep them out. What to do? Make a few quick changes, that's all. Whether you're dining at home or in a restaurant, these simple swaps will save you countless calories and grams of fat and sodium.

Instead of	Try
Alcoholic cocktails	Club soda with lime, tomato juice, mineral water; a wine spritzer; a tall drink such as a rum and Diet Coke
Bacon	Canadian bacon
Beef (Prime or Choice)	USDA "Select" grade and cuts like sirloin, flank, loin, round, or leg
Butter, margarine, or oil for baking	Applesauce or pureed prunes
Canned fish	Draining oil and rinsing fish before eating, or getting water packed
Canned vegetables	Using fresh or frozen (unsalted). If you use canned vegetables that contain added salt, rinse them off before eating or cooking—this reduces the sodium by about one-third.
Chips	Baked tortilla, potato, or corn chips; pretzels or unbuttered popcorn
Cleaning your plate	Resigning your membership in the Clean Plate Club or take less (smaller portions)

Instead of	Try
Condiments (ketchup, mustard, commercially prepared sauce)	Low-sodium versions, limited amounts of the regular kind, or make your own
Creamer (nondairy)	Powdered nonfat milk, or low-fat or skim milk
Egg yolk	2 egg whites for each yolk, or ¼ cup egg substitute for each egg
Fat-based sauces	Sauces made with nonfat or low-fat yogurt, tomato-based sauces, wine sauces
Fatty meats (prime ribs, luncheon meats such as salami, bologna, etc.); chicken or turkey with skin	Lean meats, chicken or turkey with skin removed
Frying/sautéing/refrying	Steaming, poaching, roasting, broiling, grilling, boiling, microwaving
Going to the restaurant hungry	Eating some raw veggies or fruit or drinking tomato juice or a tall glass of flavored water at home before you go so you won't be ravenous at the restaurant; ordering a salad or beverage when you arrive; trying to shift your focus by enjoying your companions, the ambience etc.
Ice cream	Nonfat or low-fat yogurt, ice milk, sherbet
"Larger than life" portions at the restaurant	When the food arrives, immediately cut it in half and remind yourself anything beyond your half is off-limits. Or, once you cut it, immediately ask the waiter or waitress to pack it up.

Instead of	*Try*
Ordering whatever is on the menu	Requesting sauce on the side, broiling instead of frying, or whatever else may be easier on your waistline
Salad dressing	Fat-free or reduced-fat dressing, or flavored vinegars, including wine, balsamic, and apple cider
Salt (to season foods)	Fresh or dried herbs, lemon juice
Sour cream-based dips	Nonfat- or low-fat–based sour cream or yogurt dips
Spontaneous mealtime decisions (especially in restaurants)	Planning ahead; eating lightly at other meals; choosing restaurants that serve "your" kind of food
Turkey (self-basting)	Turkey (regular)
Yogurt (made from whole milk)	Yogurt (nonfat or low-fat)

9

❧

Exercise: Your Secret Weapon
for Staying Healthy,
Vibrant, and Slim

It's official! Those headlines you've read for years about the benefits of exercise are all true. Exercise is the powerful key to unlocking health, warding off certain diseases, getting and maintaining a slim body, and keeping stress at bay. No pill, potion, or prescription can do nearly as much for your heart, your lungs, your energy and blood pressure levels, and your overall sense of well-being as lacing up a pair of sneakers, putting on some comfortable sweats or shorts . . . and getting that body moving! Whether you've been moderately to very active all your life or you've spent most of your time avoiding anything more strenuous than loading the dishwasher, there's good news: It's never too late to begin a workout program. What's more, exercise does you and your body a world of good at every stage of your life but most especially during menopause, when it can be a tremendous aid in alleviating your menopausal symptoms.

Doubt it? Here are the ways in which regular exercise can help you look and feel better:

- *Exercise boosts your cardiovascular health* by protecting against heart disease by reducing blood pressure, raising levels of "good" HDL cholesterol, and improving circulation.

- *Exercise helps build and maintain bone health and strengthen joint health.* In combination with a calcium- and nutrient-packed diet, strength training, and, to a lesser extent, weight-bearing aerobic activities like walking, running, and jogging, increase calcium absorption by the bones. This can help prevent fractured bones, so common in inactive, poorly nourished older women. One-third of women over sixty-five have had at least one vertebral fracture, while one-third of those over eighty have fractured a hip. Strength training helps maintain or even increase bone density and the muscles supporting your bones. In addition, exercise strengthens back and joint muscles, making it less likely that you'll injure yourself doing everyday chores and activities.
- *Exercise helps keep the adrenal glands healthy.* Why is this important? Because if the body's supply of estrone (the main form of estrogen available to you now during menopause) is diminished slowly and gradually—which is generally what happens when the adrenal glands are functioning properly and you have an appropriate amount of body fat for the conversion to take place—your menopausal symptoms, including hot flashes, will be minimal.
- *Exercise helps to reduce mood swings, depression, and stress.* Exercise increases your tissue response to insulin, which helps to stabilize blood sugar levels and mood. And it's been found that moderate activity lasting 20–30 minutes causes the brain to release endorphins, the natural opiates that produce a so-called exercise "high." In addition, norepinephrine, another brain chemical known to help reduce depression, is also released during exercise. Exercise also eases tension and so helps you feel more relaxed.
- *Exercise helps relieve insomnia, as well as produces a deeper, more restful sleep* so that you can get fewer hours of sleep and feel as refreshed.
- *Exercise helps you sustain your motivation and boosts your energy levels,* because you're taking charge of yourself, setting goals, and seeing positive results. Little wonder you wind up feeling happier and more *self-confident.*
- *Women often report an improved sex drive and sexual functioning* as a result of regular exercise, partly because it pro-

vides you with more energy and suppleness and partly because Kegel exercises (described in Chapter 4) can improve vaginal muscle tone. *Kegel exercises can also improve bladder control and help alleviate and perhaps prevent urge and stress incontinence.*

- *Smoother, healthier skin is another result of regular exercise.* That's because exercise increases blood circulation to the skin, keeping it soft, supple, and moist. Working out also spurs the skin to produce collagen, the fibrous protein that enables skin to bend and stretch and then spring back into place.

- *Exercise aids digestion*, which may become more problematic with age, and helps to *relieve constipation.*

All these benefits, and I haven't even touched on the terrific things exercise does for your body weight! Study after study has shown that simply making dietary changes—even the smartest ones—won't give your weight-loss program the necessary boost and staying power you get from adding some aerobic exercise. Exercising *aerobically*—meaning, by utilizing oxygen, in ways that involve slow and steady *movement* of large muscle groups in your body and getting your heart rate up—helps burn the calories you eat every day and reduce the amount of your body fat. Thus, by incorporating an exercise plan into your life, you'll be able to eat more while maintaining a lower weight.

Your body will also benefit enormously from a program of strength training. If you're turning up your nose at the thought of lifting weights *at your age*, don't—you're definitely *not* going to turn into a menopausal Arnold Schwarzenegger. A modest routine using free weights at home and perhaps some machines at your local Y or gym will do wonders for your body shape and for toning and tightening your body as you drop pounds and decrease body fat—all of which is crucial during menopause. Remember that as you age, your lean body mass declines by 2–3 percent with every decade, so that even if you weigh now what you weighed at age 21, chances are that your body *shape* may be very different because it may have more fat and less muscle mass. Strength training shifts that ratio so you build or maintain your muscle. Since muscle is denser and more compact than fat and takes up less space, even if you have recently accumulated your body fat around your waist, you can look better, have a trimmer waistline, and minimize the middle-age spread syndrome by engaging in a program of regular strength training. You can see and feel inches lost, even if your weight stays the same.

Another added plus . . . strength training increases your muscle mass, or amount of lean tissue. Because muscle tissue burns calories quicker than fat tissue does, if you have more muscle, you increase the calories you expend. So it not only affects your body shape but your body weight as well.

What's more, exercise helps you keep your weight down by keeping your appetite down. Alan Titchenal, Ph.D., who is an instructor in the Department of Food Science and Human Nutrition at the University of Hawaii, explains that aerobic activities like walking, running, or jogging tend to decrease appetite for a period of time after the exercise is over. And when you *do* sit down to your next meal or snack, it will probably be a healthy one—after all, you won't want to undo all your exercise efforts.

So now that you know all the ways in which exercise is a boost to your health and your weight-loss program, let's get started!

DESIGNING AND LAUNCHING YOUR EXERCISE PLAN

Before you begin any exercise program, make sure to get your doctor's okay.

THE BENEFITS OF EXERCISE

Next, you need to get yourself psyched up to start working out, especially if you haven't really done it on any regular basis before now. I've already offered you a host of reasons for exercising, but the critical issue is for you to identify the benefits that you feel exercise will offer you.

From the following list, check off the reasons that are most important to you *right now*.

__lose weight
__lost fat
__increase muscle

__tone specific parts of the body
__trim waistline
__lower blood pressure
__increase cardiovascular health
__protect against developing cancer
__improve lipid profile (increase HDL cholesterol)
__maintain bone strength and mass
__keep joints lubricated
__prevent injuries, such as muscle strain
__promote circulation
__help regulate blood sugar
__improve vaginal, urethral, and bladder control
__improve digestion
__help alleviate hot flashes
__improve skin tone
__relieve insomnia
__improve mood
__decrease hunger
__alleviate stress and tension
__increase sex drive
__improve feelings of well-being and self-esteem
__feel sense of accomplishment
__other

Whether you checked off a dozen reasons or just a couple, keep this list close at hand so you can review it every day. You might want to make a copy of it and post it on your bedroom mirror, say, or on your car dashboard. When you feel your exercise motivation slipping, take another look at the list to remind yourself why you are exercising. Also evaluate whether you have already benefited—have your health, weight, and moods already improved thanks to your new exercise program? That should help keep you on track.

MAKE IT FUN

In order for exercise to be effective, it's got to become a part of your life, not just something you pick up every so often, like that crafts project you probably won't complete until the turn of the century. How do you ensure that your exercise program is something you actually *want* to do? By making it *fun*. After all, exercise doesn't have to be a drag . . . not when there are so many pleasant ways to get your daily workout.

Take a few minutes right now to think about the ways you enjoy being active. No matter how sedentary you insist you are, surely you like biking on a nice day . . . or swimming . . . or bowling . . . or ballroom dancing . . . or even just walking around the park or the mall. Each of these is a perfectly fine way to get your exercise. Or consider an activity you've always wanted to try but never seem to find the time for, such as tap dancing or a jazz exercise class. Not only will exercising make you feel and look better, but if done with other people, it becomes a social event as well.

Now, take the short self-test that follows. Answering these questions should help you determine the type of activity you'll most enjoy and the best time to exercise:

I like to exercise alone.	__True __False
I think I will stay more motivated if I join a class or a gym.	__True __False
I prefer working out first thing in the morning, before my day gets crazy.	__True __False
I like to unwind at the end of the day, so a brisk walk with a family member, friend, or even the dog will probably suit me best.	__True __False
I'm always looking to try something new, so I'm going to explore a new sport as well.	__True __False
I'm pretty set in my ways, so I'll most likely stick to some familiar activity like walking or biking.	__True __False

Now's the time to decide what seems most appealing to you and the best time to exercise. Remember, if you choose an activity you like and who you do it with, it won't *feel* like exercise—it'll simply feel like fun. And if you find a time that works nicely into your schedule you'll enjoy the time, rather than feeling that exercise is another pressure.

EXCUSES, EXCUSES!

You're at the very beginning of your workout program, and it all seems new and exciting. But the day will come in the not-so-distant future when you might be tempted to chuck the whole thing. Perhaps you're not feeling a lift in spirit yet, or your weight hasn't been coming off as fast as you had hoped. Maybe the weather's bad, and the last thing you want to do is go out for your daily walk. Whatever your excuse to put your exercise on hold . . . don't! You've got to stay committed to your plan in order to see the results you want. So how will you deal with the excuses you'll come up with? By "busting" your excuse with a logical response and an alternative plan of action.

Following are some typical excuses you might come up with for yourself, each followed by an apt "excuse-buster":

Excuse: "I'm just too busy! I don't have time to exercise today."
Excuse-buster: "Making time for my exercise is important. I can easily work thirty minutes of walking into my day today if I simply walk for fifteen minutes during my lunch hour, and then get off the bus one stop earlier and spend fifteen minutes walking home."

Excuse: "Why should I even bother? I've tried to exercise in the past and I've always lost interest."
Excuse-buster: "If I analyze why I quit exercising before, I realize that it was because running hurt my knees. Now I'm going to pick an activity that's less stressful and more pleasant, like brisk walking or biking."

Excuse: "Look! It's raining! How can I exercise?"
Excuse-buster: "I can exercise indoors. I can use the stationary bicycle right in my house, the one I've been using to hang my clothes on, or I can do some exercise using a videotape, or I can

go for a walk around the mall. I won't let the weather interfere with my exercise program."

A LITTLE GOES A LONG WAY

If you're still not ready to commit to working out, maybe it's because you've read in the past that you need to do a vast amount of exercise to do your weight and heart any good. The conventional wisdom used to be that unless you did a full twenty- to-sixty-minute session, three to five times a week, you weren't really getting much in the way of benefits. But all that's changed. Now, a whole host of respected organizations, including the American College of Sports Medicine, the President's Council on Physical Fitness, the American Heart Association, and the U.S. Centers for Disease Control and Prevention, agree that you *don't* have to work up a heavy sweat to reap the rewards of physical activity. A few short spurts of moderate activity here and there totaling thirty minutes or so, spread throughout the day, will add up to an effective workout if you do it on a regular basis.

The activities have to be considered of "moderate intensity," and they can be anything from walking up some stairs, gardening, playing Frisbee with the dog . . . even chasing after a lively grand-child or two! Your typical thirty minutes of daily activity might be broken down like this:

- a five-minute brisk walk to the bus
- a fifteen-minute walk during lunchtime
- five minutes of walking up and down the stairs at work
- five minutes of raking the leaves after dinner

Your goal is to *make regular activity part of the way you live each day*, rather than something you have to grit your teeth to do. And you'll find that, the more active you become, the more you'll want to keep it up, not only from five minutes of motion here and there but with planned activities like sustained aerobic (cardiovascular) exercise and strength training. If you're extremely sedentary, even the slightest additional activity will increase your energy and give your weight-loss efforts an amazing boost.

AEROBIC EXERCISE

Okay, so you've decided that you're going to make exercise part of your weekly routine. You've chosen the sport or activity you're going to do, at least initially—remember, you can always switch to another one, or vary activities during the week, to prevent boredom from setting in.

But it's not enough to jump into action, no matter how enthusiastic you may be right now. Your aerobic workout actually has *five* equally important components:

1. warming up
2. stretching
3. aerobic activity
4. cooling down
5. stretching

1. Warming Up *(5 minutes)*

No matter what sport or activity you do—and this will also hold true for strength training, which I'll be discussing shortly—it's critical to begin every session with a five-minute warm-up, to get your muscles and joints warm and your cardiovascular system ready for action. A warm-up is simply a slow-paced version of the activity you'll be doing, but this simple trick will make your exercise workout easier and will reduce your risk of injury while working out. So, if you'll be walking, just start walking at a slow pace, or if you'll be biking, start out on a flat surface or a slight decline, and pedal along slowly.

2. Stretching *(5 minutes)*

You need to stretch right after warming up to keep your body agile and your joints limber during exercise. Like warming up, stretching, even for just five minutes, helps you avoid injury. That's because regular stretching will cause your muscles to lengthen, giving you a greater range of motion. One of the added bonuses of launching your new exercise program is that, through a regular program of stretching, you should see a greater flexibility in your connective tissue—muscles and tendons—and if your

joints are stiff and painful, stretching will in time help alleviate
your pain.

Some stretching tips, especially if you're just starting out:

- Get your doctor's okay first, especially if you've been inactive, recently underwent surgery, or have problems with joints or muscles.
- Keep your body relaxed both before the stretch and as you hold the stretch.
- Always move *slowly* and without bouncing.
- Breathe deeply while stretching in order to increase the amount of oxygen going to your muscles. Don't hold your breath—that might increase your blood pressure.
- Pay attention to your posture while stretching.
- Perform each stretch two or three times, increasing the time you hold each stretch. For example, hold a stretch for twenty seconds during Week 1, then thirty seconds during Week 2, then forty seconds during Week 3. The longer you hold a stretch, the better, especially if an area feels tight. Do extra stretching wherever muscles feel particularly tight. Achieving greater flexibility is a function of time.
- Don't push yourself too far too quickly. The moment you feel any pain, *stop*.

SAMPLE STRETCHES TO TRY

Vary your stretches, but do the ones that are most appropriate
for the exercise you plan to do. For instance, if you'll be running,
you'll want to focus on leg stretches, and if you'll be doing upper-
body strength training or playing any racquet sports, you'll want
to stretch your shoulders, arms, and chest.

Standing Body Stretch (stretches shoulders, arms, and back).
   1. Stand with feet about 12 inches apart, heels flat on the floor, knees slightly bent, stomach muscles held tight.
   2. Place your arms directly overhead, parallel to one another, stretching upward, reaching as high as you can.
   3. Hold the position for 15–30 seconds.

4. Lower arms to your sides and relax shoulders. Hold this position.
5. Repeat 2 or 3 times. Each time you repeat it, increase the stretch slightly by gently pulling yourself a little farther into it. It should feel a bit more intense, but not painful. Don't overstretch.

Standing Medial Shoulder Stretch (stretches shoulders and triceps)

1. Stand with feet shoulder width apart, with knees relaxed and slightly bent.
2. To stretch your shoulder, with your left hand gently pull your right elbow across your chest toward your left shoulder. Hold the stretch for 15–30 seconds.
3. Repeat Step 2 using right hand and left elbow.
4. Repeat 2 or 3 times. Each time you repeat it, increase the stretch slightly by gently pulling yourself a little farther into it. It should feel a bit more intense, but not painful. Don't overstretch.

Standing Upper Body Stretch (stretches chest, anterior shoulder)

1. Stand with feet hip width apart, arms relaxed and at your sides, knees slightly bent, stomach muscles tight.
2. Clasp your hands behind you, interlacing your fingers, keeping your arms straight.
3. Lift your arms behind you, toward the ceiling. Keep your chest out and head straight ahead; don't bend over. Hold the stretch for 15–30 seconds.
4. Repeat 2 or 3 times. Each time you repeat it, increase the stretch slightly by gently pulling yourself a little farther into it. It should feel a bit more intense, but not painful. Don't overstretch.

Standing Calf Stretch (stretches calf muscles)

1. Face the wall, standing about an arm's length away.
2. Looking straight at the wall, place both palms on the wall at shoulder height.

3. Step forward with your left leg, leaving your right leg back. Keep both legs straight, with toes pointing to the wall and heels on the floor.

4. Bend your left knee (front leg) slightly, while slowly moving hips forward and keeping lower back straight. Make sure your right heel remains flat on the floor. Hold the stretch for 15–30 seconds.

5. Repeat the stretch by stepping forward with your right leg, and moving your left leg back.

6. Repeat 2 or 3 times. Each time you repeat it, increase the stretch slightly by gently pulling yourself a little farther into it. It should feel a bit more intense, but not painful. Don't overstretch.

Seated Hamstring Stretch (stretches lower back, back of legs, and hamstrings)

1. Sit on floor with legs directly out in front of you.

2. Press your knees against the floor, and flex your feet so that your toes are pointing to the ceiling. You may feel the stretch in the back of your legs. If so, hold this position.

3. Reach your hands out toward your feet, to the point where you feel your knees want to bend (but don't let them!). Hold the stretch for 15–30 seconds.

4. Repeat 2 or 3 times. Each time you repeat it, increase the stretch slightly by gently pulling yourself a little farther into it. It should feel a bit more intense, but not painful. Don't overstretch. If you do a straight-leg stretch such as this without first bending and straightening legs, you can strain your lower back. Also, you need to be sure stomach is in while stretching forward, to support your lower back.

Standing Gluteus Stretch (stretches several muscles of the buttocks)

1. Stand, facing a sturdy chair or table.

2. Place the ball of your right foot on the table or chair seat, while keeping your left leg straight, feet flat on the floor, toes pointing straight ahead.

3. Bend your right knee, slowly moving your hips forward. Feel the stretch, and hold it for 15–30 seconds.
4. Repeat with left leg.
5. Repeat 2 or 3 times. Each time you repeat it, increase the stretch slightly by gently pulling yourself a little farther into it. It should feel a bit more intense, but not painful. Don't overstretch.

Standing Quadriceps Stretch (stretches quadriceps [front of thighs])
1. Stand facing a wall, legs together. Place your right palm against the wall for support.
2. Bending your left leg behind you, slowly reach back with your left hand and grasp your left ankle, gently pulling your heel as close to your buttocks as possible. Keep thighs parallel. Hold the stretch for 15–30 seconds.
3. Repeat with right leg.
4. Repeat 2 or 3 times. Each time you repeat it, increase the stretch slightly by gently pulling yourself a little farther into it. It should feel a bit more intense, but not painful. Don't overstretch.

Standing Back Stretch (stretches back muscles)
1. Stand with feet 12 inches apart, knees slightly bent, abdominal muscles tightened.
2. Raise your arms to shoulder height, palms facing outward.
3. Place one palm over the other and press your palms away from the body.
4. Repeat 2 or 3 times. Each time you repeat it, press farther away from body.

*3. Aerobic Activity **(30–60 minutes)***
As I've discussed, aerobic activity—anything that gets you moving and your heart pumping—is great for helping you feel good and for burning calories, which can help you slim down. It's best if the aerobic portion of your workout lasts a *minimum* of 20 minutes (although 30 minutes or more is preferable to gain the full cardiovascular benefit).

As for the number of calories burned, Elly Munsinger, fitness consultant and AFAA fitness practitioner, states: "People used to think if you exercised for 20 minutes, you started burning fat, rather than carbs for energy. What we now know is something different. For the beginner exerciser, as the intensity of the activity increases, the fuel of choice changes from fats to carbs, not the other way around. That's great because carbs burn off 5.05 kcals per liter of oxygen, while fat burns off 4.7 kcals per liter of oxygen. So there is a calorie benefit to this."

Yet once you become more conditioned, you then start burning *more* fat rather than carbs, per liter of oxygen, because you don't have to work as hard.

While the choice of activity is yours, you should take it easy if you're just beginning to exercise. You want this to be a program that *lasts a lifetime*, so start slow and build gradually. If you're over forty, have any history of fractures, or have lost some height as a result of bone loss, then you should probably stick to what's called low-impact aerobics—such activities as low-impact dancing, cross-country skiing (as opposed to downhill), and brisk walking (instead of jogging or running). These activities can be just as much fun as high-impact aerobics without nearly the potential for injury.

How much should you exercise? That all depends on your current level of fitness and activity. Which of the three descriptions below best describes you?

Low: You normally move around very little. If given the choice between taking the stairs or the elevator, you always opt for the elevator. You rarely get involved in activities that increase your breathing or heart rate either at work or at home.

Moderate: You're fairly active. It's typical for you to engage in some "lifestyle activity," such as gardening or vigorous housework, and/or some regular sports or exercise, such as biking or brisk walking, totalling about thirty minutes a day, three times a week.

High: You're very active. You do some sort of fairly vigorous activity at least thirty minutes a day, every day.

Now that you've identified your fitness level, use the chart that follows to help you create your personalized exercise program. I've used three sample activities—walking, cycling (outdoors or on a stationary bike), and swimming.

To reap the maximum benefit of exercise, Elly Munsinger recommends for cardiovascular training that beginners aim for three to five days a week. Start with 10 minutes of cardiovascular activity and gradually increase your time. After about three weeks, increase to five times a week, with cardiovascular activity lasting about 30 minutes. For those who are currently exercising, increase to five to six times a week. It's important to always give your body a rest. "Seven days of exercise is just too much. Risk of injury increases to 50% if you exercise seven days a week," according to Munsinger.

	Week	Walking	Cycling	Swimming
L O W	1	5–10 minutes	5–10 minutes	5–10 minutes
	2	10–5 minutes	Outdoor cycling: 10-15 minutes Stationary bike: Pedal— 5–10 minutes Rest— 2 minutes Pedal— 5 additional minutes	10–15 minutes
	3+	15–20 minutes	15–20 minutes	15–20 minutes
M E D	1	30 minutes	20 minutes	20 minutes
	2	35 minutes	Outdoor cycling: 25 minutes Stationary bike: Pedal— 20 minutes Rest— 2 minutes Pedal— 5 additional minutes	25 minutes
	3+	40 minutes	30 minutes	30 minutes

	Week	Walking	Cycling	Swimming
H **I** **G** **H**	1	40 minutes	30 minutes	30 minutes

	2	45 minutes	Outdoor cycling: 35 minutes
			
			Stationary bike:
			Pedal—
			    30 minutes
			Rest—
			    2 minutes
			Pedal—5 additional minutes
				35 minutes

	3+	50 minutes	40 minutes	40 minutes

What should you be aiming for? Build up to 30–40 minutes per session (or up to 60 minutes per session if your initial fitness/activity rating was high). Don't forget to set aside time for your warm-up and stretching program!

For aerobic exercise, to make sure you're not overdoing it, take the "talk test"—that is, you should exercise hard enough so that you perspire but are still able to *comfortably* talk or sing while working out. For resistance training, beginners can start with a session once a week and build up to three times a week.

How to Increase the Challenge: Once you've been at the thirty-to-forty-minutes-per-session level for a number of weeks or months, you may want a new fitness challenge—and good for you if you do! If you're working out three times a week, you can shoot for five. Or, add more resistance to your routine. For example, take your walk or bike uphill, or if you swim, add some buoyant devices to make swimming more challenging.

You might also want to alternate types of exercise—perhaps by swapping some part of your normal walking routine for some biking or swimming. This is known as cross-training. Not only does cross-training give your workout some variety, but it also improves your aerobic capacity, so that your body uses oxygen better. Of you may consider interval training, whereby you add some short, quick bursts of speed throughout your typical routine. So, if you're biking, pedal as fast as you can for fifteen or twenty seconds a few times during your ride. You can do the same thing while walking or swimming.

4. Cooling Down (5 minutes)
After you've been working out aerobically and your heart rate has been elevated for twenty or thirty minutes, you want to *slowly* get your pulse back down to its resting rate. That's why a five-minute cool-down is so important. It also helps you avoid stiff muscles. All you need to do to cool down is a few minutes of slow walking or slow pedaling as you slowly breathe in and out.

5. Stretching (5 minutes)
To wrap up your exercise session, you need to stretch out the warm muscles and joints that were involved in the aerobic activity. A few minutes of stretching will reduce soreness and relax your muscles, which generally tighten after exercise. Choose your stretches from those described above.

STRENGTH TRAINING

Not so very long ago, it was unthinkable for women—especially women past a certain age—to lift weights. Strength training was for the likes of Arnold Schwarzenegger and Sylvester Stallone, not you! Anyway, who wanted to have big, bulging muscles? But little by little women started getting into the act, going to the gym and pumping iron, not so much to develop big muscles but to get strong. Even Madonna was into strength training and *she* didn't look like a weight lifter. Still, it seemed like an activity for body-builders.

Now we know different. Today strength training (also called weight training or resistance training) is generally acknowledged to be a key to lifelong health. As you age you lose muscle mass, and building muscle strength through a regular program of strength training may help prevent this and many of those age-related problems you may now be concerned about: osteoporosis, musculoskeletal injury, and the loss of independence that often accompanies limited body strength and mobility. In fact, recent experiments involving nursing home residents who participated in strength training programs have yielded some remarkable results. Many participants showed an amazing increase in muscle strength, after which they were able to regain some independence in doing everyday activities.

Strength training is of particular importance to post-menopausal women. One survey now underway, called the Framingham (Massachusetts) Heart Study, reveals the shocking fact that half of the inactive women sixty-five and older can't lift even ten pounds! Women usually start losing muscle mass more rapidly as they age. This age-related muscle mass loss will be compounded if you've been dieting to lose weight most of your life and have not been exercising concurrently—even on the healthiest of diets. But if you begin a program of strength-training, your muscle and bone mass can be restored and preserved, putting you at far less risk for sprains and debilitating fractures.

As with most exercise, strength training can be done by anyone, regardless of age or current level of fitness, as long as you go slowly and follow directions. How does it work? Strength training is the application of resistance—lifting free weights, using strength-training machines, or using your own body weight—against your muscles and, in so doing, you are forcing your muscles to work harder than usual by pushing, pulling, or lifting more than you ordinarily would. Do this often enough, with an exertion that approaches your maximum possible effort, and your muscles become strengthened (not bulky!) and toned. Not only will you look better and feel stronger but this additional muscle mass will enable your body to burn calories more efficiently. And you may notice that your shape changes as well. Your stomach, back, and arms may become trimmer as you build more muscle. To maintain these benefits, however, you have to keep up your strength-training program. (For every pound of muscle you develop through exercise, you burn about 50–100 additional calories a day.) And, if you have a higher percentage of muscle to fat, you burn calories more efficiently so you can lose excess weight or maintain your current weight without having to slash your calorie intake dramatically.

If you think you need a lot of fancy equipment or have to drag yourself to the gym five times a week to do strength training, think again. While you *do* need some instruction (provided here are a few of the basics, which should be supplemented by a session with an exercise physiologist or certified personal trainer), you can work out at home using simple objects, such as inexpensive exercise bands or your own weights.

Before you begin any strength-training program, follow these guidelines:

- Get your doctor's okay.
- Plan on doing strength training no more than three times a week, about twenty minutes per session to start. Later on, after perhaps three or four months, if three sessions is too difficult because of the time commitment, etc., you can drop down to two sessions a week and maintain muscle strength.
- Give yourself a day off in between strength-training sessions, so your muscles have a chance to repair themselves. Use the days off to do your aerobic exercise—or just take them as days of rest.
- Just as with aerobic exercise, be sure to warm up, stretch, and cool down when you do strength training.
- And as with your aerobics activities, be sure to *breathe*. Breathe out as you do the work (exhale as you exert yourself) and breathe in as you return to the resting position as you do your strength-training workouts. Do *not* hold your breath during any part of the exercise.

STRENGTH TRAINING FOR BEGINNERS

If you've never tried strength training before, you probably have lots of questions. You should find the answers below:

Q. Will I start looking big and bulky like some of the male weight lifters if I do strength training?

A. Not at all. What makes a male weight lifter look big and "masculine" has a lot to do with the presence of the male hormone testosterone, which is primarily responsible for male musculature. Since as a woman you have significantly less testosterone than a man, you really don't have to worry about this. In addition, you can keep your body from bulking up too much by using lighter weights and simply increasing the number of reps you do, instead of doing fewer reps with heavier weights.

Q. What's the best way to get started?

A. If you like being surrounded by other people, your best bet is to enroll in a strength-training class, where you may use bands or light weights, or be taken through some calisthenic exercises that

The Language of Strength Training

If you're new to strength training, you may not be familiar with the lingo. Here are some key words and phrases you should know before you begin:

anaerobic: literally "without oxygen." Strength training is anaerobic exercise, as opposed to aerobic ("with oxygen") exercise like walking, biking, and swimming.

"burn": the feeling of heat in a muscle or group of muscles when you are exercising it. You know you've succeeded in isolating a muscle group when you feel the burning sensation there, which indicates that the area isn't getting enough oxygen. This is a normal part of anaerobic activity.

contraction: the tightening of a muscle.

"maxing out" (or working to the point of failure): doing exercise to the point where the muscles are so fatigued that it is extremely difficult to do one more repetition.

repetition ("rep"): one complete exercise movement, from start to finish. Thus, when you lift the weight up and down, you've completed one rep.

rest: a break between sets used for muscle recovery.

set: a certain number of continuous repetitions. Eight to twelve reps usually comprise one set.

will strengthen your muscles. Taking a low-impact aerobics class can also help—usually some portion of the class is devoted to calisthenics. If you prefer working out alone, you can rent a strength-training video that, like a class, will use light weights, bands, and calisthenics. When choosing a tape don't simply reach for one starring your favorite actress or singer. Instead, look for one that's approved by the Aerobics and Fitness Association of America (AFAA) or the American College of Sports Medicine (ACSM).

After you feel like you've mastered the class or tape, you can then move on to machines.

Q. Help! I'm overwhelmed by all the machines at the gym. What should I do?

A. Ask if there's an exercise physiologist or certified personal trainer available to explain the machines to you and help you set up a program that's right for your particular level. It's possible that he or she will encourage you to start with the machines first rather than free weights because there is less risk of injury with the machines. The trainer should watch and correct your form with every exercise.

Q. How much weight should I lift?

A. According to Kathy Hager, R. N., M. S., president of Health and Fitness Concepts, Inc., if you're using machines, start with the first plate (each plate is about 10 pounds), and see how it feels. Try to lift or press it for 8–12 reps. If it seems as though you're working your muscles and you feel a "burn" at the end of the set, this is the right weight for you. If you don't feel as though your muscles are being challenged, keep adding more weight, a plate or two at a time, until it feels just right.

If you're using free weights, go to a sporting goods store, and try lifting 5-pound weights 8 times within 30–50 seconds. Is it reasonably comfortable? If so, then it's probably a good weight for you. If it feels too easy—as though you could easily lift it many more times—select a slightly heavier weight and try lifting that 8 times within 30–50 seconds. Sporting good stores will have both dumbbells and weights. You can attach the weights to your body with Velcro closures. Unlike dumbbells, which are only used for upper-body work, Velcro weights can be strapped to your arms for upper-body work or to your ankles for lower-body exercises. You can also make your own weights using clean plastic detergent or milk containers that you fill with water or sand. You can make them heavier as your strength-training program progresses.

Q. How many sets should I do?

A. Elly Munsinger suggests that the goal here is to reach a "burn" or "failure," which means that you are reaching your maximal intensity. First, try to complete a set of 8–12 reps with an appropriate weight. If you find that you do a set of reps and don't feel a burn, add more weight.

Although many instructors recommend 3 sets of 8–12 reps, Munsinger states that stimulating a muscle multiple times to maximal intensity shows *no additional benefit*. However, doing *multiple types* of an exercise for the same muscle group will help strengthen the muscles, by changing the angle of the pull.

Q. What would be a typical routine to follow at the gym?

A. One menopausal client who was at risk for osteoporosis and had fifteen pounds to lose began strength training. She followed this program, outlined by her exercise physiologist, which took her about forty-five minutes:

Exercise	Body Part	Reps	Sets
(Dumbbell)			
bench press	chest	8–12	3
Dumbbell press	shoulders	8–12	3
Back pulldown	back	8–12	3
Leg press	legs	8–12	3
Leg extension	thighs	8–12	3
Leg curl	hamstrings	8–12	3
Dumbbell arm curl	biceps	8–12	3
Triceps extension	triceps	8–12	3
Abdominal crunches	abdomen	8–12	3

A BASIC STRENGTH-TRAINING PROGRAM

Quadriceps (knee) Extension
1. Sit upright in a chair, feet flat against the floor, with a 2.5-pound weight around each ankle.
2. Holding the sides of the chair seat for balance, slowly extend one leg straight out in front of you.
3. Breathe out as you raise your leg and breathe in as you lower your leg.
4. Slowly lower the leg to the starting position, and repeat within one second.
5. Repeat for a total of 3 sets, 8–12 reps per set. When you do

repetitive reps, change the angle of the pull for the muscle group you are working on to continue to build strength. Rest about 60–90 seconds between sets. Then switch to other leg.

Hamstring (back of thigh or posterior thigh) Curl
1. Strap or cuff a weight around each ankle.
2. Facing the back of a chair, with your feet shoulder width apart and toes pointing forward, stand with chest lifted, shoulders relaxed and eyes straight ahead.
3. Holding the top of the chair for support and keeping knees slightly bent, flex one foot and slowly lift it off the floor toward your buttocks. You should feel the muscles in your outer thigh contract.
4. Return to starting position.
5. Repeat for a total of 3 sets, 8–12 reps per set. Rest about 60–90 seconds between sets. Then switch to other leg.

Hip Extension
1. Strap or cuff a 2.5-pound weight around each ankle.
2. Facing the back of a chair, with your feet shoulder width apart and toes pointing forward, stand with chest lifted, shoulders relaxed, and eyes straight ahead.
3. Holding the top of the chair for support and keeping knees slightly bent, flex one foot and slowly slide that foot backward, extending your leg toward the wall behind you. Your heel should be lifted off the floor but your toes should remain in contact with the floor.
4. Return to starting position.
5. Repeat for a total of 3 sets, 8–12 reps per set. Rest about 60–90 seconds between sets. Then switch to other leg.

Shoulder Exercise (Anterior Shoulder)
1. Sit upright in a chair, feet flat on the floor.
2. Hold a dumbbell in each hand, with your hands hanging downward along the side of the chair, palms facing in.
3. Slowly raise one arm at a time, straight out in front of you. Lower to your side and repeat for a total of 3 sets, 8–12 reps per arm. Breathe out as you raise your arm and breathe in as you lower your arm.

4. Raise both arms straight out in front of you, to shoulder level. Lower slowly back down to your sides. Repeat for a total of 3 sets, 8–12 reps each. Rest about 60–90 seconds between sets. Keep breathing out as you raise your arms and breathe in as your lower your arms.

Shoulder (Posterior)
1. Sit upright in a chair, feet flat on the floor.
2. Hold a dumbbell in each hand.
3. Drop torso forward, almost to knees.
4. Slowly raise one arm at a time out to the side, so that elbow is same height as shoulder. Lower to side and repeat for a total of 3 sets, 8–12 reps per arm. Breathe out as you raise your arm and breathe in as you lower your arm.
5. Raise both arms to your sides, to shoulder level. Slowly lower back down to your sides. Repeat for a total of 3 sets, 8–12 reps each. Rest about 60–90 seconds between sets. Keep breathing as you raise your arms and breathe in as you lower your arms.

Shoulder (Medial)
1. Sit upright in chair, feet flat on the floor.
2. Hold a dumbbell in each hand.
3. Slowly raise both arms out to the side, so that elbow is same height as shoulder. Then, bend both arms at your elbow, so your fingers are pointing to the floor. Lower both arms to side and repeat for a total of 3 sets, 8–12 reps. Breathe out as you raise and bend your arms and breathe in as you lower your arms.

Upper Trapezius Exercise
1. Sit upright in a chair, feet flat on the floor.
2. Hold a weight in each hand, palms facing forward.
3. Raise your arms up, as if you are in a stickup, fists raised to the ceiling. Keep elbows bent and at shoulder level.
4. Bring elbows together in front of you, then bring them back to the original position. Breathe out as your elbows come together, and breathe in as they return to original position.

5. Repeat for a total of 3 sets, 8–12 reps per set. Rest about 60–90 seconds between sets.

Bicep (arm) Curl
1. Sit on a chair, with back firmly against back of chair. Keep shoulders back and chest lifted.
2. Hold a dumbbell in each hand. Keeping elbows close to your waist, grasp dumbbells so the palms of your hands face forward.
3. Slowly bring one dumbbell up toward your shoulder, then slowly lower it to the starting position.
4. Breath out as you curl the dumbbell up, breathe in as you return to starting position.
5. Repeat for a total of 3 sets, 8–12 reps per set. Rest about 60–90 seconds between sets. Then switch to other arm.

Bent-Knee Push-Ups (for chest, shoulders, and upper arms)
1. Get down on the floor on your hands and knees. Walk your hands forward so that your hips are straight and diagonal to the floor, and you are feeling the weight of your body mostly on your hands.
2. Lower your body toward the floor but do not touch the floor, so the weight of your body remains mostly on your hands; then push back up. Avoid locking your elbows.
3. Repeat for a total of 3 sets, 8–12 reps per set. Rest about 60–90 seconds between sets.

Abdominal Crunches (for stomach and abdominal strength, better support of internal organs, and better bladder control)
1. Lie on your back on the floor, one hand comfortably behind your head, with your fingertips spread wide to support your neck. Place your thumb from your other hand on the top of your abdominal muscle and the middle finger on the bottom of your abdominal muscle.
2. Bend your knees, keeping your heels flat on the floor.
3. As you inhale, contract the abdominal muscle so that your thumb and middle finger move toward each other and your

head and shoulders lift slightly of the floor. Hold this position for 15–30 seconds. Exhale.

4. Lower your upper body to starting position.
5. Repeat 10 times. Over the next 1 or 2 months, build up to 50 of these "crunches" a day.

EXERCISE BANDS

Some women like working out with exercise bands instead of weights or machines. Bands are available at sporting goods stores as well as at surgical supply stores. The surgical kind can be cut to various lengths and thicknesses depending on how challenging you want to make the exercise (different lengths and thicknesses mean greater or lesser resistance against your body). The nice thing about bands is that they're inexpensive and can be carried anywhere. Here are a few guidelines for using them:

- Cut two or three different lengths of bands. Where you need a circular band, you'll need to tie the ends together. Before you start to work out, do a firm pull-test to make sure the knot is secure. (To perform the exercises that follow, you'll need one five-foot-long band and another five-foot band tied together to make a circle.)
- Wear sweats or leg warmers rather than shorts to prevent irritation to your skin while working out with bands. You may also want to wear lightweight gloves.
- Don't neglect your warm-up, stretches, and cool-down.
- Remember to *breathe* while doing these exercises! Don't hold your breath.

Seated Quadriceps (for legs)
1. Sit in a chair, feet flat on floor.
2. Place the circle band around the left front chair leg.
3. Place your left foot through the loop, so that the band is resting on your ankle. (Better yet, keep it around the toe of your sneaker to prevent it from slipping up your leg.)
4. Holding on to the seat of the chair for support, raise and

lower your left leg. Breathe out as you raise your leg and breathe in as you lower your leg.

5. Repeat for a total of 3 sets, 8–12 reps per set. Rest about 60–90 seconds between sets. Repeat with other leg.

Seated Hip Flexors (for hips)

1. Sit in a chair, feet flat on floor.
2. Place circle band under right foot, keeping foot tight to the floor. Stretch band so it encircles your left knee.
3. Raise left knee toward your chest, then lower it. Breathe out as you raise your leg and breathe in as you lower your leg.
4. Repeat for a total of 3 sets, 8–12 reps per set. Rest about 60–90 seconds between sets. Repeat with other leg.

Standing Hamstrings (back of thighs)

1. Stand facing the back of a chair, your feet about 12 inches apart, toes pointing forward.
2. Hold on to the top of the chair for balance.
3. Place the circle band around one leg of the chair and your left ankle. Keep your knees together and your back straight.
4. Bend your left knee and raise your left foot back, toward your buttocks, keeping right leg straight (don't lock knee). Hold it and feel the stretch.
5. Lower left leg to starting position.
6. Repeat for a total of 3 sets, 8–12 reps per set. Rest about 60–90 seconds between sets. Repeat with other leg.

Standing Outer Thigh

1. Stand with your left side toward the back of a chair.
2. Hold on to the top of the chair with left hand for balance.
3. Place the circle band around your ankles.
4. Lift your right (outside) leg as far back as you can. Hold it and release.
5. Lower right leg to starting position.
6. Repeat for a total of 3 sets, 8–12 reps per set. Rest about 60–90 seconds between sets. Repeat with other leg.

Standing Shoulders (for medial muscles)

1. Anchor one end of the straight band under your right foot.
2. Gripping the other end of the band with your right hand, lift your right arm out to your right side, raising it as close to shoulder level as possible. Hold it and release. Maintain good posture.
3. Return to starting position.
4. Repeat for a total of 3 sets, 8–12 reps per set. Rest about 60–90 seconds between sets. Repeat with other leg.

Standing Shoulder Raises (for posterior muscles)

1. Anchor one end of the long band under your right foot.
2. Gripping the other end of the band with your right hand, pull it upward toward your chest while bending your right elbow. Hold. Maintain good posture and don't lean forward into the pull.
3. Repeat for a total of 3 sets, 8–12 reps per set. Rest about 60–90 seconds between sets. Repeat with other arm.

Standing Bicep (front of the upper arm) Curl

1. Anchor one end of the long band under your right foot.
2. Grip the other end with your right hand. The band should be tight and your palms should face upward.
3. Bend arm at the elbow and pull your hand up toward your shoulder. Hold. Release slowly.
4. Return band to starting position.
5. Repeat for a total of 3 sets, 8–12 reps per set. Rest about 60–90 seconds between sets. Repeat with other arm.

Standing Tricep (back of upper arm) Press

1. Grip the circular band with your right hand, knuckles facing out. Place band near your chest while keeping your right elbow bent.
2. Grip the lower end of the band with your left hand, knuckles facing out, and hold at waist level.
3. Lower left hand toward the floor, keeping arm straight but relaxed. Hold it and feel the stretch.

4. Repeat for a total of 3 sets, 8–12 reps per set. Rest about 60–90 seconds between sets. Repeat with other arm.

Lying Chest Exercise
   1. Lie on the floor. Place band under your chest, with the two sides of the band extending out near your shoulders.
   2. Grip the right side of the band with your right hand, and the other with your left hand. Raise both arms to a 90-degree angle, with palms facing forward. Slowly bring your thumbs towards each other until they meet. Squeeze pectoralis muscle as thumbs move to middle. Hold it and then release.
   3. Return to starting position.
   4. Repeat for a total of 3 sets, 8–12 reps per set. Rest about 60–90 seconds between sets.

CAROLINE'S STORY

I haven't had a period in two years, my blood pressure is high for the first time in my life, and I gained about 18 pounds during menopause—I was about 187 pounds and 5'4" when I started working with Judy. My eating habits didn't really change when I started menopause, but I put on weight more easily than before. I also noticed that the shape of my body changed—I put on more fat on my stomach and arms, places that had never gotten any heavier when I put on weight in the past. I think my rise in blood pressure might have been due to the excess weight.

I recognized the fact that exercise was critical to losing weight, getting my blood pressure under control, and toning up. I started exercising—now I do race-walking almost every day. First I did 10 minutes a day, and then I added 1 minute every day. Now I'm up to 40 minutes, which is comfortable for me. My weight has gone down, but I really noticed changes when I took my body measurements. My waist went down 4 inches, and my body fat went down by 3 percent after sticking with the CPP program and exercising regularly for several months. And my blood pressure is back to normal.

10

Managing Your Response to Stress

Even if you weren't going through menopause . . . even if you weren't focusing your energies on trying to ensure future good health, or on losing weight, this could *still* be a stressful time in your life. A woman's mid-to-late forties and fifties are typically a period marked by change, both good and not-so-good, some of which may affect her for the rest of her life.

Stop for a moment and ask yourself how many of these events have occurred to *you* within the last year or two:

- divorce
- remarriage
- caring for one or more seriously ill parents
- the death of one or both of your parents
- caring for your seriously ill husband
- the death of your husband
- the death of a good friend
- the last of your children leaving home
- the marriage of one of your children
- the return of your adult child to your home to live
- the birth of one or more grandchildren
- money difficulties
- moving to a smaller home

- losing your job
- launching your own business
- starting early retirement
- change in your health or your own chronic illness
- fears about aging and death

As you can see, stress comes in many forms. And you can view stressors— those demands placed on you by others, by yourself, or by circumstances outside your control—as points on a continuum, with the negative stressors on one end and the positive stressors on the other. Both types of stress get your adrenaline going and spur you into action so that you focus on matters at hand. The key is not to let stress at *either* end of the continuum get the better of you because that can lead to burnout, constant upset, or falling back into bad habits you've worked so hard to change. Since many of life's stressors are unavoidable, learning how to deal with them effectively as they occur is critical, especially once you understand what a toll stress can take on your body.

STRESS: THE FIGHT-OR-FLIGHT RESPONSE

You may recall the earlier discussion on the importance of keeping the adrenal glands healthy and well functioning, to ensure as smooth a transition into menopause as possible. Stress has a definite impact on the adrenal glands, and if you're exposed to constant stress and don't handle it effectively, that can be a drain on the adrenals.

During times of stress these glands manufacture larger-than-normal amounts of the hormones adrenaline (also called epinephrine) and norepinephrine, thus triggering a whole chain of bodily responses. As these hormones travel through your bloodstream to your heart and blood vessels, your heart gets the signal to beat more rapidly and your blood vessels get the signal to constrict. Your hands and feet get cold as blood is directed away from them. Blood is also directed away from the digestive tract, so that even if you're eating healthy food, it's not being digested as well. Your metabolism speeds up, mainly because of fatty acids being released from your fat stores, and you become more alert. Short-term stress also causes increased secretion of the hormone cortisol by the adrenal glands. If the stress is ongoing, the increased secretion of cortisol can cause the breakdown of some of your proteins. These proteins are converted to glucose. The newly formed glucose ensures adequate fuel supply to the brain and heart.

Long-term stress can cause your body to lose some vital body protein, as well as some potassium, phosphorus, calcium, and other vitamins and mineral, which may exacerbate your current menopausal symptoms, including headaches, depression, fatigue, and decreased interest in sex. And because "the fight-or-flight" response to stress can cause tissue repair to shut down temporarily, continual stress may put you at greater risk for osteoporosis and fractures. The good news is that, soon after the stress response has been turned on, it can be turned off. The chemicals that have been released are metabolized and your body functions return to normal—*if* you can calm your mind and body down. That's admittedly a big *if*, but you can do it!

HANDLING STRESS: GETTING STARTED

When some women are stressed out, they stop eating. This can only further stress your system. Others, however, turn to those comforting foods to try to calm themselves down—which also adds additional stress—even though they know all too well that eating to numb their feelings is just a short-term solution at best. Eventually, they're left with two sources of stress: the original stressor *and* the bad feelings about themselves because of the excess food they ate. In fact, they may end up with yet a *third* problem—namely, a menopausal symptom brought on by their eating. Did you know, for instance, that a binge can intensify your hot flashes? That's why if you eat unhealthy foods in response to stress, you may be a) aggravating your menopausal symptoms and b) undermining, and not supporting, your weight-loss efforts.

To change this behavior, or any other unhealthy habit, it's important to gather some baseline information on the sources of stress in your life, as well as how they affect your body. Start by taking the inventory below.

RECOGNIZING STRESS

As successful as you may be in making lifestyle changes, there are going to be times when your moods and life's usual ups and downs try to take over—and your impulse may be to turn to food. That's when you need to pause and step back to see what's going on in terms of what is causing your stress and how you are responding. If you suspect that you're getting stressed out as exhibited by the way you feel or the sloppiness of your habits, ask yourself the following:

1. WHAT ARE YOUR STRESSORS?

First, try to identify what situations or people (including yourself!) in your life might be responsible for the stress you're feeling. Check off all those items that apply to you:

__Major life stressors, such as divorce; death of a spouse; separation from children; loss of friends due to death, retirement, or relocation; coping with an ill parent; your own illness; fears of aging/death, etc.

__Money problems

__Relationship conflicts, such as those with a spouse, an adult child, a boss or coworker, friend, or neighbor

__Time management problems (too much to do with too little time; too little to do)

__Minor ongoing hassles, such as being mistakenly billed on your credit card for someone else's purchase, traffic hassles, long lines at the bank, etc. (Don't underestimate these! They can add up and send you over the edge.)

__Getting in your own way, such as not resolving an internal conflict; not being able to let go of situations that are spurring on your anger (or any negative emotion); not accepting yourself for what you are, but focusing on what you are not.

2. WHAT ARE YOUR SYMPTOMS?

Now, think about the way you are responding to the stressors in your life. Are you experiencing any of following symptoms? Many of them may be the result of your response to the stress in your life. Check off all those that apply:

Lifestyle Habits

__I use food as a tranquilizer when life becomes too much to handle.

__I overeat at mealtime.

__I overeat between meals.

__I feel as though I'm obsessed with food and eating.

__I skip a meal, then I gorge at the next meal.

__I eat anything that's around, even foods I don't like.

__I don't plan what I'm going to eat in advance.

__I plan what I'm going to eat, but abandon my plan at the drop of a hat.

__I don't keep foods in the house that will help me stay on track with my health goals and weight-loss efforts.

__I actively seek out foods that I know I should try to limit, like chocolate.

__If given a choice, I sleep instead of exercise.

__My routine activity is at a bare minimum.

__I've given up my regular exercise program.

__I frequently have a drink to relax.

__I smoke cigarettes to relax.

Physical Habits

__I bite my nails.

__I drum my fingers.

__I grind my teeth.

__I pick at my fingernails.

__I sigh a lot.

__I twist/pull my hair.

Illness

__My asthma has been triggered by stress recently.

__I have digestive problems—indigestion, heartburn, constipation, or diarrhea.

__I have muscle aches/pains.

__I have sexual problems.

__I break out in eczema, hives, or acne.

__I'm losing more hair than usual.

Moodiness

__I feel anxious.

__I feel depressed.

__I feel frustrated.

__I feel hopeless.

__I feel restless.

__I feel irritable.

Behavior/Emotional Changes

__I'm not sleeping well.

__I feel I overreact.

__People say I overreact a lot.

__Lately I've been making many mistakes/having accidents.

__I have emotional outbursts.

3. WHERE IS THE STRESS IN YOUR BODY?

Now that you know your stressors, locate the tension in your body and where it tends to settle by doing a body scan. In this exercise you will be mentally traveling through your body, exploring all your body parts, and as you move from one area to another, ask yourself whether or not you feel tension. Follow these steps.

1. Find a quiet, comfortable place to sit.
2. Start concentrating on your breathing. Breathe relaxation *in*, breathe tension *out*.
3. Close your eyes.
4. Start with your toes. Do you feel any tension in your toes? Your calves? Knees? Thighs? Buttocks?
5. Move to your lower back. How does that feel? What about your stomach? Your chest? Your shoulders?
6. Move down to your hands. How do your fingers feel? Your lower arms? Your upper arms?
7. Move to your neck—does it feel tense? What about your

facial or jaw muscles? Your mouth? (Are your teeth clenched?) Tongue? (If it's resting on the floor of your mouth, that's a sign of relaxation.) Your eyes? Your forehead?

8. If you're having trouble telling where the tension in your body lies, try doing the Progressive Muscle Relaxation found on page 223.

START A STRESS-AWARENESS DIARY

To help you identify what triggers your responses to stress, begin tracking the times when you tend to feel most stressed, the event(s) that act as triggers, and the way you respond/react to the stress. Make a copy or two of the following Stress-Awareness Diary and keep it up-to-date for two full weeks.

		Stress-Awareness Diary	
Day	*Time of Day*	*Stressful Event*	*Response/Reaction*

It's not enough to just jot down what stresses you out and when—you've got to spot your patterns early in order to change them. For example, do you find that every time you get into an argument with someone at work, you get a headache within a half hour? The key is to identify the stressor and your typical response as quickly as possible, and to adjust your reaction by using the relaxation techniques I describe in this chapter.

STRESS-MANAGEMENT RELAXATION EXERCISES

All exercises designed to relieve stress and promote calm—whether they originated in Eastern or Western cultures—have four important factors in common:

1. a quiet environment
2. being in a comfortable position
3. adopting a passive attitude, a let-it-happen attitude, so that you free your mind of thoughts
4. continuously repeating a calming word or phrase, or "passively" concentrating on your breathing throughout the exercise to help you become focused

Following is a variety of exercises. The exercises range from dealing with stress through actual relaxation techniques, such as muscle relaxation and deep breathing, to managing stress by managing your emotional response or your attitude to it such as thought stopping and positive self-talk techniques. You'll also find introductions to such useful techniques as meditation and creative visualization. To learn which activities work for you, it's best to try each one for a full week and practice it *at least* once each day.

Progressive Muscle Relaxation
Before you begin, follow these suggestions:

- As you relax, try to keep your mind free of thoughts. (This is called passive concentration.)
- When tensing each muscle group, hold the tension for 5–7 seconds.
- When relaxing each muscle group, relax for 10–30 seconds.

- Make sure you feel the contrast between tension and relaxation before you move on to the next muscle group.
- Repeat the tensing and relaxing of each body part twice. If one area of your body is particularly tight, repeat up to 5 more times.
- On the other hand, you should be careful not to overtighten any muscle group. (For example, overtightening the toes or feet can cause muscle cramping.)
- Don't hold your breath. Remember to *keep breathing*.

To Do Progressive Muscle Relaxation:
1. Get into a comfortable position and close your eyes.
2. To start the process, curl the toes of both feet under. Feel the tension in your calves. Hold for 5 seconds, then gradually release to the count of 10. Take a slow, deep breath. Repeat.
3. Curl the toes of both feet upward. Feel the tension in your lower legs. Hold for 5 seconds, then gradually release to the count of 10. Take a slow, deep breath. Repeat.
4. Press your knees together as tightly as you can. Hold for 5 seconds, then relax to the count of 10. Repeat.
5. Tighten the muscles of your buttocks and thighs. Hold this position for 5 seconds, then relax for 10 seconds. Repeat.
6. Tighten your stomach muscles. Hold for 5 seconds, then relax for 10 seconds. Repeat.
7. Arch your back by pressing your shoulders toward each other behind you. Hold the tension for 5 seconds, then relax for 10 seconds. Repeat.
8. Clench both hands into fists. Feel the tension in both fists, hands, and forearms. Hold for 5 seconds, then relax for 10 seconds. Repeat.
9. Bend your elbows upward and make a fist to tense the muscles of your upper arms. Hold for 5 seconds, then relax for 10 seconds. Repeat.
10. Now, tense a series of facial muscles. Wrinkle your forehead as tightly as you can. Squint your eyes hard. Clench your jaw, biting hard. Press your tongue to the roof of your

mouth. Do all of these simultaneously for 5 seconds. Relax for 10 seconds. Repeat.

BREATHING EXERCISES

Proper breathing is an effective way to reduce or alleviate anxiety, tension, and mild depression.

Breathing Awareness

The first thing you need to know about your breathing is whether you are doing it from your abdomen (correct) or from your chest (incorrect). To find out, lie on the floor, with your legs straight in front of you, your arms at your sides, and your eyes closed. Breathe in and out, placing your hand on the part of your body that rises and falls. If it's your chest, it's a sign that you're not breathing fully or making proper use of your lower lungs. After doing the following exercises several times, retest your breathing to be sure you've shifted to your abdomen.

Deep Breathing

Try this exercise once or twice a day. In these 5 minutes you should feel much more relaxed. If you have more time or feel particularly stressed, continue each session for a full 10–20 minutes.

1. Sit in a comfortable position in your favorite chair. Close your eyes.
2. Place one hand on your abdomen and the other on your chest.
3. Inhale slowly and deeply through your nose, into your abdomen, so your hand pushes outward and upward as you inhale. Your chest should move only slightly, and only when your abdomen moves.
4. Exhale slowly through your mouth.
5. Take long, slow, deep breaths. "Passively" focus on the sound of your breathing and /or on your abdomen rising and falling.

MEDITATION

Meditation is focusing your attention on the present moment so you learn to restrain and control your mind and experience the here and now. Researchers have found that by concentrating on one thing and learning to relax or "quiet" your mind and body, you become more aware of what's going on both inside and outside of you. During this process your body starts to relax—your heartbeat and breathing rate slow down; blood lactate levels, which are related to stress and fatigue, fall; and there's increased alpha activity in the brain, another sign of relaxation.

Meditation has been used successfully in the treatment and prevention of high blood pressure, heart disease, stroke, and migraines, as well as to help reduce obsessive thinking. Many of my clients find it very helpful to meditate every day. They tell me it keeps them more centered, focused, and less overwhelmed. They report that they dwell less on the past and obsess less about the future. And they find that they're better able to stick to any lifestyle change they are working on—such as changing the types of foods they eat, how much they eat—or changing anything they set out to accomplish.

The following exercise is based on the Relaxation Response, developed by Dr. Herbert Benson, the author of a book by the same name and associate professor of medicine at Harvard Medical School.

Start off with a 5-to-15-minute session, and eventually build up to thirty minutes. To keep track of the time, you might want to listen to an instructional meditation audiotape or one featuring relaxing music or sounds of nature, and when it clicks off you know your "formal" relaxation time is over.

1. Sit in a chair in a relaxed position, knees comfortably apart and hands resting on your lap. (You can also sit cross-legged on the floor. Place a cushion under your knees for greater comfort.)
2. Choose a short word or phrase to concentrate on—the words "one" and "om" are popular. Start breathing; breathe relaxation *in*, breathe tension *out*. Say the word you've chosen aloud or silently to yourself each time you exhale. Or else,

rather than a word, as you exhale, you can simply concentrate on your body—for instance, your abdomen as it falls.

3. Gently close your eyes. Become aware of your breathing. Keep breathing in relaxation and breathing out any tension. Breathe slowly and steadily. Say your chosen word as you breathe out.

4. If you notice during your breathing that your mind is drifting to past thoughts or future events, gently bring yourself back to your word or your breathing. Tell yourself that you can return to those thoughts later.

5. Spend 5–10 minutes doing this. When your session is over, sit quietly for a couple of minutes without using your chosen word. When you're ready, open your eyes.

EATING MEDITATION

If you're experiencing weight-related difficulties, part of your problem may be your inability to stay "present" or be focused on what's going on *right now*. You may be obsessing about what you said to your significant other yesterday, or how well you will handle the banquet tomorrow evening. Your mind is constantly darting here and there, full of worries or plans or details. These thoughts aren't necessarily bad, but they do cause you to miss out on a lot of the joy of the *now*.

Many people try to escape what's uncomfortable for them in the present by overeating. Not only is that merely a temporary escape, but it also leaves you with that out-of-control feeling and the consequences of your unwise eating—menopausal symptoms and/or extra weight. What's more, at such times it's very unlikely that you're even appreciating the food itself. And when you don't *know* what you're eating it's hard to be satisfied, and you're apt to just keep shoveling in more. It becomes a vicious cycle.

To get in touch with what you're eating, do the following eating meditation. Select a food that you really enjoy. You'll need to sit at a table with the food you've chosen, plus a plate, silverware, and a set of chopsticks. (If you don't have chopsticks, do the exercise through point 6.)

1. Sit at the table, with the food on the plate in front of you. Take several slow breaths. Notice the food—the color, the shape, the smell. Does it look appealing? Do you feel like digging into it *right now?* Get in touch with your feelings about this food.

2. Begin eating, using the appropriate silverware (save the chopsticks for later). Pay attention to your hand moving the food closer to your mouth. Just before you put it in your mouth, take another moment to look at it and smell it. Does it make your mouth water?

3. Put the food in your mouth, paying particular attention to the amount.

4. Start chewing. Notice whether you're chewing quickly or slowly. Are you already going for your next bite while you're still chewing the last one? Do you taste the food, or just getting ready to put more in your mouth? Where is your arm between bites?

5. Feel yourself swallow. Become aware of how the muscles in your esophagus contract and relax as they push the food to your stomach. Where do you feel the food after you've swallowed—in your stomach? In your chest?

6. Now, switch hands and eat with your nondominant hand. Go over all the steps outlined above. Does the awkwardness heighten your awareness of the food and your eating behaviors?

7. Now, try eating with the chopsticks. Do they slow you down? Did you taste the food?

The next time you sit down to eat, try to carry over some of your newfound awareness. Don't gobble down the food. Make each meal or snack a true *experience.* You may be eating different or less food these days, but remember, *eating is still meant to be a pleasure.* Take the time and give it the attention so you can enjoy it.

VISUALIZATION

Visualization, or visual imagery, means conjuring up pictures in your mind's eye—ideally, pleasant, relaxing images that will help you gain a feeling of control and peace. Daydreams and memories are all types of visualizations. The next time you feel tense, instead of reaching for some food, try one of the following exercises:

Creating Your Own Special Place
1. Sit in a comfortable chair.
2. When you're ready, close your eyes.
3. Think about an enjoyable vacation you've had or a place you've visited and loved. Or, think about a place you'd like to visit and all the details of that place that make it special. For instance, if it's the mountains, "see" the white clouds, the clear blue sky, the larger-than-life mountains. "Feel" the cool breeze, "smell" the clean air, and "hear" the sound of a waterfall running down the mountain and some birds singing. Place yourself in the scene with someone wonderful. Enjoy the scene for about 5 minutes.
4. When you're ready, open your eyes. Keep this visualization tucked in your mind, and draw upon it again whenever you want to relax.

THOUGHT-STOPPING

You're so tense or anxious that all you can think of is . . . food! You can't (or don't want to) move your thoughts away from eating something *now*. Your mind is racing with thoughts like:

- "I'm afraid that my partner won't think I'm as attractive as I once was now that I'm menopausal."
- "I'm worried that the next time I'm at a party, I'll lose control of my eating."

But you *can* eliminate your negative thoughts. Thought-stopping is a technique in which you first concentrate on these thoughts, then consciously stop them, and then move on to a relaxation exercise or some deep breathing. There are four steps:

1. The moment you become aware of being lost in a destructive thought, close your eyes and imagine the stressful situ-

ation. Give yourself a minute or two to play out the situation in your mind.

2. Then, command yourself to stop by doing one of the following:

- shouting "Stop!" aloud or mentally
- giving yourself "time out" from the thought—have a "time-out chair" and physically move yourself to that place.
- snapping a rubber band that you wear around your wrist.
- making a loud noise—turning the radio on at full blast, or banging some pots together—to interrupt the thought.
- counting backward from five to zero.

Empty your mind. If the upsetting thought returns, immediately repeat one of the actions above. In time, all you'll need to do to effectively stop the thought is to quietly say or think the word "Stop!"

3. Now, think of a positive, assertive thought with which to replace the negative thought. For example:

UNPRODUCTIVE THOUGHT: "I'm afraid that my partner won't think I'm as attractive as I once was now that I'm menopausal."

THOUGHT SUBSTITUTION: "I'm going to make sure I continue to look as good as I can. And now that I don't have to worry about getting pregnant, our sex life will be better than ever."

UNPRODUCTIVE THOUGHT: "I'm worried that the next time I'm at a party, I'll lose control of my eating."

PRODUCTIVE THOUGHT: "When I walk into the party, I'll immediately get a club soda with lime, then seek out someone fun to talk with."

4. Do the deep-breathing technique or the Relaxation Response immediately.

Remember, you didn't develop that negative thought overnight, so you won't get rid of it that quickly either. The thought may return, and you'll simply have to repeat the process. The main goal is to prevent the thought from turning into a destructive act, like eating a food that's unhealthy for you, overeating, or avoiding exercise.

POSITIVE SELF-TALK

You know that little nagging voice in your head—the voice that's always making you feel awful about something? One day, for example, that voice will say: "Why did you eat that brownie? You don't even *like* brownies! Great! Now you'll be fatter than ever!"

The trick is to learn how to talk back to that voice through positive self-talk. For example, instead of letting that voice bully you into feeling bad, talk back to it with a comment like, "You're right. I made a mistake. That brownie didn't help solve my problem. I'm just going to have to be more careful." A mistake can actually become a positive experience if you learn from it.

Take a moment and think about some of the negative things you typically say to yourself. Do you criticize yourself too harshly? Do you call yourself names? Jot down those words or phrases on the lines below, followed by something positive you can say in response. Next time you talk to yourself unkindly, remind yourself that it's important to be your own best friend.

NEGATIVE THOUGHT _____

POSITIVE AFFIRMATION _____

NEGATIVE THOUGHT _____

POSITIVE AFFIRMATION _____

NEGATIVE THOUGHT _____

POSITIVE AFFIRMATION _____

ASSERTIVENESS

Another way to deal effectively with stress is to stand up for what you believe in—firmly but politely. Let's say your friend calls. He'd like to stop by for coffee tonight and asks you to have some cake on hand. From past experience you know that his habit is to make this request—but he never eats the cake because he's not as hungry as he thought he'd be. You then ask him to take the cake home (and out of your sight!), but he refuses, so you're stuck with it . . . but not for long! You usually wind up eating the cake, partly because you want it and partly because you're angry at *him*.

This time, you decide to handle things differently, more assertively. Instead of blithely giving in to his demand, you could:

- buy some kind of dessert you don't much like and won't be tempted to eat
- take him out to a coffeehouse instead, where he (and you) can order whatever you like.
- say, "I have a problem with keeping dessert around the house. How about some fruit instead?"
- just buy the fruit, and skip the discussion

Whatever it takes, be assertive. If you feel a little anxious about becoming more assertive, start slowly. If a situation isn't working for you, change it so that it does. You can be in the driver's seat—if you choose to be.

OTHER STRESS-BUSTERS

Exercise/Recreational Activities
Exercise is a great stress reducer. Not only does it produce mood-enhancing endorphins, but it also clears your mind and redirects your attention to something positive. The net result is that you generally feel more "up" and are able to put the troublesome situation in better perspective. Similarly, doing other, less-physical activities you enjoy—playing bridge, reading a mystery, working on a hobby, listening to music—will shift your focus, distracting you and helping you relax. Exercising or doing other activities with friends—those activities that have a social component—may also be very nurturing, producing a feeling of "fullness," and preventing feelings of loneliness and isolation.

Sleep

Lack of sleep on a regular basis leads to a state of exhaustion that makes it difficult for you to manage life's stressors and your eating. Even if you're sleeping fewer hours than you used to—sleep as much as you need to and keep regular hours.

Yoga

Yoga exercises can help you relax and control your breathing. There are many good books and videotapes on the subject, as well as classes available through your local Y or community center.

Biofeedback

Biofeedback provides you with moment-to-moment information about what's going on in your body in the form of auditory and visual signals. It's a noninvasive technique used to treat many conditions, including migraines, insomnia, and high blood pressure. One commonly used biofeedback machine picks up electrical impulses from a muscle group and translates them into light flashes or beeps whenever your muscles are tense, and the flashes or beeps slow down as *you* calm down. This way, you learn what you can do specifically to relax. If you want to try it out, look in your yellow pages under Biofeedback.

Balanced Diet

All throughout the book I've emphasized the importance of eating well—for minimizing menopause symptoms, for cutting health risks, for helping to alleviate tension, and for weight loss. When you're stressed, it's common to want to eat the first thing you see to calm you down or lift you up. But as I've discussed, sugar, caffeine, and alcohol can ultimately leave you feeling more sluggish and let down. Because what you eat and how you feel are so closely linked, it's vital that you choose your foods wisely, particularly when you're overwhelmed by stress. The three eating plans outlined in this book will help you focus on your best stress-fighting options.

Humor

Perhaps the best way to help you keep things in perspective is with humor. When you're laughing, it's hard to think about what's troubling you. Laughter is a highly effective way of distancing yourself from the source of your stress, short-circuiting those all-too-common feelings of anxiety, helplessness, and hopelessness—or whatever you are feeling. If laughter has been in short supply in your life lately, spend some time seeking out those things that invariably make you chuckle—whether it's the cartoons in *The New Yorker* or a Marx Brothers movie you can rent. Do this enough and you'll soon be wondering what you were ever worried about.

A FINAL WORD . . .

The relaxation and stress-management exercises in this chapter will work only if done regularly. Ideally, you should do them five to seven days a week, in a quiet place where you won't be interrupted. After trying all the techniques, select one or two techniques that you feel have been most helpful to *you*. The key is to *practice*, so that you get steadily better at performing the exercises and so that eventually you can do them spontaneously—calling them up at a moment's notice, whenever stress strikes.

11

❦

Tracking Your Success in Journals, Diaries, and Charts

You've set three big, important goals for yourself: to take charge of your eating habits, to exercise regularly, and to manage your response to the stress in your life. Along the way, you'll be setting and achieving small goals, such as exploring new ways to take care of yourself—for example, completing three thirty-minute exercise sessions in a week or handling your stressors without food. And week by week, month by month, you'll see and feel the results of all your hard work, whether it's the wonderful feeling of being in control, or taking twenty points off your cholesterol reading, or seeing your hot flashes practically disappear, or dropping a dress size.

There's no greater feeling than knowing you're working to improve your health and well-being. And the best way to keep track of what's happening to your body and the lifestyle changes you are making is by using the charts and journals that follow.

MENSTRUAL FLOW CHART

For your convenience, I've repeated this chart, which appears in Chapter 1.

As soon as you start noticing changes in your menstrual flow—which may indicate that you're menopausal—keep track of them by using the chart below. Indicate the date your period began and jot down, each day during your cycle, whether the bleeding was "L" for light flow, "N" for normal flow, "H" for heavy flow. Also track any unusual symptoms that occur at other times of the month by indicating an "S" for spotting, or an "IB" for irregular bleeding, etc. Write down the symptoms you typically get at the bottom of the chart with an abbreviation.

LIFESTYLE JOURNAL

Keeping a written record of your lifestyle habits—what you're eating, how much you're eating, what your exercise habits are like, your moods and stress levels and how you're handling them—lets you tune in to your own life, so you can stay focused and in control. Setting mini-goals and writing them down not only helps you to plan your course of action so you stay in touch with what's important to you *right now*, but also gives you the opportunity to acknowledge when you've met those goals, so you can give yourself a much-deserved pat on the back. With such a system in place, you'll reach your goals more quickly and easily. And you get to see your patterns. When the inevitable obstacles come along, you'll know how to deal with them—because you can refer to your journal to remind yourself how you dealt with them successfully in the past.

For example, let's say your journal reveals that you generally grab something to eat soon after you get home from work—and that food isn't always the best thing for you. Don't set yourself up for failure by ignoring this pattern; instead, *plan* for it. Perhaps you can find something else to do when you get home—something you enjoy. Maybe it's sitting in your favorite chair and relaxing for five minutes. Or, if you are hungry, maybe you can reach for something that will satisfy you *and* is healthy. Perhaps some creamy nonfat yogurt, or something warm and sweet like a cup of sugar-free hot chocolate.

What about your activity level? Have you tried to add a few extra steps into your daily living? Have you begun to exercise? Are you doing it consistently? Your journal will tell you right away, as well as where you need to roll up your sleeves and get going.

Menstrual Flow Chart

Day	Symptom	Jan	Feb	Mar	Apr	May	Jun	Jul	Aug	Sep	Oct	Nov	Dec
1													
2													
3													
4													
5													
6													
7													
8													
9													

Menstrual Flow Chart

Day	Symptom	Jan	Feb	Mar	Apr	May	Jun	Jul	Aug	Sep	Oct	Nov	Dec
10													
11													
12													
13													
14													
15													
16													
17													
18													

Menstrual Flow Chart

Day	Symptom	Jan	Feb	Mar	Apr	May	Jun	Jul	Aug	Sep	Oct	Nov	Dec
19													
20													
21													
22													
23													
24													
25													
26													
27													

Menstrual Flow Chart

Day	Symptom	Jan	Feb	Mar	Apr	May	Jun	Jul	Aug	Sep	Oct	Nov	Dec
28													
29													
30													
31													

Symptoms:

Abbreviations:

How are you doing with goal setting? Remember, in order to move forward, you need a plan of action. Setting weekly goals is crucial, and you should keep them small, manageable, and meaningful to you.

HOW TO USE THE LIFESTYLE JOURNAL

Begin by making copies of the chart that follows. Make a lot of copies—you will be using one per day.

Use these pages to indicate the time of day you ate, what you ate (the food, quantity, and how it was prepared), where you were when you ate, what you were doing (were you eating alone or with others?), how hungry you were when you ate, and your mood or menopausal symptoms triggered by a food (anxious? depressed? content? hot flash?). In particular, try to keep track of how many units from each of the Food Groups (protein, starch, vegetable, fat, dairy, fruit) and add-on calories you consumed at each meal or snack so you get a sense of how much you need to eat to achieve weight control. Make copies of this journal and chart your progress each day.

In the goal-setting section, work toward the same goal for 7 days. It may seem repetitive to write the same goal day after day but by writing down your goal daily, you keep it in front of you.

Additionally, you might want to use the back of each chart to record your feelings in greater detail, which you can review in days and weeks to come. This will help you see when and if you were using food to "manage" your moods and disappointments, as well as times when you successfully got through your tough moments in positive ways, such as by going for a walk or talking to a friend.

LIFESTYLE JOURNAL

Time	Food/ Quantity and Preparation	Location/ with whom

How many units of each of the following did I eat today?

Protein _____   Fat _____

Starch _____   Dairy _____

Vegetable _____   Fruit _____

Add-on calories (specify) _____

_____

_____

DATE:

*Hunger Index**	*Mood/*
(0-3)	*Menopausal Symptoms*

*Hunger Index: 0 = Not hungry 1 = Somewhat hungry 2 = Hungry 3 = Very hungry

Did I exercise today?   __YES __NO

Activity _____

Duration_____

Goal for the Day _____

_____

_____

Did I move toward this goal today?   __YES __NO

WEIGHT/FAT LOSS AND BODY
MEASUREMENTS CHART

Another very important tool to help you keep track of your progress are the following charts on pages 245–247, which enable you to record and review your weight loss as reflected on the scale, to track your waist-to-hip ratio, your BMI, your percent body fat, and your body measurements. For the most accurate readings, weigh yourself no more than once a week, and calculate your waist-to-hip ratio, BMI, and percent body fat monthly. Also, take your measurements no more than once a month. (Although it's tempting to do so more often, it can lead to frustration since you won't see any real change, just meaningless day-to-day fluctuations.)

STRESS-AWARENESS DIARY

For your convenience I've repeated this Diary on page 248, which appears in Chapter 10.

To help you identify what triggers your responses to stress, begin tracking the times when you tend to feel most stressed, the event(s) that act as triggers, and the way you respond/react to the stress. Make a copy or two of the following Stress-Awareness Diary for future use.

BLOOD PRESSURE/CHOLESTEROL
TRACKING JOURNAL

To help you keep an ongoing record of what's happening in your periodic laboratory workups, use the chart on page 249 to track your results.

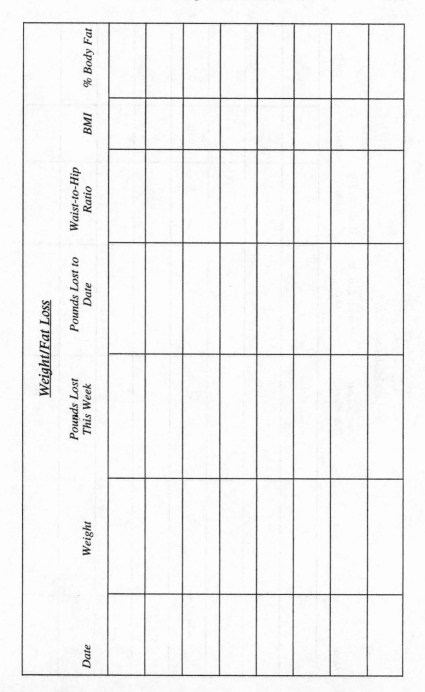

Weight/Fat Loss

Date	Weight	Pounds Lost This Week	Pounds Lost to Date	Waist-to-Hip Ratio	BMI	% Body Fat

Weight/Fat Loss

Date	Weight	Pounds Lost This Week	Pounds Lost to Date	Waist-to-Hip Ratio	BMI	% Body Fat

Body Measurements

Body Part	Date	Measurement	Inches Lost This Month	Inches Lost To Date
Chest/Bust				
Shoulders				
Arm				
Waist				
Hips				
Thighs				

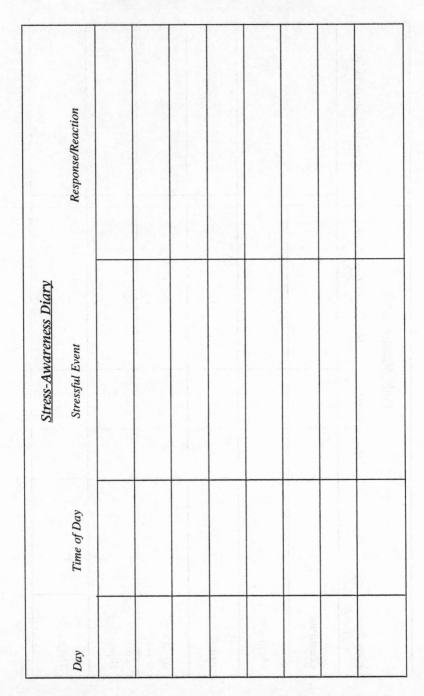

Stress-Awareness Diary

Day	Time of Day	Stressful Event	Response/Reaction

Blood Pressure/Cholesterol Tracking Journal

Date	Blood Pressure	Total Cholesterol	HDL Cholesterol	LDL Cholesterol	Total Chol/ HDL Ratio	Triglycerides	Other Lab Values

12

⁂

A Lifetime Plan for Maintaining Your Slim-Down/Shape-Up Program

Congratulations on reaching your weight loss and fitness goal! During your journey you developed many new skills to help you succeed. And while it's important to continue to apply what you've learned, it's also critical to learn a few *new* skills specific to weight maintenance and adapting to the New You. As with weight loss, weight maintenance won't just *happen*. It takes a strong belief in your own ability to succeed, plus perseverance.

WHAT IS MAINTENANCE?

Maintenance is keeping your body at a steady point or range. It might mean, for example, holding your weight to within a three-pound range, measured on the scale. Or, it might be sticking to a particular dress size.

As you know by now, to lose weight you needed to expend more energy than you took in each day. Now, your goal is to *balance* calorie input—in the form of the food you eat—with calorie output—a result of the calories burned through exercise.

ADJUSTING THE EATING PLAN TO MAINTENANCE

To help you determine what daily calorie intake level is right for *you*—and how to gradually adjust to that level—you need to follow four steps. Over the next eight weeks, they will help you establish what you should be eating to stabilize your weight.

STEP 1

Write down on the following chart what foods (either specific items or Food Group units) you are currently eating. Of course, your meals will vary from day to day, but include whatever you generally eat during a typical day.

Meal	Food and Amount	Number of Units from Each Food Group	Food Group
Breakfast			
	_____	_____	Protein/Alternatives
	_____	_____	Starch/Bread
	_____	_____	Vegetables
	_____	_____	Fat
	_____	_____	Dairy
	_____	_____	Fruit
	_____	_____	Add-On Calorie Foods
Snack			
	_____	_____	Protein/Alternatives
	_____	_____	Starch/Bread
	_____	_____	Vegetables
	_____	_____	Fat
	_____	_____	Dairy
	_____	_____	Fruit
	_____	_____	Add-On Calorie Foods

Meal	Food and Amount	Number of Units from Each Food Group	Food Group
Lunch			
	_____	_____	Protein/Alternatives
	_____	_____	Starch/Bread
	_____	_____	Vegetables
	_____	_____	Fat
	_____	_____	Dairy
	_____	_____	Fruit
	_____	_____	Add-On Calorie Foods
Snack			
	_____	_____	Protein/Alternatives
	_____	_____	Starch/Bread
	_____	_____	Vegetables
	_____	_____	Fat
	_____	_____	Dairy
	_____	_____	Fruit
	_____	_____	Add-On Calorie Foods
Dinner			
	_____	_____	Protein/Alternatives
	_____	_____	Starch/Bread
	_____	_____	Vegetables
	_____	_____	Fat
	_____	_____	Dairy
	_____	_____	Fruit
	_____	_____	Add-On Calorie Foods
Snack			
	_____	_____	Protein/Alternatives
	_____	_____	Starch/Bread

Meal	Food and Amount	Number of Units from Each Food Group	Food Group
	_____	_____	Vegetables
	_____	_____	Fat
	_____	_____	Dairy
	_____	_____	Fruit
	_____	_____	Add-On Calorie Foods

TOTALS FOR THE DAY

_____	*Protein/Alternatives*
_____	*Starch/Bread*
_____	*Vegetables*
_____	*Fat*
_____	*Dairy*
_____	*Fruit*
_____	*Add-On Calorie Foods*

STEP 2

Now that you know how much you're eating, take a look at how much you're exercising.

Exercise	# Days per Week	Minutes/Hours per Week
Routine activity	_____	_____
Stretching (flexibility)	_____	_____
Aerobic activity	_____	_____
Strength training	_____	_____

STEP 3

Now that you know how much you are eating and exercising, it's time to learn how to adjust your eating plan so you can start maintaining your weight, rather than losing.

EATING PLAN: WEEK 1

While maintaining a stable level of activity, add 100 "Add-On" calories per day (or 700 calories per week) to whichever eating plan you've been following—CPP, PPP, IMP, or the one you've designed that incorporates the best features of the others. You'll need a good calorie counter for foods like meat, poultry, fish, fresh fruits, and vegetables, which don't generally provide nutrition information on the food label. In the case of packaged foods, calorie counts will be found on the package, in the Nutrition Facts label. You can add 100 "Add-On" calories per day, or "bank" them and use 500 or 700 at one time for a splurge meal or dessert. If you do take all your additional calories in one day, it's best not to weigh yourself the next day—the scale may show a temporary weight gain.

Or, rather than splurge meals or desserts, you may consider increasing the quantity of healthy food you eat at your meal—for example, eat more pasta as a side or main dish, or an extra piece of chicken. Or have an extra piece of fruit as a snack. Remember that balance is still important—when adding foods think healthy plus what brings you eating pleasure.

Use the Maintenance Stabilization Diary on page 256 for the next eight weeks to help you determine how many calories you are able to add to maintain your current weight.

EATING PLAN: WEEK 2

After 7 days of following the plan, check in and see how you're doing.

- If you maintained your weight, stick with your current calorie level.
- If you gained a pound or more, go back to your original eating plan (CPP, PPP, or whatever), eliminating the extra add-on calories.

- If you lost weight, add another 100 calories per day (or another 700 per week, for a total of 1400 additional calories per week).

EATING PLAN: WEEKS 3–8

Weigh yourself weekly and follow the same guidelines just described.

Remember, your goal is to maintain the same weight, week after week. A good rule of thumb in determining the best calorie level for you is to find the weight you're stable at for four consecutive weeks. Then you'll know the calorie level—both the calories you take in through food and the calories you expend through exercise—that will enable you to sustain your weight long-term. If, in weeks or months to come, something in your usual routine should change—for example, an injury causes you to decrease your exercise program—then you will need to go through the process of determining a new leveling point. Once your weight has pretty much stabilized, a good rule of thumb is to keep to within a three-pound range of that number.

Don't be lulled into thinking that just because you're satisfied with your weight now, you don't need to keep track of it as closely as before. Trust me on this: You *do*. Weigh-ins (which could be cut down to monthly) or recording your monthly percent body fat or body measurements are as critical now as ever. Try to weigh yourself at the same time of day each time, wearing the same amount of clothing. And if you are tracking how your weight is impacting your health—your blood pressure, your cholesterol, etc.—use the Blood Pressure/Cholesterol Tracking Journal in Chapter 11 and watch your blood levels remain steady, or maybe even go down, as you maintain your weight.

Even after taking all the necessary precautions to stabilize your weight, there will be times when you'll see fluctuations. They're quite common and might be the result of anything from hormone-level changes to medications you may be taking to the water you drank before weighing yourself. Don't let weight fluctuations discourage you.

Use the chart that follows to monitor yourself over the next eight weeks.

Maintenance Stabilization Diary

Week	Weight (in lbs)	Average Units Selected Daily from Each Food Group*							Average Number of Maintenance Calories Added Daily	Activity		
		P	S	V	Ft	Fr	D	C		Same	Inc	Dec
1												
2												
3												
4												
5												
6												
7												
8												

*P = Protein   S = Starch   V = Vegetable   Ft = Fat   Fr = Fruit   D = Diary   C = Add-On Calories

FINDING YOUR BALANCING POINT: THE
MAINTENANCE STABILIZATION DIARY

Continue to use the Lifestyle Journal in Chapter 11 to track your eating and exercise habits. Use the space given to list add-on calories to monitor any maintenance calories you are adding. At the end of each week, for the next eight weeks, *summarize* your week by using the following Maintenace Stabilization Diary. Begin by recording the average number of units you selected daily from each food group. Then, indicate the average number of maintenance/add-on calories you selected daily. Finally, jot down whether over the course of the week your activity stayed the same, increased, or decreased, in comparison to the prior week.

STEP 4

If you're comfortably maintaining your weight and you're pleased with your current level of activity, fine. But you can, if you wish, do more exercise if you (and your doctor) feel that you're up to it. (Remember, the more calories you expend, the more you can eat.)

Refer to the following chart to see how many additional calories you'll burn through these various activities. Keep in mind that when you're doing your calorie–exercise trade-off calculations, include only the exercise that goes *beyond* what you normally do. For example, if you do *additional* vacuuming, or if you make a point of standing rather than sitting during all your phone conversations for one week, then you would count these as extra calories burned.

AVERAGE NUMBER OF MINUTES OF ACTIVITY NEEDED TO BURN 100 CALORIES

Activity	Body Weight (in Pounds)					
	128	*143*	*154*	*169*	*184*	*199*
Outdoor Work:						
Car wash and wax	29	26	23	21	19	17
Gardening:						
Digging	14	13	12	11	10	9
Hedging	22	20	18	16	14	13
Planting	16	14	13	12	11	10
Weeding	24	22	20	18	16	14

Activity	Body Weight (in Pounds)					
	128	143	154	169	184	199
Shoveling Snow	15	14	13	12	11	10
Sweeping	30	27	24	22	20	18
Window Cleaning	29	26	23	21	19	17
Indoor Work:						
Cleaning	28	25	21	19	18	17
Grocery Shopping	28	25	23	21	19	17
Mopping Floor	28	25	23	21	19	17
Scrubbing Floor	16	14	13	12	11	10
Standing Up	48	43	39	35	32	29
Sweeping Floor	30	27	24	22	20	18
Vacuuming	38	34	31	28	25	23
Washing (automated)	38	34	31	28	25	23
Leisure Activities:						
Bowling	34	31	28	25	22	20
Cycling (5.5 mph) or						
total 2.4 miles	27	24	22	20	18	16
Dancing						
Ballroom	34	31	28	25	23	21
Modern Rock	10	9	8	7	6	5
Square/Folk	15	14	13	12	11	10
Horseback Riding	23	21	19	17	15	14
Ping-Pong	24	22	20	18	16	14
Rowing (slow)	24	22	20	18	16	14
Sailing	26	23	21	19	17	15
Shuffleboard	34	31	28	25	23	21
Recreational Sports:						
Golfing (walking with						
hand-pulled cart)	20	18	16	14	13	12
Gymnastics	26	23	21	19	17	15
Handball						
Light/Moderate	13	12	11	10	9	8
Vigorous	9	8	7	6	5	5
Racquetball						
Light/Moderate	13	12	11	10	9	8
Vigorous	10	9	8	7	6	5
Skiing						
Downhill (moderate)	13	12	11	10	9	8
Tennis						
Doubles	21	19	17	15	14	13
Singles	15	14	13	12	11	10
Volleyball	34	31	28	25	23	21

Activity	Body Weight (in Pounds)					
	128	*143*	*154*	*169*	*184*	*199*
Cardiovascular Fitness:						
Aerobic dance						
Light Impact/Moderate	17	15	14	13	12	11
Heavy Impact	13	12	11	10	9	8
Bench Stepping						
11-inch Bench,						
18 Steps/Minutes	20	18	16	14	13	12
11-inch Bench,						
30 Steps/Minutes	12	11	10	9	8	7
16-inch Bench,						
18 Steps/Minutes	15	14	13	12	11	10
16-inch Bench,						
30 Steps/Minutes	9	8	7	6	5	5
Cycling (17 miles)						
Outdoors: 9.4 mph	17	15	14	13	12	11
Cycling, Stationary						
50–60 rpm: speed						
300 kgm (1.0 KP)	22	20	18	16	14	13
450 kgm (1.5 KP)	17	15	14	13	12	11
600 kgm (2.0 KP)	13	12	11	10	9	8
750 kgm (2.5 KP)	11	10	9	8	7	6
900 kgm (3.0 KP)	10	9	8	7	6	5
Jumping Rope						
70 Jumps/Min	11	10	9	8	7	6
80 Jumps/Min	10	9	8	7	6	5
125 Jumps/Min	10	9	8	7	6	5
145 Jumps/Min	9	8	7	6	5	5
Running						
12-minute Mile	12	11	10	9	8	7
8-minute Mile	8	7	6	5	5	5
6-minute Mile	6	5	5	4	4	4
Skiing, cross country						
3 mph (.7 = Total Miles)	13	12	11	10	9	8
8 mph (.9 = Total Miles)	7	6	5	5	5	4
Stair climbing	17	15	14	13	12	11
Swimming						
20 Yards/Min (Total						
Yards: 520 yd)	26	23	21	19	17	15
25 Yards/Min (Total						
Yards: 500 yd)	20	18	16	14	13	12
50 Yards/Min (Total						
Yards: 450 yd)	9	8	7	6	5	5
Walking (Track/ Treadmill)						
3.0 mph						
(Total Miles = 1.5)	30	27	24	22	20	18

Activity	Body Weight (in Pounds)					
	128	143	154	169	184	199
3.5 mph (Total Miles = 1.6)	26	23	21	19	17	15
4.0 mph (Total Miles = 1.4)	21	19	17	15	14	13
4.5 mph (Total Miles = 1.2)	16	14	13	12	11	10
Outside (road) 3.5 mph (Total Miles = 1.3)	21	19	17	15	14	13

Keep in mind that the above values are averages and are rounded to the nearest whole number and adapted from the following source: Rippe JM. *The Exercise Exchange Program*. New York: Simon and Schuster, 1992.

A Note About the Foods You're Eating Now

Remember that when you originally selected an eating plan to follow, you weren't going on a diet, but were establishing a way of eating that was right for you. The guidelines provided were just that—guidelines to help you make your own decisions about what works best for you.

And if you recall, I've emphasized the message that to be successful, any program you choose to follow has to be one you find healthy, comfortable, and enjoyable. If, for some reason, your eating plan is leaving you feeling deprived, *then you have not adapted it enough to your own needs.* Work on making changes so you're happy with your daily menu. If you don't feel as though you're eating enough of your favorites each week, perhaps you'll want to use some of your additional daily "Add-On" calories to remedy that problem. Still dissatisfied? Try new foods, and adding creativity in the kitchen. If you don't cook, try a new restaurant or a new dish in a favorite restaurant. Don't forget: the goal is to create a program you can live with and truly enjoy.

TRACKING: KEEPING YOUR WEIGHT IN CHECK

Now that you've arrived at your targeted "healthy" weight, it's important to evaluate whether this is a weight at which you're happy. Once you have established what you would like to weigh, the next important thing is to track your weight. You want to make sure your weight doesn't suddenly start creeping up and out of control. Now is the time to:

Reevaluate your chosen weight/weight range. Take a moment to think about the target weight you've picked for yourself. Is it a realistic weight, one that you believe you can comfortably maintain long-term? Is it a weight that has eliminated or greatly reduced any of the health problems you had before? And is it a weight that makes you feel good about your body? If you've now concluded that your weight is a good one for you, stay as close to it as possible within a three-pound range.

Track your weight or percent body fat. You can weigh yourself once a week, and jot down those numbers in your Weight/Fat Loss and Body Measurement Chart (Chapter 11). Or once a month or so, recompute your percent body fat, your BMI, or your waist-to-hip ratio (all explained in Chapter 5). Keep in mind that your weight may change if you increase your level of exercise—you'll burn more calories and perhaps build more muscle. Because muscle weighs more than fat, the scale may actually show that you've gained some weight, while at the same time your tape measure shows that you've lost some inches since muscle is more compact, and takes up less space than fat. What's happening? You are adding muscle, not fat, so it's possible that you may see a corresponding improvement in your waist-to-hip ratio. Also, if you are doing strength training, your measurements may increase in the areas of your body where you're building muscle.

Keep up your Lifestyle Journal. This will let you know right away when moods or a troublesome situation may lead you back to some bad habits. Try to keep the Maintenance Stabilization Diary I've discussed for the first eight weeks. Then start using the Journal in Chapter 11. If you don't like keeping a journal, after week 12, when your weight has stabilized, aim to keep records at least one week per month.

Try on your "reference outfit." By now you should have selected a favorite outfit that's comfortable and fairly form-fitting and that indicates when you've had a weight change. Slip into the outfit periodically to make sure your weight's where it should be. Anytime the outfit feels a bit snug, it's likely you've put on a few pounds and need to do something about it quickly.

SUCCESSFUL WEIGHT MAINTENANCE: IT'S MORE THAN JUST EATING AND EXERCISE

Weight loss and weight maintenance are similar in that they both require concentration, dedication, and perseverance. In exchange, you receive a tremendous reward: feeling healthy and feeling good about yourself (and your body) as you slowly take control of your destiny.

But as you know by now, there *are* some fundamental differences between losing weight and maintaining it. While the time it takes to reach your desired weight is limited, weight maintenance is a lifelong effort.

That's something Lynn learned.

LYNN'S STORY

My menopause started about 4 or 5 years ago. When I came in to see Judy about losing weight, I weighed 207 pounds—I'm 5' 2½". When I started working 15 years ago I was 140 pounds, but each year another 10 pounds would creep up on me. My three children still live with me at home, and they bring food into the house all the time. Mallomars, peanuts, chocolate-covered jelly rings . . . these are all foods that got me in trouble. But I shouldn't blame the kids—I know I ate to comfort myself. When I got stressed, I ate. Like the day I got my evaluation at work and found out I wasn't perfect. I shoveled the food down to try to deal with that reality.

But I've changed. I went on the CPP program and I started to do exercise, even though I resisted it at the beginning. And I've lost a lot of weight—I'm now down to my desired weight of 145 pounds! I've also discovered some low-calorie foods that take the edge off my hunger as well as provide some comfort foods—sugar-free Jell-O and sugar-free hot chocolate. I've also gotten used to the exercise part of it (although I'll probably never love it). This is the first time I did the combination of reduced food intake and exercise, and it's *amazing* the difference in my body shape at 145 pounds now compared to when I weighed 145 in the past. Before I couldn't fit into a size Medium; today I can.

Now I have come to realize: *I have to do this forever*. At first, I found that a harsh reality—I was envious of those women who didn't have to work so hard to stay slim. But I've changed my mind-set of eat-it-all-now-and-tomorrow-I'll-diet. Now I keep telling myself, what I don't eat today, I can always eat—within reason—tomorrow.

Getting to my goal weight has been scary—men are noticing me now! But it's been worth it.

What's more, weight loss can present you with the fairly instant gratification of seeing a smaller number on the scale or having your clothes feel loose. During weight maintenance your focus is on long-term gratification; the goal is to see the same number, week after week, or the same (or less!) percent body fat, month after month.

Just as you've learned to deal with the challenges of going through the weight-loss process, you're now facing a new set of challenges that accompany your efforts to sustain your weight. Below, you'll see some issues you may be facing these days. Some will sound very familiar; others will be new. Take the time to read each section so you can determine which areas you need to focus on, and do the activities, all designed to help you get in touch with yourself. During this process, be gentle with yourself. It will take you some time to adjust. Move at your own pace, not one you think you "should" be moving at. In fact, let go of *all* your "shoulds" and let your inner wisdom be your guide.

ATTITUDES/BELIEFS

Do you believe you have the ability to maintain your weight or fitness levels now? If you believe you can do something, you WILL. Maintain an optimistic attitude and you will succeed.

DEALING WITH CHANGE

These days you may be asking yourself, "Who am I?" Suddenly, the New You may seem like a stranger. Suddenly, there are so many issues to deal with. You might even be looking back fondly at your weight-losing days, thinking that they were easy compared with what you're experiencing now. If you love stability in your life, you may find this a challenging time. But if this new phase of your life is making you uptight, it won't do so for very long, provided you face your challenges squarely and work them through.

The key to dealing with change is to prepare for it as much as you can—anticipate how any change might affect you and do what you might do to handle it so you can minimize the negatives. But let's be realistic: there will be some changes that you can neither anticipate nor control. After all, there is only so much of life that any of us can dictate. When a particular situation is out of your control, the best you can do is to let go of how you *wanted* things to be and go with the flow of what *is*. Adapt. Work within the existing framework. Just take deep breaths along the way and keep your achievements and goals in mind.

FEELINGS

During the weight-loss process you learned to *deal* with your feelings and emotions, rather than stuffing them down with food. In so doing, you gained self-confidence, as well as greater control over your eating. In order to be successful at *lifetime* weight control, you need to continue to manage and *feel* your feelings, particularly as new and challenging ones crop up.

Understand that feelings, in and of themselves, are neither good nor bad. They simply are. That's why it's important not to judge your feelings but rather acknowledge them and meet them head-on, rather than deny their existence. As you get in the habit of coming up with constructive ways to deal with your feelings, you will be able to see your challenges as opportunities.

Following are some specific feelings you may be experiencing these days, along with some ways, old and new, to handle them.

Anxiety/fear/vulnerability. Are you feeling insecure about keeping your weight off and your fitness program going strong? Do you keep recalling past episodes of weight yo-yoing and fear that it's just a matter of time before you're back to square one?

Or perhaps you feel anxious about new social pressures. Maybe for the first time in a long time—or even for the first time in your *life*—men are looking at you appreciatively. Suddenly you may be feeling more "exposed"—after all, there's no fat to hide behind.

Maybe you're feeling anxious about everything you have to do. Maybe you had put your life on hold until you reached your desired weight, saying things like, "I'll deal with my problems at work after I lose weight" or "I'll reevaluate my relationship with Bob when I reach my desired weight" or "I'll think about doing some volunteer work after I'm thinner and in better shape." Well . . . the time has come! You can't delay anymore—and the sooner you actually deal with the situation at hand, the better you'll feel.

Disappointment. Did you have certain expectations about how your life would change once you entered The Thin World? For instance, you may have believed that losing weight would automatically improve your sexual relationship with your partner, or that the constant bickering would end. Perhaps, to your disappointment, that hasn't happened. Or, it's possible that you thought that, once you were thinner, men would be lining up to ask you out. Maybe that didn't happen either.

Rather than judge yourself about how you're feeling, stop and simply *feel* the feeling. Focus on it, and sit with it for a while. For example, if you're feeling sad because your weight loss and new shape didn't bring the attention you'd hoped for, feel the sadness while letting go of the actual incident. Then, think about ways to change the situation. If you want to meet more men, let your friends know that. Start reading personal ads. Take a class in a subject that interests you. Once you've decided how to change the situation, take *action*, in small, comfortable steps. It's scary, sure, but little by little, your dream will become a reality. Do *not* waste your energy catastrophizing, making your molehills into mountains. If you keep things in perspective and act on your desires, you'll see many positive changes.

Karen was one client who first experienced disappointment at her new weight but took positive steps to turn this feeling around.

KAREN'S STORY

I've always been shy and quiet. I thought that if I lost weight, I would feel better about my body and a new, "bubbly" person would emerge, the kind of person others would want to be around.

I started out at 212 pounds, and I thought my metamorphosis would occur when I got down to 150—that was my magic number. I would finally let myself out of my own prison! I was really excited and determined. So . . . I lost the weight and I *did* discover I was a different person in a lot of ways. I felt more self-confident, since I had set my mind to do something and I had accomplished it. For the first time in years, I felt great about my body. I no longer cringed when I walked past a mirror at home and saw myself without clothes. In fact, I would actually stop and admire myself!

I was riding high when I was by myself, but with others I found I still felt a little uncomfortable. Here I thought that with my beautiful face and my beautiful new body, people would flock to me, wanting to be my friend—men in particular. I was certain that once I lost weight, I would be "discovered." But that didn't happen, and I didn't understand why.

I started feeling really down, and I decided to see a therapist. I made up my mind that I was going to nip this in the bud and not use food to numb myself, as I had in the past. In therapy I learned that my shyness had nothing at all to do with my weight—I learned I couldn't blame everything on my weight. I had to get to the root of my problems, and little by little, that's what I've been doing.

Empowered. This may seem strange in a list that includes anxiety and disappointment, but feeling empowered—knowing that the power lies within you, that you can no longer fool yourself or others by acting helpless or hopeless if you fail to always make the best choices—can be scary. It can be terrifying to realize that you're in the driver's seat, with no one to blame but yourself if things go right or wrong!

It may feel overwhelming now, but you'll soon get used to the feeling of empowerment—it's a good one. And in time, with practice, you'll learn to use your power to make better and better choices that work for you.

Good. Have you stopped a second to get in touch with how you feel about yourself now? For starters, you must feel great about yourself because you set a weight loss and fitness goal and just accomplished it. What other qualities do you like about yourself? To get in touch with them, take some time now to consider your strong points.

ACTIVITY: FEELING GOOD ABOUT YOURSELF— GETTING IN TOUCH WITH YOUR GOOD QUALITIES

Check off all responses below that apply to you:

__I'm honest with myself.

__I'm honest with others.

__I take care of myself/I tend to my needs.

__I'm considerate of others.

__I'm responsible.

__I'm persistent.

__I'm a good lover.

__I have a positive outlook on life.

__I'm supportive of others.

__I feel attractive.

__I set my mind to do something and I get it done.

__I have many friends.

__I'm flexible/I can adapt to any new situation.

__I have many nonfood interests.

__I care about others.

__I ask for help when I need it.

__I deal with problems directly and assertively.

__I de-emphasize food in my life.

__I'm creative.

__I'm a caring parent.

__I'm a considerate daughter.

__I maintain a healthy lifestyle.

__I'm intelligent.

__I consider myself well-rounded.

__I like my body, in particular the following body parts:

__face

__hair

__height

__weight

__body firmness

__breasts

__waist size

__stomach

__hips

__thighs

__buttocks

__calves

__others (specify)

_____

_____

In reviewing those items you've checked, are you surprised by just how many there are? Remind yourself of them in the future, when you may be inclined to dump on yourself. It's time to focus on what you like about yourself. You've earned it!

LAPSES

One thing is a given: things won't always go as smoothly as you'd like, and lapses will occur. Sometimes, it will be easy to eat wisely and maintain your active lifestyle. Other times you may find yourself caving in, eating inappropriately, and "forgetting" to exercise.

Figure out what triggers in your life tend to lead you to stray from your good habits, and what actions you can take to counteract them. If you find that you have deviated, look at the event as a valuable opportunity to learn. Question what went wrong. Were you too rigid, not allowing yourself to change your plan of action when the need arose? Were you getting sloppy by not paying attention to your internal clock? In the activity that follows, you'll get to review your high-risk situations and your list of nonfood ways to handle them.

Whatever has happened, deal with yourself in a positive, constructive way. Don't let one incident undermine your self-confidence, because that may only lead to an episode of unplanned eating (relapse) or continuously eating unhealthy foods. Find out what your weak link is—and break the chain now. Then, look forward. Visualize yourself effectively handling the same or a similar situation in the future. Just as Olympic athletes visualize themselves giving gold-medal performances at the start of an event, you should "see" yourself succeeding in challenging situations.

The next two activities will help you identify past patterns that have led to lapses and help you figure out strategies for success.

ACTIVITY: LAPSES—IDENTIFY YOUR PAST WEIGHT MAINTENANCE OBSTACLES

If you've been a yo-yo dieter, it's important—now that you're at a healthy weight and level of fitness you've worked hard to achieve—to understand what in the past went wrong (and right!) with your weight maintenance. What you want to do is to keep any negative patterns from repeating hemselves now. Check off any of the reasons below that applied to you.

After I reached my desired weight in the past, I . . .

__stopped making wise food choices.

__stopped exercising/exercised only sporadically.

__didn't realize it was *my choice* to keep the weight off or gain it back.

__didn't think enough things changed in my life as a result of my new weight and fitness, and I was disappointed.

__believed I could return to my old habits and still maintain my weight and shape.

__couldn't deal with new problems that cropped up without turning to food.

__still disliked my body.

__was overwhelmed by all my feelings, positive and negative, and didn't know how to deal with them without food.

__really didn't believe I could maintain my weight and fitness program, so I decided I wouldn't even try.

__felt more vulnerable as men started paying more attention to me and I couldn't handle the attention.

__didn't realize that maintenance would still require work and I didn't feel like working at it.

__made some unwise food choices and I started exercising errat- ically. I felt I had "blown" it, and I started bingeing and stopped exercising. This lapse led to repeated lapses, after which I couldn't get my food or exercise back on track.

__still "saw" myself as a fat, out-of-shape person.

__was still obsessed with food and thought that, rather than just fantasize about eating, I would do it.

__stopped getting compliments and lost my motivation.

__didn't know how to relax without food.

__got sloppy about keeping track of my weight and slowly regained it.

__Other (specify)_____

_____

Are any of the items you checked off *still* issues for you? You'll need to resolve them if you hope to maintain your new weight. Once a week, select one item you checked above. Think about some ways in which you might change the situation. Start work- ing on it. Ask yourself why you're still concerned about this mat- ter, especially in light of your recent accomplishment.

ACTIVITY: LAPSES—IDENTIFY YOUR HIGH-RISK SITUATIONS

High-risk situations are those that may tempt you to overeat or make inappropriate food choices. For example, do you find that you're so tired after work (the *situation*) that you eat larger por- tions than you should (the *risk* the situation creates)? Or maybe being with a group of friends or colleagues makes you uncom- fortable (the *situation*), and because you're not always sure of what to say, you eat instead (the *risk* the situation creates). Or maybe you eat whenever confronted by a stressful situation—say, just before a job interview.

Once you've identified the situations and their corresponding risks, determine the *action* you will take the next time you encounter such a situation. This gives you control—you can plan your course of action and not permit your thinking to get clouded by what's going on. If you're a yo-yo dieter, don't forget to include the items you checked above.

Situation	Risk the Situation Creates	Action I Will Take to Deal Effectively with the Situation

Review the high-risk situations to make sure you've identified those times you feel you have little or no control. Be on the alert for situations you *think* you can manage but somehow still find you "handle" with food. Similarly, don't create problems that don't truly exist. Otherwise, you wind up using a lot of energy on needless worry and never move on to other things.

STRESS

To help you deal with all the new and positive changes you're going through, practice your relaxation techniques. Being in a relaxed state will help you stay focused on what's important and what you want to do.

SUPPORT

Take some time to reexamine your support system. Are you continuing to take care of yourself by asking for and receiving support from others? Have you found new friends and acquaintances who are good at providing encouragement, people you can talk to about what you may be going through now?

Also, are you being supportive of *yourself*? Are you gentle (yet firm) with yourself when you've had relapses? Have you learned to gently discipline yourself as the need arises? You should be a good parent to yourself, "teaching" yourself the difference between right and wrong at those times your behavior proves disappointing or damaging to you. Giving yourself support will make it easier for you to get back on track quickly.

MOTIVATION

While this may be a very exciting time, it may also be a little scary. If in the past you depended on friends and family for your motivation—one nice compliment on your weight loss and workout program could keep you going for a week!—that may not be happening nearly as much now. Now you've got to look to *yourself* for constant motivation, and making this transition can be challenging—but it can be done.

Since it's mainly up to you to stay motivated . . . how do you do it? By focusing on the *positive*. Take time out *now* to feel good about your appearance and your accomplishments. Look in the mirror and really *admire* what you see. Or pull out your "before" and "after" pictures and see just how far you've come.

Keep the good feelings going. When you go shopping for clothes, select outfits that accent your best features. If you've got nice curves, don't be afraid to wear figure-hugging clothes. Knowing how good you look in them will keep your motivation high. Celebrate yourself and your achievements on a regular basis. At least once a month, renew your commitment to yourself to eat well, exercise, and keep stress under control. Treat yourself lovingly and you'll be naturally inclined to do what's best for you and your body.

Whatever your feelings now, keep in mind that they're normal. Don't beat yourself up for your feelings, but at the same time, don't let yourself succumb to them and fall into a motivational slump. Don't forget, the power lies within you.

TRUSTING YOURSELF . . . FOR A LIFETIME

Your body, your internal cues . . . they have very important things to teach you day by day. If you haven't been doing it all along, start to *listen* to your body and pick up on your internal cues.

Remember how much you learned during your weight-loss journey? About what to eat . . . how exercise affects not just your weight but also your moods and your feeling of well-being . . .

how what you eat affects your menopausal symptoms . . . how letting your appetite take control can make you feel bad both physically and mentally? Stay in constant touch with these important lessons you've learned, so you can continue to build on them through your life's journey.

A FINAL NOTE

The key to a good quality of life is making empowering choices. And you do that by knowing what your options are, getting in touch with what works for you, and choosing the path that brings you your desired results.

I sincerely hope that this book has made clear what your options are so that you can make wise choices to help you feel and look good, both inwardly and outwardly. By now you're probably aware that through a greater understanding of what is happening to your body, you can actually listen to your body and work in greater harmony with it. If you can . . .

- eat healthfully to nourish your body and mind
- exercise to keep your bones, heart, and body strong
- learn how to manage your response to life's stresses rather than have them control you
- maintain a positive attitude
- stop to take a "mentalpause" during menopause and reflect on where you've been and where you are going
- recognize that persistence is key to everything you hope to accomplish in life

. . . then you'll be able to do whatever you set your mind to do, because the magic lies within *you*.

If you'd care to share your own menopause story, I'd love to hear from you. Thank you.

Judy E. Marshel
25 Park Place, Suite 1R
Great Neck, New York 11021

Appendix A

❦

Trim-Down/Shape-Up Menu Suggestions and Shopping Tips

In Chapter 8 you decided which one of the three weight-loss plans would be best for you to start with. To make life even easier, following are seven days' worth of meals and snacks as well as tips for how to set up your kitchen. The menu suggestions are for two of the eating plans, the Carbohydrate-Packed Plan (CPP) and the Protein-Packed Plan (PPP). (Because the Indulge In Moderation Plan [IMP] is one you design yourself, there are no specific menus suggested here).

In this restaurant-style menu, all the breakfasts are interchangeable with one another, and all lunches are interchangeable, as are the dinners and snacks. All meals within a given category (for example, all breakfasts) are similar in nutrient content, although there might be a slight variation because of the ranges given in the number of selections recommended daily from some Food Groups. For example, you may have either 4–6 Starch selections per day on the CPP, and 2–3 Starch selections daily on the PPP.

As you'll see, each meal contains interesting and varied selections from several of the six Food Groups, plus the bonus Add-Ons. You'll also notice some additional food items here that are not included in the Food Groups. They're included to give you even more food choices within each category. So add these to your Food Groups as well as any of your favorite foods that aren't included.

Try to vary your selections as much as possible from day to day, so you can keep your meals interesting and nutritionally balanced. As you make your choices, keep in mind the basic principles of healthy eating: limit eggs yolks to 4 per week and the higher-fat meat and cheese selections to 2–3 times per week each. Always go for the whole-grain item, rather than the refined "white." And aim for a couple of fish meals a week that are high in Omega-3 fatty acid, the heart-healthy fish oils (salmon, sardines, etc.).

First, decide on an item you want—say, a cereal-and-milk breakfast. You can either follow these menus exactly or make substitutions within a category. Next, check the Food Group information that appears in Chapter 8 for the food in the menu. After each menu the number of Protein, Starch, Fat, Vegetable, Fruit, Dairy, and/or Add-On Calories are listed.

Notice that an amount is not listed for vegetables since you can have four *or more* servings per day. For optimum health, you should have at least four servings a day, but the amount beyond that is up to you!

Don't like something in the menu? Refer to the Chapter 8 Food Groups to see what a suitable substitute might be if you want to make a swap. For example, yogurt is on the same list as milk, so you could exchange one for the other. Check the serving sizes. Here, one cup of yogurt equals one cup of skim milk, but serving sizes aren't always equal, so make adjustments as necessary. Select one item from Breakfast, Lunch, Dinner *and* Snack Ideas each day.

THE CARBOHYDRATE-PACKED PLAN (CCP)

BREAKFAST IDEAS

Berry and Cinnamon Raisin Toast, made with 1 slice cinnamon raisin bread, toasted, topped with 1 tablespoon blueberry spreadable fruit. (**1 Starch, 1 Fruit**)
Low-fat soy or skim milk, 1 cup (**1 Dairy**)

Breakfast Shake, made with 1 cup nonfat fruit-flavored yogurt, with ¾ cup sliced strawberries and 2–3 ice cubes, blended in blender until thick and smooth (**1 Dairy, 1 Fruit**) Apple-cinnamon–flavored rice cakes, 2 (**1 Starch**)

Wheat 'n' Nut Butter, made with 2 slices reduced-calorie whole wheat bread, toasted, spread with 1 tablespoon nut butter (almond or peanut), topped with 2 tablespoons raisins (**1 Starch, 1 Protein, 1 Fruit**)
Soy or Skim milk, 1 cup (**1 Dairy**)

Fruity Cheese and Crackers made with 4 melba toast slices topped with 1 slice (1½ oz.) nonfat hard cheese and 1 small apple, sliced (**1 Starch, 1 Dairy, 1 Fruit**)

Yogurt-Blueberry Crunch Parfait made with ¾ cup blueberries and 1 cup nonfat plain yogurt topped with 1 oz. (about ¾ cup) cold cereal (**1 Fruit, 1 Dairy, 1 Starch**)

Cinnamon Oatmeal Delight made with ½ cup cooked oatmeal sprinkled with a dash cinnamon (**1 Starch**)
Soy or Skim milk, 1 cup (**1 Dairy**)
Orange juice, ½ cup (**1 Fruit**)

Cereal Banana Roll-Up, made with 1 small banana covered with 1 tablespoon peanut butter rolled in 1 oz. (about ¼ cup) low-fat granola cereal. Slice banana and eat. (**1 Fruit, 1 Protein, 1 Starch**)
Soy or Skim milk, 1 cup (**1 Dairy**)

LUNCH IDEAS

Turkey Sandwich, made with 2 oz. turkey with tomato slices and shredded lettuce on 2 slices reduced-calorie whole wheat bread with carrot and celery sticks (**2 Protein, Vegetables, 1 Starch**)

Tuna and Veggie Platter, made with 2 oz. drained canned tuna on spinach leaves with sliced tomato, green pepper rings, and radishes (**2 Protein, Vegetables**)
Breadsticks, 1 oz. (**1 Starch**)

Vegetable-Cheese Omelet, made with 3 egg whites (or 1 egg) with 1 slice low-fat Swiss cheese and sliced mushrooms and onions, sautéed in 1 tsp. canola oil (**2 Protein, Vegetable, 1 Fat**)
Toasted bagel, ½ small (**1 Starch**)

Cucumber, tomato, and red onion slices with wine vinegar (**Vegetables**)

Greek Salad, made with 2 oz. feta cheese mixed with lettuce, tomato, cucumber, and 5 olives (2 Protein, Vegetables, 1 Fat)
Bread sticks, 1 oz. (1 Starch)

Pita Chips with Chickpea Dip (Hummus), made with 1 small (1 oz.) whole wheat pita, split, quartered, and toasted, dipped into hummus, made with ⅔ cup cooked chickpeas that have been mashed and combined with 1 teaspoon sesame oil, 1 teaspoon sesame seeds with dash lemon juice and garlic (**1 Starch, 2 Protein, 1 Fat, 15 Add-On Calories**)
Salad with alfalfa sprouts, chopped lettuce, and tomato (Vegetables)

Egg Salad Stuffer, made with 2 hard-cooked eggs or 6 cooked egg whites chopped, combined with chopped onion, celery, grated carrots, and 2 teaspoons reduced-calorie mayonnaise placed in 1 small (1 oz.) whole wheat pita pocket (**2 Protein, Vegetables, 1 Fat, 1 Starch**)
Salad with cucumber slices, green pepper rings (**Vegetables**)

Vegetable Cottage Cheese with Flatbread/Crispbread, made with ½ cup cottage cheese that has been mixed with chopped red and green pepper, radishes, cucumber, and fresh chives, spread on 1 oz. flatbread/crispbread (**2 Protein, Vegetables 1 Starch**)

Baked Potato and Cheese, made with 1 small baked potato topped with 2 slices (2 oz.) low-fat Cheddar cheese, topped with cooked, chopped broccoli (**1 Starch, 2 Protein, Vegetables**)

DINNER IDEAS

Beef Kebab made with 2 oz. cooked lean beef cubes with whole mushrooms, tomato cut into wedges, zucchini cut into thick slices, threaded on skewers and brushed with 2 tsp. canola oil, broiled (**2 Protein, Vegetables, 2 Fat**)
Brown rice, 1 cup cooked (2 Starch)
Broiled tomato, sprinkled with herbs (Vegetables)

Roast Beef Sandwich, made with 2 oz. lean roast beef on 1 large (2 oz.) whole wheat roll and topped with lettuce leaves and tomato, sliced (**2 Protein, 2 Starch, Vegetables**)
Small green salad tossed with ½ tablespoon salad dressing, 5 olives, and 1 oz. croutons (**Vegetables, 2 Fat, 1 Starch**)

Baked potato, 1 large (**2 Starch**)
Flounder, 2 oz., sprinkled with paprika and lemon, baked (**2 Protein**)
Acorn Squash, ½, sprinkled with cinnamon, baked (**1 Starch**)

Small green salad tossed with 1 tablespoon salad dressing (**Vegetables, 2 Fat**)
Steamed broccoli (**Vegetables**)

Parslied Noodles, made with 1½ cup cooked noodles, 1 tablespoon chopped parsley, and 2 teaspoons sesame oil (**3 Starch, 2 Fat**)
Veal chop, 2 oz., grilled (**2 Protein**)
Steamed asparagus (**Vegetables**)
Small green salad with vinegar and herbs (**Vegetables**)

Lean beef patty, 2 oz., broiled on 1 large (2 oz.) whole wheat bun with onion and tomato slices (**2 Protein, 2 Starch, Vegetables**)
Small green salad tossed with 1 tablespoon salad dressing (**Vegetables, 2 Fat**)

Cooked spaghetti, 1½ cups, mixed with ½ cup tomato sauce (**3 Starch, Vegetables**)
Broiled salmon, 2 oz., with lemon wedge (**2 Protein**) Mixed vegetable salad made with chopped carrots, sliced mushrooms, alfalfa sprouts, and cut spinach leaves, tossed with 1 tablespoon salad dressing (**Vegetables, 2 Fat**)

Chicken Stir-fry made with 2 oz. chicken breasts, cut into strips, sliced mushrooms, sliced onions, and red pepper rings, stir-fried in 2 teaspoons sesame oil and low-sodium soy sauce (**2 Protein, Vegetable, 2 Fat**)
Brown rice, cooked, 1½ cups (**3 Starch**)

SNACK IDEAS (ANYTIME)

Crudités with Yogurt-Herb Dip, made with crudités (cucumber, carrot sticks, and broccoli florets) dipped in a "dip," made of 1 cup plain nonfat yogurt mixed with 1 teaspoon each dill and chopped parsley (**Vegetable, 1 Dairy**)
Apple, 1 (**1 Fruit**)

Reduced-Fat Dairy Shake, 1 packet (**1 Dairy**)
Cherries, 12 (**1 Fruit**)

Blueberry-Yogurt Parfait, made with ¾ cup blueberries mixed with 1 cup plain nonfat yogurt (**1 Fruit, 1 Dairy**)

Grapes and Cheese, made with 12 large grapes (seedless) served with 1½ oz. nonfat hard cheese (**1 Fruit, 1 Dairy**)

Reduced-Fat Pudding, prepared, ½ cup (**1 Dairy**)
Cranberry Cooler, made with ½ cup cranberry juice mixed with ½ cup club soda. Squeeze in both a twist of lemon and lime. (**1 Fruit**)

Fruit Salad and Yogurt, made with 1 cup nonfat plain yogurt spooned over ½ cup combined sliced bananas, berries, and orange slices (**1 Dairy, 1 Fruit**)

Strawberry Shake, made with ¾ cup sliced strawberries, 1 cup soy or skim milk, and 2–3 ice cubes, processed in blender until smooth (**1 Fruit, 1 Dairy**)

NOTE: If you are still hungry, at any time, have some fresh veggies dipped in salsa or nonfat dressing, a dish of sugar-free flavored gelatin, or low-sodium bouillon. Or maybe your "hunger" is really thirst—have a glass of water and find out!

THE PROTEIN-PACKED PLAN (PPP)

BREAKFAST IDEAS

Cheese omelet, made with 3 egg whites and 1 oz. low-fat Swiss or soy cheese, cooked in nonstick skillet with vegetable oil spray (**2 Protein**)
Grapefruit, ½ (**1 Fruit**)

Dutch Apple Yogurt, made with 1 cup plain nonfat yogurt mixed with ¼ cup unsweetened applesauce, 1 tablespoon raisins, ¼ teaspoon each vanilla and cinnamon (**2 Protein, 1 Fruit**)

Low-fat cottage cheese, ½ cup (**2 Protein**)
Melon balls, 1 cup (**1 Fruit**)

Turkey sausage, 1 link (**2 Protein**)
Apple, 1 small (**1 Fruit**)

Low-fat Swiss or soy cheese, 2 oz. (**2 Protein**)
Pear, 1 small (**1 Fruit**)

Ricotta-Pineapple Crush, made with ½ cup low-fat ricotta cheese and ½ cup canned crushed pineapple in its own juice, drained (**2 Protein, 1 Fruit**)

Strawberry Shake, made with 1 cup soy or skim milk, ¾ cup sliced strawberries, and 2–3 ice cubes, blended in blender until thick and smooth (**2 Protein, 1 Fruit**)

LUNCH IDEAS

Grilled turkey burger made with 4 oz. turkey patty topped with tomato slices and lettuce leaves (**4 Protein, Vegetables**)

"Tomato" Cheese Melt, made with 4 slices tomatoes topped with tomato sauce topped with 2 slices (2 oz.) low-fat mozzarella or soy cheese, broiled (**Vegetables, 2 Protein**)
Tossed salad with ⅔ cup cooked garbanzo beans with vinegar and herbs (**Vegetables, 2 Protein**)

Tuna salad, made with 4 oz. tuna mixed with 2 teaspoons reduced-fat mayonnaise with 1 tablespoon each chopped onions and celery (**4 Protein, 1 Fat, Vegetables**)
Carrot sticks (**Vegetables**)

Cheese-Stuffed Tomato, made with 1 medium tomato, quartered, topped with 1 cup low-fat cottage cheese that has been mixed with finely chopped scallions, carrots, green pepper, and radishes (**Vegetables, 4 Protein**)
Carrot sticks (**Vegetables**)

Turkey "Roll" Salad, made with 4 slices (4 oz.) turkey, each slice spread with mustard, rolled around cucumber spears and placed on lettuce leaves (**4 Protein, Vegetables**)

Salad with tomato slices, sliced shredded lettuce, and alfalfa sprouts with vinegar and herbs (**Vegetable**)

Grilled Chicken Strips, made with 4 oz. chicken, cut into strips, of placed on mixed green salad (**4 Protein, Vegetables**)
Celery sticks (**Vegetables**)

Salmon and Vegetable Platter, made with 4 oz. salmon with slices of tomato, green pepper rings, and sliced radishes on lettuce leaves (**4 Protein, Vegetables**)

DINNER IDEAS

Broiled flank steak, 4 oz. (**4 Protein**)
Baked potato, 1 large (**2 Starch**)
Steamed zucchini (**Vegetables**)
Small tossed salad with 1 tablespoon salad dressing (**Vegetables, 2 Fat**)

Chef's Salad, made with 1 oz. **each** ham, roast beef, low-fat Swiss cheese, and 1 sliced, hard-cooked egg (or 3 cooked egg whites, chopped), shredded lettuce, a tomato, cut in wedges, and cucumber slices and sprinkled with 1 tablespoon Russian Dressing (**4 Protein, Vegetables, 2 Fat**)
Roll, 1 large (2 oz.) (**2 Starch**)

Chicken, 4 oz., baked (**4 Protein**)
Cooked noodles, 1 cup, cooked, mixed with tomato sauce
(**2 Starch, Vegetables**)
Small green salad tossed with 2 teaspoons olive oil and vinegar
and herbs (**Vegetables, 2 Fat**)
Steamed green beans (**Vegetables**)

Broiled flounder, 4 oz. (**4 Protein**)
Peas, 1 cup (**2 Starch**)
Steamed carrots (**Vegetable**)
Spaghetti squash, ½ cup, drizzled with tomato sauce (**Vegetables**)
Small green salad with 1 tablespoon salad dressing (**Vegetables, 2 Fat**)

Veal chop, 4 oz. (**4 Protein**)
Ear of corn, 1 large (**2 Starch**)
Steamed zucchini (**Vegetables**)
Small green salad tossed with 1 tablespoon salad dressing (**Vegetables, 2 Fat**)

Tofu Stir-fry, made with 8 oz. tofu marinated in low-sodium soy
sauce and garlic and stir-fried in 2 teaspoons olive oil with sliced
mushrooms, broccoli, onions, and pea pods (**4 Protein, 2 Fat, Vegetables**)
Cooked brown rice, 1 cup (**2 Starch**)

Open-faced Tuna Melt, made with 3 oz. water-packed tuna,
drained, on 2 slices whole wheat bread, topped with 1 oz. of Swiss
cheese, broiled (**4 Protein, 2 Starch**)
Small green salad, tossed with 1 tablespoon salad dressing (**Vegetable, 2 Fat**)

SNACK IDEAS (ANYTIME)

Nonfat plain yogurt, 1 cup, mixed with crushed pineapple,
½ cup, in its own juice, drained (**1 Dairy, 1 Fruit**)
Soy or skim milk, 1 cup (**1 Dairy**)

Crudités with Yogurt-Herb Dip, made with crudités (cucumber,
carrot sticks, and broccoli florets) dipped in a "dip" made from 1

cup plain nonfat yogurt mixed with 1 teaspoon each fresh dill and chopped parsley (**Vegetables, 1 Dairy**)
Grapes, 12, frozen (**1 Fruit**)
Soy or Skim Milk, 1 cup (**1 Dairy**)

Thick Orange Shake, made in a blender with 1 packet reduced-fat vanilla-flavored milk and ½ cup orange juice, processed in blender until smooth, with 2–3 ice cubes added, one at a time (**1 Dairy, 1 Fruit**)
Soy or Milk, low-fat (1%), 1 cup (**1 Dairy**)

Reduced-fat pudding, prepared, ½ cup (**1 Dairy**)
Coconut Banana, made with 1 small banana rolled in 1 teaspoon fresh lemon juice and then in 2 teaspoons coconut, toasted, frozen for several hours (or overnight) before eating. (**1 Fruit, 20 Add-On Calories**)
Soy or Milk, low-fat (1%), 1 cup (**1 Dairy**)

Nonfat Swiss or soy cheese, 1½ oz. (**1 Dairy**)
Apple, 1 small, sliced (**1 Fruit**)
Hot chocolate, made with 2 teaspoons unsweetened cocoa mixed in 1 cup soy or low-fat (1%) milk and then heated on stove or microwaved 1½–2 minutes, with 1 packet sugar substitute stirred in or otherwise sweetened to taste. (**1 Dairy, 10 Add-On Calories**)

Nonfat plain yogurt, 1 cup, mixed with ¾ cup blueberries (**1 Dairy, 1 Fruit**)
Soy or Milk, low-fat (1%), 1 cup (**1 Dairy**)

Hot cocoa, reduced-fat, 1 packet (**1 Dairy**)
Banana, 1 small (**1 Fruit**)
Yogurt, nonfat fruit-flavored, 1 cup (**1 Dairy**)

Piña Colada Tropical Smoothie, made with 1 cup nonfat yogurt (tropical flavor) processed in blender with ½ small ripe frozen banana and ¼ cup frozen pineapple chunks, with ½ teaspoon coconut extract. (**1 Dairy, 1 Fruit**)
Soy or Milk, skim, 1 cup (**1 Dairy**)

SETTING UP YOUR KITCHEN

How do you keep away from temptation? By keeping temptation away from *you*! A fridge full of the wrong kinds of foods only makes your life—and your weight-loss attempts—tougher than they need to be. So now that you're ready to start eating differently, take the time to make a clean sweep of your kitchen. Today's the day to get rid of all those foods that hinder your efforts and to stock up on staples that are not only healthy and tasty but that make quick-fix meals a snap.

If you live with other people—a partner or grown children or siblings—it's admittedly going to be a bit harder to arrange the kitchen *precisely* your way. There may be some grumbling as you prepare to toss that pint of cookie-dough ice cream or cannister of cashew nuts, and understandably so: you can't force others to eat your way (even if it's good for them). So give them a chance to clean up the leftovers themselves, or have a few friends over and serve them the last of the tempting foods. If you *must* keep a few high-fat/high-calorie foods around the house for your loved ones, at least you can make it harder to give in to temptation by storing those items in the *back* of the fridge or the cabinet, in a plastic container so you can forget they're even there. And as you start to stock up on items you'll need for yourself now, keep an eye out for things you *all* like. Who knows? Your mate may come to enjoy cinnamon raisin bread and nonfat mozzarella as much as you.

SHOPPING TIPS

- If you're using the PPP or CPP restaurant-style menu suggestions as a guide, take this book with you to the market so you can be sure you bring home all the foods you'll need for the week. If you are planning your own menus, use the Lifestyle Journal in Chapter 11 to plan your week's menu.

- Shop with a list . . . even if you're just "running in" for a few midweek items. Again, it will help you avoid bringing home those foods you should be avoiding.
- Don't shop when you're hungry. You'll be more likely to pick up troublesome foods when your stomach is growling than just after a meal. Even if you have a carrot or a glass of water before leaving home, you'll be better able to resist temptation at the market.
- Shop alone, if you are the kind of person who is easily talked into buying what you hadn't planned on. That way, you won't be talked into buying things you don't need or want by well-meaning friends.
- Experiment. Sticking to the same old meals and menus can be a recipe for weight-loss failure. Periodically, go through magazines like *Cooking Light* or a low-fat cookbook for new dishes to try, and be sure to add needed ingredients to your weekly shopping list.
- Don't forget to check dates on dairy and meats to ensure freshness.

KITCHEN STAPLES

Try always to have these items on hand. It will make it simpler for you to follow your eating plan and they'll be a lifesaver on those days when you just can't get out to go shopping. As you discover the foods you prefer—and the ones that work best for your weight loss—you can fine-tune this list.

CANNED/BOTTLED/PACKAGED GOODS:

- canned salmon
- canned water-packed tuna
- reduced-sodium chicken and vegetable bouillon
- vegetable oil (preferably expeller-pressed)
- fat-free or reduced-fat salad dressing and mayonnaise
- peanut or almond butter

- tomato sauce
- sugar-free gelatin
- all-fruit preserves (spreadable fruit)
- raisins
- pineapple (in its own juice) or other canned fruit
- sugar-free puddings
- sugar-free milk beverages
- sugar-free hot chocolate
- mineral water
- vegetable cooking spray

CEREAL/GRAINS/PASTA/BREAD
(Select whole-grain products wherever possible.)

- bagels, rolls, English muffins, whole wheat pita
- reduced-fat whole wheat bread
- melba toast
- any pasta
- low-fat microwave popcorn
- brown rice
- any low-sugar/low-fat cold or hot cereal (ideally whole-grain varieties)

DAIRY PRODUCTS/EGGS

- soy, skim milk, low-fat (1%) milk or buttermilk
- nonfat yogurt (plain or fruited)
- egg whites or egg substitutes
- butter or margarine (from liquid vegetable oil)
- cottage cheese (2% or less fat) or ricotta (part-skim or non-fat)
- nonfat or low-fat cheddar, mozzarella, Muenster, Swiss, etc.

PROTEIN

- chicken/turkey
- fish and shellfish
- lean beef
- beans, including garbanzos, kidney, lima, lentils, etc.
- tofu
- low-fat/low-sodium processed meats such as roast beef, ham, or turkey

FRUITS AND VEGETABLES

- any fresh, frozen, or canned fruits and vegetables, including fruit and vegetable juices

SEASONINGS/CONDIMENTS/SPICES, INCLUDING . . .

- chives
- cinnamon
- dill
- dry mustard
- garlic
- ginger
- ketchup (low-calorie)
- lemon juice
- mustard
- parsley
- pepper
- red-wine vinegar
- salsa
- sesame seeds
- soy sauce (reduced-sodium)
- Tabasco
- vanilla
- Worcestershire sauce

KITCHEN EQUIPMENT

- food scale
- measuring cups and spoons
- nonstick skillet and/or baking pans
- steamer
- blender or food processor
- wok
- microwave

Appendix B

⚜

A Few Highlights about Food Labels

How do you know what's in a supermarket can or box? By reading the label, of course. And how do you know what's in the *food* in that can or box? By reading the Nutrition Facts panel, which has, since May 1994, been found on virtually every processed food. The handy-dandy Nutrition Facts panel has replaced earlier models, and it is bigger and easier to understand. The panel highlights the ingredients most important to your weight loss and your overall health—such as calories, fat, sodium, and fiber—and the serving sizes within particular categories of food are now standardized and logical (no more "1.3 cups per serving"; everything is nicely rounded off).

But before you start to plan your meals around these labels, you need to keep a few facts in mind. For one thing, the panel now includes the number of calories per serving and the number of calories from fat. It also includes total fat, with the breakdown listing the amount of saturated, polyunsaturated, and monounsaturated fat; the amount of cholesterol, sodium, total carbohydrate (including dietary fiber and sugar), and protein. The % Daily Value for the above-listed nutrients and Vitamin A, Vitamin C, Calcium, and Iron are also listed. The % Daily Value tells you how a serving of a food fits into a 2000-calorie-per-day reference diet. The numbers in this column range from 0%–100%. You can use% Daily Value to see how high or low in specific nutrients this food is.

For example, take a one-ounce bag of pretzels. The Nutrition

Facts panel might indicate that Total Fat is "1.5 grams fat." The % Daily Value column may indicate that the Total Fat has a % Daily Value of 2%. This means that the 1.5 grams of fat found in the pretzels uses up 2 percent of your daily fat limit or Daily Value. How do you interpret that? As a general rule, any food with a Daily Value of 20 percent or more is considered high in that nutrient, and any with 5 percent or less is considered low in that nutrient. So these pretzels are considered a low-fat food. Your goal is to select foods with high % Daily Values for fiber, vitamins, and minerals, but low % Daily Values for fat, cholesterol, and sodium.

One additional, important note: all the information currently found in the "% Daily Value" column on the Nutrition Facts panel is for individuals consuming 2000 calories a day. Women on a weight-loss program will be eating fewer calories, so frequently if you add up the % Daily Value from all the foods you eat, they may not total 100%. Keep in mind that your own nutrient needs may be less or more than the Daily Values on the label, based on your calorie intake.

You'll also need to pay attention to what the descriptive words referring to weight loss and health *really* mean. Manufacturers' product descriptions must conform to standardized government values, and these include:

- "sugar-free" (less than 0.5 grams per serving)
- "reduced sugar" (at least 25% less sugar per serving than the reference food)
- "calorie-free" (fewer than 5 calories per serving)
- "low-calorie" (40 calories or fewer per serving, and if the serving is 30 grams or less or 2 tablespoons or smaller, per 50 grams of food)
- "reduced (or fewer) calorie" (at least 25% fewer calories per serving than the reference food)
- "fat free" (less than 0.5 grams of fat per serving)
- "saturated fat-free" (less than 0.5 grams of saturated fat per serving and the level of trans fatty acid does not exceed 1% of total fat)
- "low-fat" (3 grams or fewer per serving, and if the serving is

30 grams or less or 2 tablespoons or smaller, per 50 grams of food)

- "low-saturated fat" (1 gram or less of saturated fat per serving and not more than 15% of calories from saturated fatty acids)
- "reduced (or less) fat" (at least 25% less per serving than the reference food)
- "reduced (or less) saturated fat" (at least 25% less per serving than the reference food)
- "cholesterol-free" (fewer than 2 mg of cholesterol and 2 grams or fewer of saturated fat per serving)
- "low-cholesterol" (20 mg or less and 2 grams or less of saturated fat per serving and if the serving is 30 grams or less or 2 tablespoons or smaller, per 50 grams of food)
- "reduced (or less) cholesterol" (at least 25% less and 2 grams or less of saturated fat per serving than the reference food)
- "sodium-free" (fewer than 5 mg per serving)
- "low-sodium" (140 mg or fewer per serving, and if the serving is 30 grams or less or 2 tablespoons or smaller, per 50 grams of food)
- "very low sodium" (35 milligrams or less per serving, and if the serving is 30 grams or less or 2 tablespoons or smaller, per 50 grams of food)
- "reduced or less sodium" (at least 25% less per serving than the reference food)
- "high-fiber" (5 grams or more per serving. Foods making this claim must meet the definition for low-fat, or the level of total fat must appear next to the high-fiber claim)
- "good source of fiber" (2.5 to 4.9 grams per serving)
- "more or added fiber" (at least 2.5 grams or more per serving than the reference food)

Selected Glossary

androgen. Hormones that have a masculinizing effect. They are produced by both men and women, but they are much more dominant in men.

androstenedione. A hormone produced mainly by the adrenal glands that is converted to a form of estrogen called estrone by the fat cells of the body. This hormone becomes the main source of menopausal estrogen.

antioxidants. Nutrients including vitamins C, E, and betacarotene and minerals such as selenium that are found in fruits, vegetables, and whole grains that counteract the harmful effects of "free radicals" and thereby may reduce one's risk of heart disease and certain cancers.

bioflavonoids. Water-soluble substances found in many fruits and vegetables that are antioxidants as well as enhance vitamin C activity. Specific bioflavonoids—such as rutin, quercetin, hesperidin, and catechin—perform different functions.

body mass index (BMI). A formula to determine a person's health risk based on the amount of his or her body fat determined by weight and height.

botanical. A substance (e.g., botanical extract) made from or containing plants.

calorie. A measure of energy available to the body. When you eat something, the number of calories it contains corresponds to the number of units of energy it provides the body. For example, a slice of bread provides the body about eighty calories. When you exercise, the number of calories burned corresponds to the number of units of energy removed from the body. For example, if you walk one mile you burn approximately 100 calories. For weight loss to occur, you need to do a combination of taking in fewer calories, through reducing food intake, *and* burning more calories, by exercising.

cholesterol. A waxy, fatlike substance produced by the liver and used by the body to manufacture hormones, digestive juices, nerve endings, etc. Despite its benefits, when present in the body in excessive amounts, which may be because the body is manufacturing an excess amount and/or you are consuming a fat- and cholesterol-rich diet, it can cause the arteries to accumulate plaque (fat, calcium, and other debris) and increase one's risk of heart disease.

climacteric. The ten to fifteen years during which the ovaries gradually stop producing eggs. These years mark the time of transition from reproductive to post-reproductive age.

endometrium. The lining of the uterus, which is shed each month during menstruation.

ERT/HRT (estrogen replacement therapy/hormone replacement therapy). A program for replacing the body's hormones, which decline during menopause, with natural or synthetic hormones. ERT/HRT can be given in a variety of forms and may be useful in preventing or minimizing such potential long-term menopausal symptoms as osteoporosis and heart disease and other early symptoms associated with menopause such as hot flashes, vaginal dryness, etc.

essential fatty acid. An essential fatty acid is a polyunsaturated fat that can't be manufactured by the body, such as linoleic acid, which must be obtained through foods.

essential nutrient. An essential nutrient is a nutrient that must be obtained through food because the body manufactures it in amounts that are insufficient for good health. Certain proteins as well as carbohydrates are examples of essential nutrients.

estrogen. A class of female sex hormones, found in both men and women, but in much larger proportions in women. It's produced mainly by the ovaries and needed for the development and maintenance of certain female secondary sex characteristics, including the growth of breasts and the regulation of the menstrual cycle. It also may protect against heart disease and osteoporosis. Estrogen production from the ovaries diminishes significantly during menopause and essentially stops after menopause.

estrone. A weak form of estrogen made from the hormone androstenedione, produced mainly by the adrenal glands. This is the main form of estrogen available during menopause.

Fallopian tube. One of a pair of narrow tubes from the uterus that opens near the ovary, acting as a duct for the sperm and eggs.

fiber. A mostly unabsorbable component of food that is useful in alleviating constipation, lowering cholesterol, aiding digestion, and possibly preventing colon cancer. It comes in two forms, soluble and insoluble.

follicle. The protective layer of cells surrounding each egg in the ovaries that produces estrogen during the menstrual cycle.

follicle-stimulating hormone (FSH). A hormone secreted by the pituitary gland, FSH stimulates egg follicles in the ovary to grow (one follicle becomes dominant) and produce estrogen in the ovaries.

"free radicals." Naturally occurring substances manufactured by body processes as well as found in air pollution, ultraviolet sunlight, tobacco smoke, certain foods, and too much exercise. Free radicals can damage cell membranes and body tissues, possibly resulting in premature aging, heart disease, cancer, cataracts, and other conditions.

high-density lipoproteins (HDLs). Components of blood cholesterol that are beneficial because they move cholesterol from the cells to the liver, to be removed from the body. For this reason HDLs are known as "good" cholesterol, since they protect against heart disease.

hormone. From the Greek word "hormaein," which means "to excite." Hormones are secreted by the glands and their role is to regulate particular organs and tissues. For example, the hormone estrogen helps control the growth and function of the uterus and breasts and affects many other parts of the body.

hypothalamus. The coordinating center of the brain that directs other glands. For example, the hypothalamus directs the pituitary gland to release FSH during the first stage of the menstrual cycle.

hysterectomy. The surgical removal of the uterus, which may or may not be done in conjunction with removal of one or both of the ovaries.

IU (international units). Units used to measure certain vitamins and minerals, including vitamins A, D, and E.

lipoprotein. A part-lipid (fat) part-protein substance that carries fat in the blood.

lipoprotein (a). A type of fat found in the body resembling LDL (low-density lipoprotein), which has recently been considered a strong risk factor in heart disease. A level greater than 0.3 grams per liter of blood raises the risk of heart disease.

low-density lipoproteins (LDLs). Undesirable components of blood cholesterol that clog arteries with cholesterol and, when present in large amounts, can increase the risk of heart disease. LDLs are known as "bad" cholesterol.

luteinizing hormone (LH). A pituitary hormone that stimulates the rupture and release of the egg from the follicle into the Fallopian tube. After rupturing, the egg follicle develops into a structure called the corpus luteum, which produces large amounts of progesterone.

menopause. From the Greek words "mens," or monthly, and "pausa," or stop. It is the permanent cessation of menstruation and, with that, fertility. Menopause has officially occurred when twelve consecutive months have passed without a menstrual period. For most American women, it takes place at around age fifty-one.

oophorectomy. The surgical removal of one or both of the ovaries.

osteoporosis. The thinning and weakening of the bones that often occurs due to aging and menopause, and can increase your risk of fracture.

perimenopause. A transitional state that lasts from several months to several years, it begins with the first signs of change in a woman's menstrual periods and ends with the termination of her fertility. Perimenopause is the result of the natural decline in female hormone production. This is the time when women notice the most physical changes—fluctuations in menstrual cycle and flow, hot flashes, thinning of the vaginal walls, vaginal dryness, weight and body shape changes, and mood swings—although not all symptoms are experienced by all women.

phytochemicals. Plant compounds that are found in such foods as soybeans, cruciferous vegetables (such as cabbage and broccoli), and tomatoes, and which protect against some diseases, including cancer.

phytoestrogens. Plant compounds that possess some estrogen-like properties and, for that reason, are recommended in the belief that they may help ameliorate menopausal symptoms such as hot flashes. These compounds are found in such foods as soybeans, tofu, boiled beans, and yams. Certain herbs recognized for their phytoestrogen action include dong quai, alfalfa, black cohosh, fennel, and anise.

postmenopause. The months and years that follow menopause, when ovarian function ceases.

progesterone. From the Greek word meaning "for pregnancy," it's a female hormone secreted by the corpus luteum during the second half of the menstrual cycle. Progesterone is involved in promoting the growth of the uterine lining prior to menstruation.

progesterone challenge test. A screening test administered for irregular bleeding to test for endometrial cancer or hyperplasia. Generally ten milligrams of progestin is given daily for seven days, with the woman's response determining whether further testing such as an endometrial biopsy or a D and C is necessary.

progestin. A synthetic form of the female hormone progesterone, used in HRT.

surgical menopause. The menopause a woman experiences when she has undergone certain surgical procedures, such as having both ovaries removed, or when she has a hysterectomy and, although her ovaries remain intact, the blood supply to her ovaries has been cut off. She will then immediately experience some or all of the usual menopausal symptoms she would have experienced later during "natural" menopause.

triglyceride. A compound composed of three fatty acid molecules attached to a molecule of glycerin. Fats are usually stored in the tissues in the form of triglycerides. The level of triglycerides circulating in the blood helps to measure the risk of heart and circulatory disease. If triglycerides are elevated, they can contribute to heart disease. If your blood values are higher than 150 mg/dl, you are at greater-than-average risk for heart disease.

unopposed estrogen or estrogen dominance. A state in which there is an imbalance of the progesterone/estrogen levels, resulting in smaller-than-necessary amounts of progesterone. Excessive amounts of estrogen in the body may lead to endometrial and breast cancer, as well as other conditions.

waist-to-hip-ratio. A way to use one's waist and hip measurements to determine one's susceptibility to health risks, based on the location of the fat in one's body.

Resources

NEWSLETTERS

A Friend Indeed: For Women in the Prime of Life
A Friend Indeed Publications, Inc.
Janine O' Leary Cobb
Box 1710
Champlain, NY 12919-1710
or
Box 515
Place du Parc Station
Montreal, Quebec H2W 2P1
Canada
(514) 843-5730

Harvard Women's Health Watch
164 Longwood Avenue
Boston, MA 02115
(617) 432-1485

Health After 50: The Johns Hopkins Medical Letter
550 N. Broadway, Suite 1100
Johns Hopkins University
Baltimore, MD 21205

Hot Flash
The National Action Forum for Midlife and Older Women, Inc. (NAFOW)
c/o Jan Porcino
Box 816
Stony Brook, NY 11790-0609

Midlife Women's Network
5129 Logan Avenue South
Minneapolis, MN 55419-1019
(800) 886-4354

Network News
Newsletter of National Women's Health Network
1325 G Street NW
Washington, DC 20005

Nutri-Health-Weigh Currents for Menopausal Women
c/o Judy Marshel
25 Park Place
Great Neck, NY 11021
(516) 487-2755

Nutrition and Healing
P.O. Box 84909
Phoenix, AZ 85071
(800) 528-0559

Older Women's League
666 11th Street, NW,
Suite 700
Washington, DC 20001
(202) 783-6686

Women's Health Connection
P.O. Box 6338
Madison, WI 53716-0338
(800) 366-6632

TOLL-FREE HEALTH AND NUTRITION HOTLINES

The American Seafood
Institute: (800) EAT-FISH

High Carbohydrate Fiber
Nutrition Research Foundation:
(800) 727-4HCF

Meat and Poultry Hotline, U.S.
Department of
Agriculture: (800) 535-4555

National Center for Nutrition
and Dietetics: (American
Dietetic Association)
(800) 366-1655

University of Alabama at
Birmingham:
(800) 231-DIET

PRODUCT INFORMATION/ SPECIALTY PHARMACIES

Bajamar Women's Healthcare
(800) 255-8025

Belmar Pharmacy
(800) 525-9473

Madison Avenue Associates
(800) 558-7046

Natural Ovens of Manitoc (for information on flax oil):
(414) 758-2500

Women's International Pharmacy:
(800) 279-5708

SUPPORT GROUPS/SELF-HELP CLEARINGHOUSES

(For help in finding or forming a
mutual self-help group, call the following and you will be provided with
a listing of regional self-help clear-
inghouses, which may have listings
of local support or menopausal
groups in your area.)

American Self-Help Clearinghouse
St. Clares-Riverside Medical Center
6 Hinchan Avenue or
25 Pocono Road
Denville, NJ 07834
(201) 625-7101

National Self-Help Clearinghouse
25 W. 43rd Street
New York, NY 10036

National Self-Help Information
Clearinghouse
U.S. Department of Health and
Human Services
(800) 336-4797

Nutri-Health-Weigh for Menopausal
Women
Menopause Groups for Nutrition,
Health and Weight

25 Park Place
Great Neck, NY 11021
(516) 487-2755

MENOPAUSE
RESOURCES/HEALTH
INFORMATION ORGANIZATIONS

Call or write to the following to get a current list of publications, doctors specializing in menopause, referral services, and workshops.

Acupuncture

American Association of Acupuncture and Oriental Medicine (AAAOM)
4101 Lake Boone Trail,
Suite 201
Raleigh, NC 27607-6518
(919) 787-5181

Allergies

American Academy of Allergy and Immunology
611 E. Wells Street
Milwaukee, WI 53202
(800) 822-2762
(414) 272-6071

Alternative Medicine

American Association of Naturopathic Physicians
P.O. Box 20386
Seattle, WA 98102
(206) 323-7610

American Holistic Medical Association
2002 Eastlake Avenue East
Seattle, WA 98102
(206) 322-6842

Alzheimer's Disease

Alzheimer's Association
919 North Michigan Ave.
Suite 1000
Chicago, IL 60611-1676
(800) 272-3900

Alzheimer's Disease Education and Referral Center
P.O. Box 8250
Silver Spring, MD 20907-8250
(301) 495-3311

Cancer

American Cancer Society, Inc.
1599 Clifton Road, NE
Atlanta, GA 30329-4251
(800) ACS-2345;
(404) 320-3333

National Breast Cancer Coalition
P.O. Box 66373
Washington, DC 20036
(202) 296-7477

National Cancer Institute
Public Inquiries Office
9000 Rockville Pike
Building 31, Room 10A24
Bethesda, MD 20892
(800) 4-CANCER;
(301) 496-5583

Depression

Depression Awareness, Recognition and Treatment Program
National Institute of Mental Health
D/ART Public Inquiries
5600 Fishers Lane,
Room 15C-05
Rockville, MD 20857
(301) 443-4513

Dermatology

American Academy of Dermatology
930 N. Meacham
Schaumburg, IL 60173-4965
(708) 330-0230

Diabetes

American Diabetes Association
National Service Center
1660 Duke Street
Alexandria, VA 22314
(800) ADA-DISC;
(800) 232-3742

National Diabetes Information
Clearinghouse
P.O. Box NDIC
9000 Rockville Pike
Bethesda, MD 20892

Digestive Disorders

Intestinal Disease Foundation, Inc.
1323 Forbes Avenue, Suite 200
Pittsburgh, PA 15219
(800) 800-5776

National Digestive Disease Information Clearinghouse
P.O. Box NDDIC
9000 Rockville Pike
Bethesda, MD 20892
(301) 468-6344

Endometriosis

Endometriosis Association
8585 N. 7th Place
Milwaukee, WI 53223
(800) 922-3636

Headache

National Headache Foundation
5252 N. Western Avenue
Chicago, IL 60625
(800) 843-2256;
(312) 878-7715

Heart Disease

American Heart Association (AHA)
7272 Greenville Avenue
Dallas, TX 75231-4596
(800) 242-1793

Citizens for Public Action on Blood
Pressure and Cholesterol
7200 Wisconsin Avenue, Suite 1002
Bethesda, MD 20814
(301) 907-7990;
Fax: (301) 907-7792

National Heart, Lung and Blood
Institute
Information Center
P.O. Box 30105
Bethesda, MD 20824-0105
(301) 951-3260

Herbs

The American Botanical Council
P.O. Box 201660
Austin, TX 78720

Homeopathy

Homeopathic Educational Services
2124 Kittredge Street
Berkeley, CA 94794
(510) 649-0294

National Center for Homeopathy
1500 Massachusetts Avenue,
NW

Washington, DC 20005
(202) 223-6182

Hysterectomy

Hysterectomy, Education, Resources
and Services (HERS)
422 Bryn Mawr Avenue
Bala Cynwyd, PA 19004
(215) 667-7757

Incontinence

Continence Restored, Inc.
785 Park Avenue
New York, NY 10021
(212) 879-3131

Help for Incontinent People
P.O. Box 544
Union, SC 29379
(800) BLADDER

Insomnia

The American Sleep Disorders Association
1610 14th Street, Suite 300
Rochester, MN 55901
(507) 287-6006;
Fax: (507) 287-6008

The National Sleep Foundation
122 S. Robertson Boulevard,
Third Floor
Los Angeles, CA 90048

Menopause

American Menopause Foundation
350 5th Ave.
Suite 2822
New York, NY 10118
(212) 714-2398

Center for Climacteric Studies
University of Florida
222 S.W. 36th Terrace,
Suite C
Gainesville, FL 32607
(904) 372-5600;
Fax: (904) 376-3716

North American Menopause Society
(NAMS)
University Hospital of Cleveland
Department of OB/GYN
2074 Abington Road
Cleveland, OH 44106
(216) 844-3334

Massage

American Massage Therapy
Association
820 Davis Street, Suite 100
Evanston, IL 60201
(708) 864-0123

Mental Health

American Mental Health Counselors
Association
5999 Stevenson Avenue
Alexandria, VA 22304
(800) 326-2642;
(703) 823-9800

American Psychiatric Association
1400 K Street, NW
Washington, DC 20005
(202) 682-6000;
Fax: (202) 789-2648

American Psychological Association
750 1st Street, NE
Washington, DC 20002
(202) 336-5500

National Institute of Mental Health
Mental Health Public Inquiries
5600 Fishers Lane,

Room 15C-05
Rockville, MD 20857
(301) 443-4513 (publications)
Fax: (301) 443-0008

National Mental Health Association
  (NMHA)
Information Center
1021 Prince Street
Alexandria, VA 22314–2971
(800) 969-6642;
(703) 684-7722

Osteoporosis

National Osteoporosis Foundation
1150 17th Street NW,
Suite 500
Washington, DC 20036
(202) 223-2226;
(800) 223-9994

Sex

American Association for Sex Edu-
  cators, Counselors and Therapists
  (AASECT)
CALL only: (312) 644-0828

Stress

The American Institute of Stress
124 Park Avenue
Yonkers, NY 10703
(914) 963-1200

Thyroid

The Thyroid Foundation of America,
  Inc.
Massachusetts General Hospital
Ruth Sleeper Hall, Room 350
Boston, MA 02114
(617) 726-8500;
Fax: (617) 726-4136

Urinary Tract

American Urological Association
1120 N. Charles Street

Baltimore, MD 21201
(410) 727-1100

Bladder Health Council
1120 N. Charles Street
Baltimore, MD 21201

RESOURCES/GENREAL HEALTH

Alliance for Aging Research
2021 K Street NW, Suite 305
Washington, DC 20006
(202) 293-2856

American Association of Retired
  Person (AARP)
Women's Initiative
601 E. Street, NW
Washington, DC 20049
(202) 434-2277

American College of Obstetricians
  and Gynecologists (ACOG)
Resource Center
409 12th Street, SW
Washington, DC 20024-2188
(202) 638-5577

American Dietetic Association
  (ADA)
216 W. Jackson Boulevard, Suite 800
Chicago, IL 60606
(800) 366-1655;
(312) 899-0040

American Geriatics Society
770 Lexington Avenue, Suite 300
New York, NY 10021
(212) 308-1414

American Health Foundation
320 E. 43rd Street
New York, NY 10017
(212) 953-1900;
Fax: (212) 687-2339

American Medical Association
515 N. State Street
Chicago, IL 60610
(800) 262-3211;
(312) 464-5000

American Society on Aging
833 Market Street, Suite 512
San Francisco, CA 94103
(415) 882-2910

Boston Women's Health Food
Collective
240 Elm Street
Somerville, MA 02144
(617) 625-0271

Congressional Caucus for
Women's Issues
2471 Rayburn Building
House of Representatives
Washington, DC 20515
(202) 225-6740

Food and Drug Administration
Office of Consumer Affairs
5600 Fishers Lane, HFE 88
Rockville, MD 20857
(301) 443-3170

Harvard Medical School
Health Publications Group
Department HRT-REP
P.O. Box 380
Boston, MA 02117

Melpomene Institute
1010 University Avenue
St. Paul, MN 55104
(612) 642-1951

National Association for Human
Development
1424 16th Street, NW

Washington, DC 20036
(202) 328-2192

National Council Against
Health Fraud
Resource Center
3521 Broadway
Kansas City, MO 64111
(800) 821-6671

National Health Information Center
P.O. Box 1133
Washington, DC 20013-1133
(800) 336-4797

National Institute of Aging (NIA)
Information Center
P.O. Box 8057
Gaithersburg, MD 20898-8057
(800) 222-2225

National Institutes of Health (NIH)
9000 Rockville Pike
Bethesda, MD 20892
(301) 496-4461;
Fax: (301) 496-0017

Office of Disease Prevention and
Health Promotion
National Health Information
Center
P.O. Box 1133
Washington, DC 20013-1133
(800) 336-4797;
(301) 565-4167

National Women's
Health Network
1325 G Street, NW
Washington, DC 20005
(202) 347-1140;
Fax: (202) 347-1168

National Women's Health Resource
Center (NWHRC)
2440 M Street, NW, Suite 201

Washington, DC 20037
(202) 293-6045

Office of Research on
  Women's Health
National Institutes of Health
Building 1, Room 201
Bethesda, MD 20892
(301) 402-1770

Older Women's League (OWL)
666 11th Street, Suite 700
Washington, DC 20001
(202) 783-6686

Sex Information and Education
  Council of United States
130 W. 42nd Street,
Suite 2500
New York, NY 10036
(212) 819-9770

Wider Opportunities for Women
  (WOW) National Commission on
  Working Women
1325 G Street, NW,
Lower Level
Washington, DC 20005
(202) 638-3143

EXERCISE INFORMATION

Aerobics and Fitness Foundation
15250 Ventura Boulevard,
Suite 310
Sherman Oaks, CA 91403
(800) BE-FIT-86

American College of Sports Medicine
401 W. Michigan Street
Indianapolis, IN 46202-3233
(317) 637-9200

National Association of Governors'
  Councils on Physical Fitness and
  Sports (NAGCPFS)

Pan American Plaza
201 S. Capitol Avenue, Suite 440
Indianapolis, IN 46225
(317) 237-5630

President's Council on Physical Fitness and Sports
450 5th Street, NW,
Suite 7103
Washington, DC 20001
(202) 272-3421

Women's Sports Foundation
342 Madison Avenue,
Suite 728
New York, NY 10173
(800) 227-3988;
(212) 972-9170

EXERCISE EQUIPMENT
MANUFACTURES

Aerobics (treadmills)
  (201) 256-9700
Concept II (rowers)
  (800) 245-5676
Life Fitness (Lifecycle stationary
  bikes; Lifestep climbers;
  Lifestride treadmills; Life rowers)
  (800) 877-3867
Nordic Trac (ski simulators)
  (800) 328-5888
Precor (climbers, ski simulators, stationary bikes, treadmills)
  (800) 477-3267
Star Trac (treadmills, climbers)
  (800) 228-6635
Tectrix (climbers, stationary bikes)
  (800) 767-8082
Tunturi (stationary bikes, climbers,
  ski simulators, treadmills, rowers)
  (800) 827-8717

Selected Bibliography

BODY COMPOSITION

Dawson-Hughes, B and Harris, S. "Regional Changes in Body Composition by Time of Year in Healthy Postmenopausal Women." *American Journal of Clinical Nutrition.* Vol. 56, 1992, pp. 307–13.

Haarbro, J; Marslew, U; Gotfredsen, A and Christiansen, C. "Post-menopausal Hormone Replacement Therapy Prevents Central Distribution of Body Fat after Menopause." *Metabolism*, Vol. 40, No. 12, Dec. 1991, pp. 1323–6.

Jensen, J; Christiansen, C; Rodbro, P. "Estrogen-Progesterone Replacement Therapy Changes Body Composition in Early Post-Menopausal Women." *Maturitas.* Vol. 8, 1986, pp. 209–16.

Krotkiewski, M; Bjorntorp, P; Sjostrom, L; Smith, U. "Impact of Obesity in Men and Women: Importance of Regional Fat Distribution." *Journal of Clinical Investigation.* Vol. 72, 1983, pp. 1150–62.

Ley, C; Lees, B and Stevenson, J. "Sex- and Menopause-Associated Changes in Body-Fat Composition." *American Journal of Clinical Nutrition*, Vol. 55, 1992, pp. 950–4.

London, S; Sacks, F; Caesar, et al. "Fatty Acid Composition of Subcutaneous Adipose Tissue and Diet in Postmenopausal U.S. Women." *American Journal of Clinical Nutrition.* Vol. 54, 1991, pp. 340–5.

McCann, S; Freudenheim, J; Darrow, S; Batt, R and Zielezny, M. "Endometriosis and Body Fat Composition." *Obstetrics and Gynecology.* Vol. 82, 1993, pp. 545–9.

Seidell, JC; Bakx, JC; DeBoer, E; Deurenberg, P and Hautvast, JGAJ. "Fat Distribution of Overweight Persons in Relation to Morbidity and Subjective Health." *International Journal of Obesity.* Vol. 9, 1985, pp. 363–74.

Wadden, TA; Stunkard, AJ; Johnston, FE; Wang, J; Pierson, RN; Van Itallie, TB; Costello, E and Peña, M. "Body Fat Distribution in Adult Obese Women. II

Changes in Fat Distribution Accompanying Weight Reduction." *American Journal of Clinical Nutrition.* Vol. 47, 1988, pp. 229–34.

CANCER

American Cancer Society: *Cancer Facts and Figures,* 1993. Atlanta, Ga: American Cancer Society.

Astedt, B. "Cancer and Other Risk Factors with Estrogen Replacement." *Acta Obstetrics and Gynecology.* Scand. Suppl., Vol. 140, 1990, pp. 46–51.

Barbone, F; Austin, H and Partridge, E. "Diet and Endometrial Cancer: A Case-Control Study." *American Journal of Epidemiology.* Vol. 137, No. 4, pp. 393–403.

"Carcinoma of the Endometrium." *ACOG Technical Bulletin.* No. 162, Dec. 1991.

Dupont, W and Page, D. "Menopausal Estrogen Replacement Therapy and Breast Cancer." *Archives of Internal Medicine.* Vol. 151, Jan. 1991, pp. 67–72.

Hankin, JH. "Role of Nutrition in Women's Health: Diet and Breast Cancer." *Journal of The American Dietetic Association.* Vol. 93, No. 9, 1993, pp. 994–9.

Henderson, IC. "Risk Factors for Breast Cancer Development." *Cancer.* Vol. 71 (suppl), 1993, pp. 2127–40.

Kerlikowske, K; Grady, D and Barclay, J, et al. "Positive Predictive Value of Screening Mammography by Age and Family History of Breast Cancer." *Journal of the American Medical Association.* Vol. 270, No. 20, Nov. 24, 1993, pp. 2444–50.

Kneale, BLG and Giles, GG. "Endometrial Cancer: Trends in Incidence and Survival: A Preventable Disease?" *Australian & New Zealand Journal of Obstetrics & Gynaecology.* Vol. 33, No. 1, 1993, p. 1.

Kopans, D; Marchant, D and Osborne, M. "Breast Cancer: Vigilance, Not Panic." *Patient Care.* November 15, 1993, pp. 135–64.

Liebman, B. "Fighting Cancer Without Fat." *Nutrition Action Healthletter.* June 1993.

Medical World News. "NCI May Shift Mammogram Stance." Dec. 1993, pp. 144–6.

Mills, P; Beeson, L; Phillips, R and Fraser, G. "Dietary Habits and Breast Cancer Incidence among Seventh-Day Adventists. *Cancer.* Vol. 64, 1989, pp. 582–90.

Satariano, W and Ragland, D. "The Effect of Comorbidity on 3-year Survival of Women with Primary Breast Cancer." *Annals of Internal Medicine.* Vol. 120, No. 2, Jan. 15, 1994, pp. 105–11.

Seely, S and Horrobin, DF. "Diet and Breast Cancer: The Possible Connection with Sugar Consumption." *Medical Hypothesis.* Vol. 11, No. 3, 1983, p. 319.

Slattery, ML and Kerber, RA. "A Comprehensive Evaluation of Family History and Breast Cancer Risk: The Utah Population Databases." *Journal of the American Medical Association.* Vol. 270, 1993, pp. 1563–68.

Vatten, L and Kvinnsland, S. "Body Mass Index and Risk of Breast Cancer." *International Journal of Cancer.* Vol. 45, 1990, pp. 440–44.

CARDIOVASCULAR DISEASE

American Heart Association. *1993 Heart and Stroke Facts*. Dallas, Texas: American Heart Association, 1992.

Amsterdan, EA and Legato, MJ. "What's Unique about CHD in Women?" *Patient Care*. November 15, 1993, pp. 21–52.

Arnold, AZ and Moodie, D. "Coronary Artery Disease in Young Women." *Cleveland Clinic Journal of Medicine*. Sep./Oct. 1993, pp. 393–8.

Chait, A; Brunzell, J; Denke, M; Eisenberg, D, et al. "Rationale of the Diet-Heart Statement of the American Heart Association." *AHA Office of Scientific Affairs*. Feb. 19, 1992, pp. 3008–29.

Colditz, GA; Willett, WC; Stampfer, MJ; Rosner, B; Speizer, FE and Hennekens, CH. "Menopause and the Risk of Coronary Heart Disease in Women." *New England Journal of Medicine*. Vol. 316, 1987, pp. 1105–10.

Ershow, AG and Skarlatos, S. "Diet and Risk Factors for Coronary Heart Disease: An Update." *Contemporary Nutrition*. Vol. 18, No. 1, 1993, pp. 1–2.

Fogarty M. "Garlic's Potential Role in Reducing Heart Disease." *British Journal of Clinical Practice*. Vol. 47, No. 2, March/April 1993, pp. 64–5.

Hubert, HB; Feinleib, M; McNamara, PM and Castelli, WP. "Obesity As an Independent Risk Factor for Cardiovascular Disease: A 26-year Follow-Up of Participants in the Framingham Heart Study." *Circulation*. Vol. 67, 1983, pp. 968–77.

Kris-Etherton, PM and Krummel, D. "Role of Nutrition in the Prevention and Treatment of Coronary Heart Disease in Women." *Journal of the American Dietetic Association*. Vol. 93, No. 9, 1993, pp. 987–93.

Kuhn, F and Rackley, C. "Coronary Artery Disease In Women." *Archives of Internal Medicine*. Vol. 153, December 13, 1993, pp. 2626–36.

Langer, R and Barrett-Connor, E. "Epidemiology and Prevention of Cardiovascular Disease in Women." *Contemporary Internal Medicine*. June 1991, pp. 50–64.

Lerner, DJ and Kannel, WB. "Patterns of Coronary Heart Disease Morbidity and Mortality in the Sexes: A 26-year Follow-Up of the Framingham Population." *American Heart Journal*. Vol. 111, 1986, pp. 383–90.

Manson, JE; Colditz, GA; Stampler, MJ, et al. "A Prospective Study of Obesity and Risk of Coronary Heart Disease in Women." *New England Journal of Medicine*. Vol. 332, 1990, pp. 882–9.

Miller, M; Moalemi, A; Seidler, A et al. "Predictors of Cardiovascular Mortality in Women: A 15-year Follow-Up Study." Abs. #2682. *Circulation*. Vol. 86 (suppl 1), No. I, 1992, pp. 674.

Orencia, A; Bailey, K; Yawn, BP and Kottke, TE. "Survival and Subsequent Coronary Heart Disease Events in Women." *ACP Journal Club*. Nov./Dec. 1993, p. 81.

Pashkow, F. "Diagnostic Evaluation of the Patient with Coronary Artery Disease." *Cleveland Clinic Journal of Medicine*. Jan./Feb. 1994, pp. 43–8.

Philpsophe, R and Seibel, MM. "Menopause and Cardiovascular Disease." *NAACOGS Clinical Issues in Perinatal and Women's Health Nursing*. Vol. 2, No. 4, 1991, pp. 441–51.

Wenger, N. "Coronary Heart Disease in Women: A 'New' Problem." *Hospital Practice*. Nov. 15, 1992, pp. 59–74.

Wenger, N; Speroff, L and Packard, B. "Coronary Heart Disease in Women: An Overview." *CVR&R*. Dec. 1993, pp. 24–41.

DEPRESSION

"Depression in Women." *ACOG Technical Bulletin*. No. 182, July 1993.

Tobias, C and Lewis, S. "Menopause and Depression: Cause, Assessment and Treatment." *Women's Psychological Health*. Vol. 2, Winter 1993, pp. 1–14.

DIET AND NUTRITION

Allen, AH. "Fact or Fad? The Latest Nutritional Breakthroughs." *Food Product Design*. May 1994, pp. 31–50.

Altura, B; Brodsky, M; Elin, R; Gums, J, et al. "Magnesium: Growing in Clinical Importance." *Patient Care*. Jan. 15, 1994, pp. 130–150.

Altura, B; Brodsky, M; Elin, R; Gums, J, et al. "Magnesium Therapy: Coming of Age?" *Patient Care*. Jan. 30, 1994, pp. 79–94.

Coniglio, J. "How Does Fish Oil Lower Plasma Triglycerides?" *Nutrition Reviews*. Vol. 50, No. 7, July 1992, pp. 195–206.

Dunne, L. *Nutrition Almanac, 3rd Edition*. McGraw-Hill, Inc., 1990.

Flodin, N. "Micronutrient Supplements: Toxicity and Drug Interactions." *Progress in Food and Nutrition Science*. Vol. 14, 1990, pp. 277–331.

Haarbro, J; Hassager, C; Jensen, SB; Riis, BJ and Christiansen, C. "Serum Lipids, Lipoproteins and Apolipoproteins during Postmenopausal Estrogen Replacement Therapy with either 19 Nortestosterone Derivatives or 17-hydroxyprogesterone Derivatives." *American Journal of Medicine*. Vol. 90, 1991, pp. 584–9.

Hamilton, EMN; Whitney, EN and Sizer, FS. *Nutrition Concepts and Controversies*. St. Paul, MN: West Publishing Company. 1991.

Krummel, D; Etherton, TD; Peterson, S and Kris-Etherton. "Effects of Plasma Lipids and Lipoproteins of Women." *Society for Experimental Biology and Medicine*. Vol. 204, 1993, pp. 123–37.

McBean, l; Chandra, R; Weaver, K, et al. "Avoiding the Adverse Effects of Zinc Imbalance." *Special Report: Zinc*. PGM Custom Communications, December 20, 1993.

McDougall, J. *The McDougall Program*. New York: Plume, 1991.

National Academy of Sciences. *Recommended Dietary Allowances 10th Edition*. Washington DC: National Academy Press. 1989.

National Research Council. *Diet and Health*. Washington, DC: National Academy Press. 1989.

Sanders, ME. "Healthful Attributes of Bacteria in Yogurt." *Contemporary Nutrition*, Vol. 18, No. 5, 1993.

Schardt, D. "The Problem with Protein." *Nutrition Action Newsletter*. Vol. 20, No. 5, June 1993, pp. 1, 5–7.

Stampfer, MJ; Colditz, GA; Willett, WC, et al. "Post-Menopausal Estrogen Therapy Study and Cardiovascular Disease: Ten-Year Follow-Up from the

Nurses' Health Study." *New England Journal of Medicine.* Vol. 325, 1991, pp. 756–62.

Tami, J; Parr, M and Thompson, J. "The Immune System." *American Journal of Hospital Pharmacy.* Vol. 43, Oct. 1986, pp. 2483–93.

Warshafsky, S; Kamer, R and Sivak, S. "Effect of garlic on total serum cholesterol." *Annals of Internal Medicine.* Vol. 119, 1993, pp. 599–605.

Wilcox, G; Wahlqvist, M, Burger, H and Medley, G. "Oestrogenic Effects of Plant Foods in Postmenopausal Women." *British Medical Journal.* Vol. 301, 1990, pp. 905–6.

"Women, Nutrition and Health." *Current Problems in Obstetrics, Gynecology and Fertility.* January 1993, pp. 11–49.

Wood, R and Serfaty-Lacrosniere, C. "Gastric Acidity, Atrophic Gastritis, and Calcium Absorption." *Nutrition Reviews.* Vol. 50, No. 2, Feb. 1992, pp. 33–40.

ENDOCRINOLOGY

Judd, HL; Judd, GE; Luca, WE, et al. "Endocrine Function of the Postmenopausal Ovary: Concentrations of Androgens and Estrogens in Ovarian and Peripheral Vein Blood. *Journal of Clinical Endocrinol Metabolism.* Vol. 39, 1974, p. 1020.

Speroff, L; Glass, R and Kase, N. *Clinical Gynecologic Endocrinology and Infertility.* Baltimore, Maryland: Williams and Wilkins, 1994.

EXERCISE

American College of Sports Medicine. *ASCM Fitness Book.* Champaign, Ill: Leisure Press. 1992.

Anderson, B. *Stretching.* Bolinas, California: Shelter Publications, 1980.

Blair, SN; Kohl, HW; Paffenbarger, RS; Clark, DG; Cooper, KH and Gibbons, LW. "Physical Fitness and All-Cause Mortality. A Prospective Study of Healthy Men and Women." *Journal of the American Medical Association.* Vol. 262, 1989, pp. 2395–401.

Forbes, G. "Exercise and Lean Weight: The Influence of Body Weight." *Nutrition Reviews.* Vol. 50, No. 6, June 1992, p. 157.

Green Birkel DA and Birkel Freitag S. *Forever Fit. A Step-By-Step Guide For Older Adults.* New York: Plenum Press, 1991.

Katch, FI and McArdle, WD. *Introduction to Nutrition, Exercise and Health.* Philadelphia: Lea and Febiger, 1993.

McArdle, WD; Katch, FI and Katch, VL: *Exercise Physiology: Energy, Nutrition and Human Performance.* Philadelphia: Lea and Febiger, 1986, p. 135.

The New Fitness Formula of the 90's. Excelsior, MN: The National Exercise For Life Institute, 1990.

Olson, MS, et al. "The Cardiovascular and Metabolic Effects of Bench Stepping Exercises in Females." *Medicine and Science in Sports and Exercise.* Vol. 23. No. 11, November 1991.

Pavlou, K; Whatley, J; Jannace, P, et al. "Physical Activity as a Supplement to a Weight-Loss Dietary Regimen." *American Journal of Clinical Nutrition.* Vol. 49, 1989, pp. 1110–4.

Rippe, JM. *The Exercise Exchange Program.* New York: Simon and Schuster, 1992.

Stutz, DS. *40+ Guide to Fitness. Forever Fit.* Yonkers, New York: Consumer Reports Books, 1994.

Wells, CL. *Women, Sport & Performance.* Second Edition. England: Human Kinetics Books, 1991, pp. 159–80.

FOOD-MOOD CONNECTION

Brzezinski, A; Wurtman, JJ; Wurtman, RJ, et al. "d-Fenfluramine Suppresses the Increased Calorie and Carbohydrate Intakes and Improves Mood of Women with Premenstrual Depression." *Obstetrics and Gynecology.* Vol. 76, 1990, pp. 296–301.

Fernstrom, JD. "Dietary Amino Acids and Brain Function." *Journal of the American Dietetic Association.* Vol. 94, No. 1, 1994, pp. 71–77.

Genazzani, AR; Petraglia, F; Facchinetti, F; Genazzani, AD; Bergamaschi, M; Grasso, A and Volpe, A. "Effects of Org OD 14 on Pituitary and Peripheral B-Endorphin in Castrated Rats and Postmenopausal Women." *Maturitas.* Vol. 7 (suppl 1), 1987, pp. 35–48.

Lieberman, H; Wurtman, J and Chew, B. "Changes in Mood after Carbohydrate Consumption among Obese Individuals." *American Journal of Clinical Nutrition.* Vol. 44, 1986, pp. 772–8.

Spring, BJ; Lieberman, HR; Swope, G and Garfield, G. "Effects of Carbohydrate on Mood and Behavior." *Nutrition Reviews.* May 1986 Supplement, pp. 51–60.

Wurtman, J. "Carbohydrate Cravings: A Disorder of Food Intake and Mood." *Clinical Neuropharmacology.* Vol. 11 (supplement), 1988, pp. S139–S145.

Wurtman, R. "Ways That Foods Can Affect the Brain." *Nutrition Reviews.* May 1986/Supplement.

HORMONE REPLACEMENT THERAPY

Brinton, L; Hoover, R, et al. "Estrogen Replacement Therapy and Endometrial Cancer Risk: Unresolved Issues." *Obstetrics and Gynecology.* Vol. 81, No. 2, Feb. 1993, pp. 265–75.

Bush, T; Gambrell, D and Miller, V. "More Reasons than Ever for HRT." *Patient Care.* Nov. 15, 1993, pp. 103–32.

Byrjalsen, I; Haarbro, J and Christiansen, C. "Role of Cigarette Smoking on the Postmenopausal Endometrium during Sequential Estrogen and Progesterone Therapy." *Obstetrics and Gynecology.* Vol. 81, 1993, pp. 1016–21.

Corson, S. "A Decade of Experience with Transdermal Estrogen Replacement Therapy: Overview of Key Pharmacologic and Clinical Findings." *International Journal of Fertility.* 1993, pp. 79–89.

Ditkoff, EC; Crary, WG; Cristo, M and Lobo, AR. "Estrogen Improves Psychological Function in Asymptomatic Postmenopausal Women." *Obstetrics and Gynecology.* Vol. 78, 1991, pp. 991–5.

"Estrogens and Disease Prevention." *Archives of Internal Medicine.* Vol. 151, Jan. 1991, pp. 17–18.

Grady, D; Rubin, S; Pettiti, D, et al. "Hormone Therapy to Prevent Disease and Prolong Life in Postmenopausal Women." *Annals of Internal Medicine.* Vol. 117, No. 12, Dec. 15, 1992, pp. 1016–34.

Hargrove, J; Maxson, W and Wentz, AC. "Absorption of Oral Progesterone Is Influenced by Vehicle and Particle Size." *American Journal of Obstetrics and Gynecology.* Vol. 161, 1989, pp. 948–51.

Harlap, S. "The Benefits and Risks of Hormone Replacement Therapy: An Epidemiologic Overview." *American Journal of Obstetrics and Gynecology.* Vol. 166, 1992, p. 1986.

"Hormone Replacement Therapy." *ACOG Technical Bulletin.* No. 166, April 1992.

Jensen, J; Christiansen, C and Rodbro, P. "Estrogen-Progesterone Replacement Therapy Changes Body Composition in Early Postmenopausal Women." *Maturitas.* Vol. 8, 1986, pp. 209–16.

Jick, H; Walker, AM; Watkins, RN, et al. "Replacement Estrogens and Breast Cancer." *American Journal of Epidemiology.* Vol. 112, 1980, pp. 586–94.

Lind, T; Cameron, EC; Hunter, WM; Leon, C; Moran, PF; Oxley, A; Gerrand, J and Lind, UCG. "A Prospective Controlled Study of Six Forms of Hormone Replacement Therapy Given to Postmenopausal Women." *British Journal of Obstetrics and Gynecology.* Vol. 86 Supplement, No. 3, 1979 3, pp. 1–29.

Lindheim, S; Legro, R; Bernstein, L, et al. "Behavioral Stress Responses in Premenopausal and Postmenopausal Women and the Effects of Estrogen." *American Journal of Obstetrics and Gynecology.* Vol. 167, 1992, pp. 1831–6.

Lobo, R. "The Role of Progestins in Hormone Replacement Therapy." *American Journal of Obstetrics and Gynecology.* Vol 166, 1992, pp. 1997–2004.

Marshburn, P and Carr, B. "Hormone Replacement Therapy." *Postgraduate Medicine.* Vol. 92, No. 4, Sept. 15, 1992, pp. 145–59.

Persson, I; Adami, HO; Bergkvist, L, et al. "Risk of Endometrial Cancer after Treatment with Oestrogens Alone or in Conjunction with Progestogens: Results of a Prospective Study." *British Medical Journal.* Vol. 298, 1989, pp. 147–51.

Samsioe, G. "Introduction to Steroids in the Menopause." *American Journal of Obstetrics and Gynecology.* Vol. 166, 1992, pp. 1980–5.

Utian, WH. "The Mental Tonic Effect of Oestrogens Administered to Oophorectomized Females. *South African Medical Journal.* Vol. 46, 1972, pp. 1079–82.

Vassilopoulou-Sellin, R. "Estrogen Replacement Therapy for Breast Cancer Survivors." *The Female Patient.* Vol. 18, Aug. 1993, pp. 41–8.

Wahl, P; Walden, C; Knopp, R, et al. "Effect of Estrogen Progestin Potency on Lipid/Lipoprotein Cholesterol." *New England Journal of Medicine.* Vol. 308, 1983, pp. 862–7.

Walsh, BW; Schiff, I; Rosner, B; Greenberg, L; Ravnikar, V and Sacks, FM. "Effects of Postmenopausal Estrogen Replacement Therapy on the Concentrations and Metabolism of Plasma Lipoproteins." *New England Journal of Medicine.* Vol. 325, 1991, pp. 1196–204.

Young, R; Kumar, N and Goldzieher, J. "Management of Menopause when Estrogen Cannot Be Used." *Drugs 40*. No. 2, 1990, pp. 220–3.

INSULIN

Weinsier, R; James, LD; Darnell, B, et al. "Lipid and Insulin Concentrations in Obese Postmenopausal Women: Separate Effects of Energy Restriction and Weight Loss." *American Journal of Clinical Nutrition*. Vol. 25, 1992, pp. 44–9.

IRON

Ascherio, A and Willett, W. "Are Body Iron Stores Related to the Risk of Coronary Heart Disease?" *New England Journal of Medicine*. Vol. 332, 1994, pp. 1152–4.

MENOPAUSE

Adlercreuta, H, et al. "Dietary Phyto-Estrogens and the Menopause."*Lancet*. Vol. 339, 1992, p. 1233.

American College of Physicians. "Guidelines for Counseling Postmenopausal Women about Preventive Hormone Therapy." *Annals of Internal Medicine*. Vol. 117, 1992, pp. 1038–41.

Beard, RJ. *The Menopause: A Guide to Current Research and Practice*. Lancaster, England: MTP Press, Vol. 30, 1976.

Brunn, RD and Brunn, B. *The Human Body: Your Body and How It Works*. New York: Random House, Inc., 1982.

Brzezinski, A and Wurtman, J. "Managing Menopause through the Transition Years." *Menopause Management*. Nov./Dec. 1993, pp. 18–23.

Ginsburg, J; Swinhoe, J and O'Reilly, B. "Cardiovascular Responses during the Menopausal Hot Flash." *British Journal of Obstetrics and Gynecology*. Vol. 88, 1981, pp. 925–30.

Greendale, GA and Judd, HL. "Menopause: Health Implications and Clinical Management." JAGS. Vol. 41, 1993, pp. 426–36.

Haddock D. A Simple Way to Manage Menopause. *Postgraduate Medicine*. Vol. 88, No. 3, 1990, pp. 131–8.

Hilton, P and Stanton, SL. "The Use of Intravaginal Oestrogen Cream in Genuine Stress Incontinence." *British Journal of Obstetrics and Gynecology*. Vol. 4, 1983, pp. 940–4.

Joint FAO/WHO/UNU expert consultation. "Energy and Protein Requirements." *Technical Reports*. Vol. 724, 1985, pp. 1–67.

Kinn, AC and Lindskoy, M. "Estrogens and Phenylpropanol-Amine in Combination for Stress Incontinence in Postmenopausal Women." *Urology*. Vol. 32, 1988, pp. 273–80.

Laufer, LR; Erlik, Y; Meldrum, Dr., et al. "Effect of Clonidine on Hot Flashes on Postmenopausal Women." *Obstetrics and Gynecology*. Vol. 60, 1982, pp. 583–6.

McKeon, VA. "Cruel Myths and Clinical Facts about Menopause." *RN*. June 1989, pp. 52–9.

McKinley, SM; Brambilla, PJ and Posner, JG. "The Normal Menopause Transition." *Maturitas*. Vol. 14, 1992, pp. 103–15.

McKinley, S and Jeffreys, M. "The Menopausal Syndrome." *British Journal of Preventive Social Medicine*. Vol. 28, 1974, pp. 108–15.

Marsh, MS and Whitehead, MI. "Management of the Menopause." *British Medical Bulletin*. Vol. 48, No. 2, 1992, pp. 426–57.

Matthews, K. "Myths and Realities of the Menopause." *Psychosomatic Medicine*. Vol. 54, No. 1, 1992, pp. 1–9.

The Medical Clinics of North America: *The Postmenopausal Woman*. Philadelphia: W. B. Saunders Company, 1987, pp. 87–93.

Menopause. National Institutes of Health/US Department of Health and Human Services, Publication No. 92–3466.

Merunier, PJ. "Prevention of Hip Fractures." *The American Journal of Medicine*. Vol. 95 (Suppl 5A), pp. 75S–78S.

Obstetrics and Gynecology Clinics of North America: *Primary Care of the Mature Woman*, Philadelphia: W. B. Saunders, Vol. 21, No. 2, June 1994.

Ravnikar, V. "Diet, Exercise and Lifestyle in Preparation for Menopause." *Obstetrics and Gynecology Clinics of North America*. Vol. 20, No. 2, June 1993, pp. 365–79.

Tataryn, IV; Lomax, P; Meldrum, DR; Bajorek, JG; Chesarek, W and Judd HL. "Objective Techniques for the Assessment of Postmenopausal Hot Flashes." *Obstetrics and Gynecology*. Vol. 57, 1981, pp. 340–4.

Wurtman, J. "Weight Gain at Menopause." *A Friend Indeed*. Vol IX, No. 4, September 1992, pp. 1–4.

OSTEOPOROSIS

Beals, RK. "Survival Following Hip Fracture: Long Term Follow-Up of 607 Patients." *Journal of Chronic Disease*. Vol. 25, 1972, p. 235.

Chamay, A and Tschantz, P. "Mechanical Influence in Bone Remodeling: Experimental Research of Wolff's Law." *Journal of Biomechanics*. Vol. 5, 1972, pp. 173–80.

Chestnut, CH 3d. "Noninvasive Techniques for Measuring Bone Mass: A Comparative Review." *Clinical Obstetrics and Gynecology*. Vol. 30, No. 4, 1987, pp. 812–9.

Heany, RP. "Thinking Straight about Calcium." *New England Journal of Medicine*. Vol. 328, 1993, pp. 503–5.

Hillner, BE; Hollenberg, JP and Paukeer, SG. "Postmenopausal Estrogens in Prevention of Osteoporosis: Benefit Virtually without Risk if Cardiovascular Effects Are Considered." *American Journal of Medicine*. Vol. 80, 1986, pp. 1115–26.

Kiel, DP; Felson, DT; Anderson, JJ; Wilson, PWF and Moskowitz, MA. "Hip Fracture and the Use of Estrogens in Postmenopausal Women: The Framingham Study," *New England Journal of Medicine*. Vol. 317, 1987, p. 1169.

Lees, B. et al. "Differences in Proximal Femur Bone Density over Two Centuries." *Lancet*. Vol. 341, 1993, pp. 673–5.

Madson, S. "How to Reduce the Risk of Postmenopausal Osteoporosis." *Journal of Gerontological Nursing.* Vol. 15, No. 9, 1989, pp. 20–4.

National Osteoporosis Foundation. *The Older Person's Guide to Osteoporosis.* Washington, DC. 1991.

Prior, JC; Vigna, Y and Alojada, N. "Progesterone and the Prevention of Osteoporosis." *Canadian Journal of Ob/Gyn and Women's Health Care.* Vol. 3, No. 4, 1991, p. 181.

Riggs, BL; Seeman, E; Hodgson, SF; Taves, DR and O'Fallon, WM. "Effect of the Fluoride/Calcium Regimen on Vertebral Fracture Occurrence in Post-Menopausal Osteoporosis." *New England Journal of Medicine.* Vol. 306, 1982, pp. 446–93.

Speroff, L; Glass, RH and Kase, NG. *Clinical Gynecologic Endocrinology and Infertility, 5th Edition.* Baltimore: Williams and Wilkins, 1994.

Stevenson, J. "Pathogenesis, Prevention and Treatment of Osteoporosis." *Obstetrics and Gynecology.* Vol. 74, No 4 (Supplement) 1990, pp. 36–9.

Wardlaw, G. "Putting Osteoporosis in Perspective." *Journal of The American Dietetic Association.* Vol. 93, No. 9, 1993, pp. 1000–6.

Wyshak, G; Frisch, RE; Albright, TE and Schiff, I. "Bone Fractures among Former College Athletes Compared with Nonathletes in the Menopausal and Postmenopausal Years." *Obstetrics and Gynecology.* Vol. 69, 1987, pp. 121–6.

PHYSIOLOGY

Barbo, D. "The Physiology of the Menopause." *Medical Clinics of North America.* Vol. 71, No. 1, Jan. 1987, pp. 11–21.

Nash, J. "Eating Behavior and Body Weight: Physiological Influences." *American Journal of Health Promotion.* Winter 1987, pp. 5–15.

National Dairy Council. "Diet and Behavior." *Dairy Council Digest,* Vol. 56, No. 4, July/Aug. 1985.

PSYCHOLOGY

Burgard, D. "Psychological Theory Seeks to Define Obesity." *Obesity & Health.* March/April 1993, pp. 25–37.

Schindler, B. "The Psychiatric Disorders of Midlife." *Medical Clinics of North America.* Vol. 71, No. 1, Jan. 1987, pp. 71–83.

Schmidt, P and Rubinow, D. "Menopause-Related Affective Disorders." *American Journal of Psychiatry,* Vol. 148, No. 7, July 1991, pp. 844–52.

Stewart, D; Boydell, K; Derzko, C and Marshall, V. "Psychologic Distress during the Menopausal Years in Women Attending a Menopause Clinic." *International Journal of Psychiatry in Medicine.* Vol. 22, No. 3, 1992, pp. 213–20.

Stewart, D and Boydell, K. "Psychologic Distress during Menopause: Associations across the Reproductive Life Cycle." *International Journal of Psychiatry in Medicine.* Vol. 23, No. 2, 1993, pp. 157–62.

Waller, K and Bates, RC. "Health Locus of Control and Self-Efficacy Beliefs in a Healthy Elderly Sample." *American Journal of Health Promotion.* Nov. 1, 1991, pp. 302–8.

SEX

Bachmann, G. "Sexual Dysfunction in Postmenopausal Women." *Geriatrics.* Vol. 43, Nov. 1988, pp. 79–83.

Iddenden, D. "Sexuality during the Menopause." *Medical Clinics of North America.* Vol. 71, No. 1, Jan. 1987, pp. 87–109.

STRESS

Benson, H. *The Relaxation Response.* New York: Avon Books, 1975.

Greene, JG and Cooke, DJ. "Life Stress and Symptoms at the Climacterium." *British Journal of Psychiatry,* Vol. 136, 1980, p. 486.

Seyle, H. *Stress Without Distress,* Philadelphia: J. B. Lippincott, 1974.

WEIGHT LOSS/MAINTENANCE

Andersson, B; Seidell, J; Terning K and Bjorntorp, P. "Influence of Menopause on Dietary Treatment of Obesity." *Journal of Internal Medicine.* Vol. 227, 1990, pp. 173–81.

Arciero, P; Goran, M; Gardner, A, et al. "A Practical Equation to Predict Resting Metabolic Rate in Older Females." *JAGS.* Vol. 41, 1993, pp. 389–95.

Berg, F. "Problem-Solving Skills Improve Maintenance after Weight Loss." *Obesity and Health.* Vol. 7, No. 4, July/Aug. 1993, pp. 68–79.

Brownell, K; Marlatt, GA; Lichtenstein, E and Wilson, GT. "Understanding and Preventing Relapse." *American Psychologist,* July Vol. 41, No. 7, 1986, pp. 765–82.

Dumesic, D and Matteri, R. "Obesity Affects Circulating Estradiol Levels in Premenopausal Women Receiving Leuprolide Acetate Depot." *International Journal of Fertility.* Vol. 38, No. 3, 1993, pp. 139–46.

Gallagher, D and Heymsfield, S. "Obesity Is Bad for the Heart, but Is Weight Loss Always Good?" *Obesity Research.* Vol. 2, No. 2, March 1994, pp. 160–4.

Kaplan, N. "Obesity: Location Matters." *Heart Disease and Stroke.* Vol. 1, 1992, pp. 148–50.

Kayman, S; Bruvold, W and Stern, J. "Maintenance and Relapse after Weight Loss in Women: Behavioral Aspects." *American Journal of Clinical Nutrition.* Vol. 52, 1990, pp. 800–7.

"Methods for Voluntary Weight Loss and Control." *Annals of Internal Medicine/Supplement.* Vol. 119, No. 7 (Part 2), Oct. 1993.

Papazian, R. "An FDA Guide to Dieting." *FDA Consumer Magazine.* Oct. 1991, No. (FDA), pp. 92–1188.

Ravussin, E and Bogardus, C. "A Brief Overview of Human Energy Metabolism and its Relationship to Essential Obesity." *American Journal of Clinical Nutrition*. Vol. 55, 1992, pp. 242S–5S.

St. Jeor, S. "The Role of Weight Management in the Health of Women." *Journal of the American Dietetic Association*, Vol. 93, No. 9, Sept. 1993, pp. 1007–12.

Schwartz, F. "Obesity in Adult Females." *AAOHN Journal*. Vol. 41, No. 10, Oct. 1993, pp. 504–9.

Wing, R; Matthews, K; Kuller, L, et al. "Weight Gain at the Time of Menopause." *Archives of Internal Medicine*. Vol. 151, Jan. 1991, pp. 97–102.

Index